Algebra for Elementary and Middle School Teachers: An Inquiry Approach

Sheryl Stump, Kay Roebuck, Joyce Bishop

Second Edition

Custom Publishing

New York   Boston   San Francisco
London   Toronto   Sydney   Tokyo   Singapore   Madrid
Mexico City   Munich   Paris   Cape Town   Hong Kong   Montreal

Cover Art: *July Morning*, by William Padien

Copyright © 2009, 2008 by Pearson Custom Publishing
All rights reserved.

This copyright covers material written expressly for this volume by the editor/s as well as the compilation itself. It does not cover the individual selections herein that first appeared elsewhere. Permission to reprint these has been obtained by Pearson Custom Publishing for this edition only. Further reproduction by any means, electronic or mechanical, including photocopying and recording, or by any information storage or retrieval system, must be arranged with the individual copyright holders noted.

All trademarks, service marks, registered trademarks, and registered service marks are the property of their respective owners and are used herein for identification purposes only.

Printed in the United States of America

10 9 8 7 6 5 4 3 2 1

2009361191

LM/MC

**Pearson
Custom Publishing**
is a division of

www.pearsonhighered.com

ISBN 10: 0-558-38777-2
ISBN 13: 978-0-558-38777-8

Algebra for Elementary and Middle School Teachers: An Inquiry Approach

Table of Contents

Preface.. **xviii**

UNIT 1: LEARNING ALGEBRA THROUGH PROBLEM SOLVING **1**

Chapter 1: Introduction to Problem Solving **1**

    1.1.   Silver Coins...9

    1.2.   Crossing the River...11

    1.3.   Cutting Through Layers...13

    1.4.   Bossy the Cow 15

    1.5.   Painted Cubes..16

    1.6.   Chickens..17

    1.7.   Staircases..19

    1.8.   Counting Handshakes 20

    1.9.   Variables 21

    1.10. Additional Problems 24

    1.11. Pedagogical Explorations..26

    1.12. Summary..29

Chapter 2: Solving Equations...**31**

    2.1.   Relational Thinking 35

    2.2.   Using Relational Thinking to Solve Equations.......................37

    2.3   Working Backward to Solve Equations 38

    2.4.   Operating with the Unknown...40

    2.5.   Farmer Brown 42

    2.6.   Additional Problems 45

Table of Contents

2.7.   Pedagogical Explorations...47

2.8.   Summary 48

UNIT 2: LEARNING ALGEBRA THROUGH PATTERNS AND SEQUENCES.....50

Chapter 3: Introduction to Patterns **50**

3.1.   Four Repeating Patterns.......................................53

3.2.   Predicting with Patterns..55

3.3.   Number Array 58

3.4.   Additional Problems 59

3.5.   Pedagogical Explorations.......................................60

3.6.   Summary...61

Chapter 4: Growing Patterns **63**

4.1.   Tile Patios 67

4.2.   Multiple Ways of Seeing 68

4.3.   Rows and Columns 70

4.4.   Toothpick Patterns 71

4.5.   More Tile Patterns...74

4.6.   Matching Rules to Patterns 77

4.7.   Pattern Block Patterns...79

4.8.   Additional Problems 81

4.9.   Pedagogical Explorations......................................85

4.10.   Summary...89

Chapter 5: Sequences **91**

5.1.   Skip Counting 96

5.2.   Describe the Rule 98

5.3.   Arithmetic and Geometric Sequences 101

5.4.   Honeybees 102

5.5.   Additional Problems 104

5.6.   Pedagogical Explorations 105

5.7.   Summary 106

UNIT 3: LEARNING ALGEBRA THROUGH FUNCTIONS AND MODELING......107

Chapter 6: Representing Functional Relationships 107

6.1.   Function Machine 113

6.2.   Jumping Jacks and Crackers 119

6.3.   From Graphs to Situations 122

6.4.   From Situations to Graphs 130

6.5.   Additional Problems 132

6.6.   Pedagogical Explorations 133

6.7.   Summary 135

Chapter 7: Linear Functions 137

7.1.   Skate Rental 142

7.2.   Matching Representations of Linear Functions 144

7.3.   Fahrenheit and Celsius 147

7.4.   Identifying Linear Functions 148

7.5.   Marbles in a Glass of Water 151

7.6.   Additional Problems 153

7.7.   Pedagogical Explorations 156

7.8.   Summary 157

Table of Contents

Chapter 8: Quadratic Functions **158**

    8.1.   Areas of Rectangles with Perimeter of 24 164

    8.2.   Graphs and Equations of Quadratic Functions 166

    8.3.   Graphs, Tables, and Equations of Quadratic Functions.......169

    8.4.   Tables with a Non-Unit Change in x...............................173

    8.5.   Slam Dunk! 175

    8.6   Covering Jar Lids with Cereal 176

    8.7.   Additional Problems 178

    8.8.   Pedagogical Explorations...182

    8.9.   Summary...184

Chapter 9: Exponential Functions **186**

    9.1.   Paper Folding..192

    9.2.   Cuisenaire Rod Trains..194

    9.3.   Exponential Functions Represented in Graphs...................195

    9.4.   Percentage Growth Rates..197

    9.5.   More Growth Factors and Decay Factors 199

    9.6.   Approximating Growth Factors......................................201

    9.7.   Disappearing Ms 203

    9.8.   Sorting Functions...205

    9.9.   Additional Problems 211

    9.10.   Pedagogical Explorations...213

    9.11.   Summary...214

UNIT 4: LEARNING ALGEBRA THROUGH GENERALIZATION AND PROOF.....216

Chapter 10: Properties of Numbers and Operations..216

    10.1.   Which Does Not Belong? 222

    10.2.   Building Rectangles with Algebra Tiles...224

    10.3.   Properties of Sets and Operations..228

    10.4.   Additional Problems 233

    10.5.   Pedagogical Explorations..235

    10.6.   Summary..237

Chapter 11: Algebraic Proof..239

    11.1.   Analyzing Children's Proofs..243

    11.2.   Department Store Discount..246

    11.3.   Changing Rectangles 247

    11.4.   Numerical Relationships..249

    11.5.   Sums of Consecutive Numbers..251

    11.6.   Additional Problems 254

    11.7.   Pedagogical Explorations..255

    11.8.   Summary..256

Algebra for Elementary and Middle School Teachers: An Inquiry Approach

Table of Contents

Preface... xviii

UNIT 1: LEARNING ALGEBRA THROUGH PROBLEM SOLVING 1

Chapter 1: Introduction to Problem Solving...1

Explore nonstandard problems with an emphasis on writing equations that use variables to describe mathematical relationships.

1.1.   Silver Coins..9

Use various strategies to solve a classic problem involving a king and his bag of silver coins.

1.2.   Crossing the River..11

Explore patterns in a situation involving children and adults who need to cross a river, and find a rule for describing the number of trips.

1.3.   Cutting Through Layers...13

Find a rule for describing the relationship among three variables. They use tables to compare this problem with Crossing the River.

1.4.   Bossy the Cow 15

Explore patterns in a situation involving a line of cows, and find a rule for describing the number of cows who get milked before Bossy.

1.5.   Painted Cubes..16

Analyze patterns in cubes that are painted on 0, 1, 2, or 3 sides, and find rules to describe the patterns.

1.6.   Chickens...17

Analyze three pictures involving three chickens to determine the weight of each chicken.

1.7.   Staircases...19

Find a rule to describe a staircase pattern.

1.8.   Counting Handshakes 20

Solve three variations of a classic problem that involves a relationship between two variables.

1.9.   Variables 21

Explore five different uses of variables that appear in school mathematics.

1.10   Additional Problems 24

1.11.   Pedagogical Explorations...26

1.12.   Summary 29

Chapter 2: Solving Equations **31**

Think about equations in new ways and examine various ways to solve equations.

2.1.   Relational Thinking 35

Use relational thinking to examine true/false number sentences.

2.2.   Using Relational Thinking to Solve Equations.............................37

Use relational thinking to solve equations.

2.3   Working Backwards to Solve Equations 38

Explore the connections between working backward to solve a problem and writing and solving a linear equation to solve the same problem.

2.4.   Operating with the Unknown..40

Compare solution processes to problems that cannot be solved by working backward but can be represented by a single equation.

2.5.   Farmer Brown 42

Compare various methods of solving a problem, some with and some without using a system of equations.

2.6.   Additional Problems 45

2.7.   Pedagogical Explorations...47

2.8.   Summary 48

UNIT 2: LEARNING ALGEBRA THROUGH PATTERNS AND SEQUENCES............**50**

Chapter 3: Introduction to Patterns..**50**

Investigate repeating patterns and use the Division Algorithm.

    3.1.   Four Repeating Patterns...53

Analyze similarities and differences among five repeating patterns.

    3.2.   Predicting with Patterns..55

Use the Division Algorithm to make predictions about repeating patterns.

    3.3.   Number Array...58

Solve a problem that involves repeating patterns in an array of numbers.

    3.4.   Additional Problems 59

    3.5.   Pedagogical Explorations...60

    3.6.   Summary...61

Chapter 4: Growing Patterns **63**

Explore a variety of growing patterns, and create both recursive and explicit expressions for describing pattern relationships.

    4.1.   Tile Patios 67

Use square tiles to extend growing patterns, make a table and describe connections between the patterns in the figures and the patterns in the table, find rules for building the nth figures, and compare techniques for counting the tiles and the resulting expressions.

    4.2.   Multiple Ways of Seeing 68

Explore multiple ways of seeing patterns. Explain why various expressions make sense as descriptions for a growing pattern.

    4.3.   Rows and Columns 70

Examine a growing toothpick pattern and find several ways to determine the number of toothpicks and express those as general formulas.

4.4.   Toothpick Patterns 71

Use two types of reasoning to explore growing toothpick patterns.

4.5.   More Tile Patterns...74

Use recursive and explicit reasoning to explore growing tile patterns. Use shading to highlight the two types of reasoning.

4.6.   Matching Rules to Patterns...77

Match growing tile patterns with the rules that describe them and construct growing tile patterns for given rules.

4.7.   Pattern Block Patterns..79

Explore the similarities and differences among several growing Pattern Block patterns.

4.8.   Additional Problems 81

4.9.   Pedagogical Explorations..85

4.10.   Summary..89

Chapter 5: Sequences **91**

Examine various types of sequences and describe them with recursive and explicit rules.

5.1.   Skip Counting 96

Explore patterns in skip-counting sequences.

5.2.   Describe the Rule..98

Explore arithmetic and geometric sequences.

5.3.   Arithmetic and Geometric Sequences................................101

Solve a problem involving arithmetic and geometric sequences.

5.4.   Honeybees 102

Explore the ancestry of honeybees and find a rule to describe the number of honeybees in a given generation.

5.5.   Additional Problems 104

5.6. Pedagogical Explorations..105

5.7. Summary...106

UNIT 3: LEARNING ALGEBRA THROUGH FUNCTIONS AND MODELING............**107**

Chapter 6: Representing Functional Relationships.......................................**107**

An introduction to functional relationships represented in tables, equations, and graphs.

6.1. Function Machine 113

Use a function machine to explore relationships between input values and output values.

6.2. Jumping Jacks and Crackers 119

Explore two real-world functional relationships by collecting data, recording the data in tables, and constructing graphs.

6.3. From Graphs to Situations 122

Interpret graphs and write stories to describe situations involving relationships between two variables.

6.4. From Situations to Graphs 130

Sketch graphs to represent situations involving two variables.

6.5. Additional Problems 132

6.6. Pedagogical Explorations..133

6.7. Summary...135

Chapter 7: Linear Functions...**137**

Explore linear relationships in real-world situations and examine the connections among tables, graphs, and equations.

7.1. Skate Rental 142

Use multiple representations to explore a linear relationship between two variables.

7.2. Matching Representations of Linear Functions 144

Match tables, graphs, and equations of linear functions.

7.3.   Fahrenheit and Celsius...147

Use the freezing points and boiling points of water to find a linear equation showing the relationship between the two temperature scales.

7.4.   Identifying Linear Functions...148

Identify linear functions in graphs, tables, equations, and real-world situations.

7.5.   Marbles in a Glass of Water..151

Explore the relationship between the number of marbles submerged in a glass of water and the height of the water in the glass and find a linear function to model the relationship.

7.6.   Additional Problems 153

7.7.   Pedagogical Explorations..156

7.8.   Summary 157

Chapter 8: Quadratic Functions **158**

Explore quadratic relationships in real-world situations and examine the connections among tables, graphs, and equations.

8.1.   Areas of Rectangles with Perimeter of 24 164

Explore the relationship between the base and area of rectangles with a fixed perimeter and represent the relationship using a table, a graph, and an equation.

8.2.   Graphs and Equations of Quadratic Functions 166

Use a graphing utility to examine connections between graphs and equations of quadratic functions.

8.3.   Graphs, Tables, and Equations of Quadratic Functions................169

Explore connections among graphs, tables, and equations of various quadratic functions.

8.4.   Tables with a Non-Unit Change in *x*...173

Explore how the table associated with a quadratic function changes when the values of x are not consecutive.

8.5   Slam Dunk! 175

Examine a table, verify that it represents a quadratic function, predict features of the graph, and find the equation.

8.6   Covering Jar Lids with Cereal 176

Explore the relationship between the diameter of a jar lid and the number of cereal pieces required to cover the bottom of the lid and find a quadratic function to model the relationship.

8.7.   Additional Problems 178

8.8.   Pedagogical Explorations...182

8.9.   Summary 184

Chapter 9: Exponential Functions **186**

Explore exponential relationships in real-world situations and examine the connections among tables, graphs, and equations.

9.1.   Paper Folding..192

Fold paper and explore relationships between the number of folds and the number of resulting regions or the size of the resulting regions.

9.2.   Cuisenaire Rod Trains..194

Use Cuisenaire rods to build as many trains as possible with a given length and find an equation to model the relationship between the length of the train and the number of different trains.

9.3.   Exponential Functions Represented in Graphs.............................195

Use a graphing utility to explore how the equations of exponential functions are related to their graphs.

9.4.   Percentage Growth Rates...197

Examine the relationship between growth factors and growth rates.

9.5.   More Growth Factors and Decay Factors.....................................199

Explore functions represented in tables to find the growth and decay factors when the independent variables are measured in increments other than 1.

9.6. Approximating Growth Factors 201

Approximate the growth factor for a set of real-world data in which the independent variable is measured in increments other than 1.

9.7. Disappearing Ms 203

Examine the pattern of disappearing Ms in a collection of M&Ms that is repeatedly tossed in a set of trials and find an exponential function to model the relationship between the trial number and the number of remaining M&Ms with an M showing.

9.8. Sorting Functions 205

Engage in a sorting activity designed to focus attention on different ways of categorizing functions and their representations.

9.9. Additional Problems 211

9.10. Pedagogical Explorations..212

9.11. Summary 214

UNIT 4: LEARNING ALGEBRA THROUGH GENERALIZATION AND PROOF 216

Chapter 10: Properties of Numbers and Operations **216**

Explore properties of numbers and operations. Express generalizations using words and algebraic symbols.

10.1. Which Does Not Belong? 222

Use words and symbols to describe patterns in numbers and operations.

10.2. Building Rectangles with Algebra Tiles..224

Use algebra tiles to build rectangles and write equations to relate the length and width of the rectangles to the area.

10.3. Properties of Sets and Operations...228

Make conjectures about binary operations defined on specific sets of numbers or objects.

10.4. Additional Problems 233

10.5. Pedagogical Explorations..235

10.6. Summary...237

Chapter 11: Algebraic Proof...**239**

Use algebra to express mathematical relationships and justify mathematical reasoning.

11.1. Analyzing Children's Proofs...243

Teachers analyze and evaluate children's proofs of the following conjecture: When you add any two even numbers, your answer is always even.

11.2. Department Store Discount...246

Explore the relationship between a discount and sales tax, make a conjecture, and write an algebraic proof.

11.3. Changing Rectangles 247

Explore relationships between the area and perimeter of various rectangles, make conjectures using words and algebra, and write algebraic proofs.

11.4. Numerical Relationships..249

Explore numerical relationships in fractions and three-digit numbers, make conjectures using words and algebra, and write algebraic proofs.

11.5. Sums of Consecutive Numbers..251

Explore sums of consecutive numbers, make conjectures about particular numbers, devise shortcuts for writing numbers as the sum of two or more consecutive numbers, and write algebraic proofs.

11.6. Additional Problems 254

11.7. Pedagogical Explorations..255

11.8. Summary...256

PREFACE

Algebra for Elementary and Middle School Teachers: An Inquiry Approach is designed for use in college classrooms with an inquiry approach to mathematics teaching and learning. This textbook provides a collection of explorations designed to engage teachers in doing mathematics. The ensuing discussions will help teachers make sense of the mathematics they are doing. Used as intended, this textbook will support the creation of a mathematical community of inquiry that encourages the development of algebraic reasoning in elementary and middle school classrooms.

This textbook responds to the call from the National Council of Teachers of Mathematics (NCTM) to implement a vision of algebra instruction that begins in the early elementary grades and focuses on algebraic reasoning through the grades. According to NCTM, understanding of algebraic concepts and procedures develops as students explore patterns, functions, variables, equality, and rate of change in the context of meaningful problem situations. In these explorations, students engage in the essential mathematical processes of problem solving, communication, reasoning and proof, connections, and representation (NCTM, 2000). This powerful image of algebra instruction poses a huge challenge for teachers who lack similar experiences in their own education.

When asked "What is algebra?" preservice teachers typically reply "Using variables, numbers, and operations in order to find an unknown number." This response is not wrong, but it represents a narrow view of algebra. It reflects the traditional mathematical experiences of most preservice teachers who first encountered algebra in middle school or high school where they learned to think of algebra as primarily rules and procedures and symbolic manipulations. Such a limited view of algebra has little appeal for students, though, as they fail to recognize its relevance to their lives. This is unfortunate because algebra is a powerful means of representing complex ideas and is considered an essential course for students who aspire to many satisfying and lucrative careers (Kaput, 1999) as well as students who wish to claim full rights of citizenship (Moses & Cobb, 2001). What can be done then, to change students' views of algebra?

Kaput (1999) indicated that the road to long-term algebra reform begins with elementary school teachers and current reform efforts already under way. The authors of this text believe that elementary and middle school teachers need meaningful algebraic experiences that will develop their own conceptual understanding and broaden their vision of algebra so that they can effectively promote the algebraic reasoning of their students. Moses (1997) observed that the content of algebra is being transformed from a discipline involving the manipulation of symbols to a way of seeing and expressing relationships, "a way of generalizing the kinds of patterns that are part of everyday activities" (p. 246). Appreciation of this aspect of algebra cannot be delivered to students or teachers in an instant, but must be cultivated over time in the context of appropriate tasks and activities. Teachers need ample opportunities to examine and extend their own understanding of important algebraic questions such as "What is a mathematical generalization?" and "How is the rate of change of a function represented in a table, a graph, and an equation?" By immersing teachers in questions like these we provide opportunities for teachers to develop knowledge and confidence so that they can lead classrooms in which algebraic reasoning can thrive. These considerations led to three principles that guided the design of this book.

Three Guiding Principles

Principle One. The first principle is that elementary and middle school teachers need a broad view of algebra that goes beyond memorizing rules and procedures and solving equations. Recommendations from various professional organizations (CBMS, 2001; MAA, 1991; NCTM, 1991) have outlined the algebraic content appropriate for teachers. This content includes investigating patterns, representing problem situations with variables, analyzing functional relationships, and investigating algebraic structure.

To incorporate this wider range of mathematical content, we have organized the content into four approaches adapted from Bednarz, Kieran, and Lee (1996). In the *Problem Solving* unit, teachers explore nonstandard problems with an emphasis on writing equations that use variables to describe mathematical relationships. They also explore various ways to solve equations. In the *Patterns and Sequences* unit, teachers investigate repeating patterns, growing patterns, and sequences that require them to identify the constant aspects of mathematical situations and describe the patterns of change. In the *Functions and Modeling* unit, teachers explore a variety of dependence relationships in mathematical and real-life situations and examine the connections among multiple representations of these relationships. Finally, in the *Generalization and Proof* unit, teachers examine the structure of mathematics, using words and symbols to express characteristics of numbers and operations that are always true and supporting their conjectures with proof.

A wide variety of problem situations challenge teachers to make sense of the situations and develop their own strategies. Explorations are often presented in an open-ended format to engage teachers in constructing their own understanding of mathematical concepts. Teachers write problem-solving reports that encourage them to reflect on their work and clarify their thinking so that they can communicate their ideas succinctly. Mention of these essential mathematical processes leads to another important principle.

Principle Two. The second principle that guided the development of this book is that teachers need to appreciate that the five process standards delineated by NCTM (2000) outline what it means to do and understand mathematics. The process standards—problem solving, communication, reasoning and proof, connections, and representation—identify processes that should permeate all mathematical work, and indeed, all mathematical instruction. The problem solving process presents school mathematics as the exploration of problems for which no clear-cut method of solution is designated. As teachers work together, they learn to communicate their ideas clearly using correct mathematical terminology and symbols, extending and refining their thinking as they work. Reasoning represents the essence of mathematical thinking and proof is the distillation of that thinking. Building connections among mathematical concepts and between mathematics and other subjects and real-life contexts not only illustrates the relevance of mathematics, but also improves the likelihood that teachers will retain what they are learning. Lastly, representation in the form of symbols, manipulatives, graphs, and tables, supports and extends the other processes by providing a basis for exploring mathematical ideas and for communicating about what is revealed. *Algebra for Elementary and Middle School Teachers: An Inquiry Approach* is designed to provide teachers with extensive experience with these processes so that they are comfortable with them themselves and prepared to incorporate them into their own teaching, which leads to our third principle.

Principle Three. The third principle that guided the development of this book is that teachers need to link the algebra they know to the algebra of elementary and middle school mathematics. Not only do teachers need their own broad and deep understanding of algebra in all its forms, but they also need a clear picture of how these mathematical ideas can be meaningfully interpreted in elementary and middle school mathematics. To help teachers build this understanding, we begin each chapter with a discussion of how the current topic is embodied at the elementary and middle school level and we include reproductions of actual pages of related activities from elementary and middle school textbooks. This helps teachers see what the mathematics "looks like" at the earlier levels. To further extend teachers' images of algebra at the early levels, we end each chapter with Pedagogical Explorations that provide additional opportunities for teachers to consider the nature of children's algebraic thinking and practices that promote it.

These three principles constitute an approach to preparing teachers to promote algebraic reasoning in elementary and middle classrooms that broadens their vision of algebra, illustrates how the NCTM standards can strengthen mathematics instruction, and that provides teachers with a vision of how they can promote algebraic reasoning in their own classrooms. We hope that the activities described here will improve teachers' preparation to teach the ideas of algebra, and consequently, improve the education of our children.

Features of this Book

NCTM Process Standards

The NCTM process standards, woven throughout this book, describe what it means to do and know mathematics. The first unit in this book emphasizes a *problem-solving* approach to algebra, incorporating a series of open-ended problems that encourage teachers to develop meaningful strategies. Later chapters also include rich problems that relate to other approaches to algebra. Discussion prompts and reflection questions encourage oral and written *communication*, providing opportunities for teachers to organize and solidify their thinking. These opportunities to communicate show that *reasoning* is valued, and the fourth unit, Generalization and Proof, explores algebraic *proof*. Prompts for reflections frequently ask teachers to make *connections* among problems and concepts. Pedagogical explorations and examples in the text highlight connections between the mathematics the teachers are studying and the mathematics in elementary and middle school textbooks. Finally, teachers are frequently encouraged to represent their ideas with mathematical symbols, and the third unit, Functions and

Modeling, particularly explores multiple *representations* of functional relationships. We believe that these five processes represent powerful mathematics.

Links to Elementary and Middle School Curriculum

Chapters frequently include references to NCTM curriculum standards for elementary and middle school mathematics and pages from elementary and middle school textbooks that illustrate how ideas associated with the chapters are presented at earlier levels. These examples confirm that the topics in this book are relevant to elementary and middle school teachers, and help teachers refine their images of the nature of algebra in the early and middle grades. It's our intention that familiarity with algebra as it is presented in elementary and middle school will help teachers recognize and capitalize on opportunities to promote algebraic reasoning.

Explorations

Explorations in the form of problems and investigations are the critical essence of this book. The explorations provide opportunities for teachers to engage in mathematical concepts *before* discussing formal terminology and techniques. These activities follow a three-phased format—Explore, Discuss, and Reflect. **Explore** denotes problem-solving activity or guided exploration. It is expected that a substantial portion of class time will be used for teachers to work in groups to solve problems and complete investigations. **Discuss** indicates interactive class discussion and some explanation designed to emphasize critical points. It is suggested that Discuss sections form the basis for class discussions. The **Reflect** phase incorporates either a problem-solving report or a set of questions to guide written reflection. This provides opportunities for teachers to organize their thinking in writing and develop ownership for the ideas. Problem-solving reports and reflections may be assigned as homework.

Additional Problems

Each chapter contains a section of Additional Problems, included to provide more opportunities for teachers to solidify concepts and experience them in other contexts. These may be assigned as homework or used to extend class discussion.

Pedagogical Explorations

Each chapter ends with Pedagogical Explorations included to further extend teachers' images of algebra in elementary and middle school. These often incorporate examples of students' thinking on the current topic, or excerpts of related research. Teachers may be asked to interpret students' thinking or devise appropriate instructional strategies to meet the needs of a situation. These activities help teachers develop more specific and personal visions of what they can do to promote algebraic reasoning in their own classrooms.

Chapter Summary

Each chapter contains a summary that includes **Terminology, Big Ideas**, and **References**. Definitions of essential **Terminology** and a summary of the **Big Ideas** of the chapter are also included here along with a list of **References**.

ACKNOWLEDGEMENTS

We are indebted to the efforts of mathematicians and mathematics educators who have conducted research on children's algebraic reasoning and created curriculum materials to develop elementary and middle school students' understanding of algebraic concepts. We hope our efforts bring some of this work to the attention of elementary and middle school teachers as they develop their own conceptual understanding of algebra.

The content of this book has been informed and improved by:
- The many students who piloted the materials and provided suggestions;
- Richard Bonacci and Kristin Burke, who provided much timely guidance and support throughout the development of the text;
- Jodi Novak, who checked the mathematics and made many important suggestions;
- Debbie Harding, who edited the copy and provided many helpful insights;
- Beth Dahlke, who provided encouragement and introduced us to the right people; and
- Beverly Hartter who made contributions to an early version of the text.

Welcome to Elementary and Middle School Teachers

This is not your ordinary algebra book! This book is for teachers—teachers who are preparing to promote algebraic reasoning in their elementary and middle school mathematics classrooms. The National Council of Teachers of Mathematics calls for a vision of algebra that incorporates important algebraic concepts such as patterns, functions, variables, equality, and rate of change beginning in the early grades. That's a tall order for teachers, especially if teachers' own experiences with algebra emphasize solving equations and manipulating symbols. This book can help you prepare to meet the challenge.

Algebra for Elementary and Middle School Teachers: An Inquiry Approach offers rich mathematical content enfolded in interesting problems and investigations. Teachers often work in groups, supporting each other as they construct deep and broad understandings of important algebraic concepts. Sample pages from elementary and middle school textbooks show teachers how algebraic concepts are presented in school books. Pedagogical explorations share examples of children's thinking about algebraic topics and provide opportunities to think about how to promote the development of elementary and middle school students' algebraic reasoning.

This textbook and this course offer you an opportunity to vastly increase your understanding of aspects of algebra that are highly relevant to elementary and middle school classrooms. With reasonable effort, you can be confident that you will leave this course much better prepared for the task that awaits you.

Notes to the Instructor

Inquiry Approach to Instruction

Preparing elementary and middle school teachers to effectively promote algebraic reasoning in their own classrooms is no small challenge! Our response to this challenge uses an inquiry approach to instruction that encourages teachers to construct their own understandings of algebraic exemplified as problem-solving, as patterns and sequences, as functions and modeling, and as generalization and proof. Discussion prompts focus attention on essential concepts, and written reflections encourage teachers to organize their thinking and strengthen communication skills.

Role of Cooperative Learning

The problems and investigations in this textbook are designed for exploration by groups of teachers. Group work promotes learning, develops communication skills, and supports on-going assessment. Cooperative learning provides structure and shared responsibility for group work, so that maximum benefits may be obtained.

Instructor's Resource

The online Instructor's Resource provides support for instructors who wish to help teachers develop the conceptual understanding, habits of mind, and confidence needed to successfully promote the algebraic reasoning of their students. The resource provides suggestions for organizing a class to promote the development of algebraic reasoning and to make the most of the problem-solving reports and other written reflections. Solutions and helpful tips are provided for problems and investigations.

We hope you enjoy teaching with this book, and we welcome your comments.

References

Bednarz, N., Kieran, C., & Lee, L. (Eds.). (1996). *Approaches to algebra: Perspectives for research and teaching.* Dordrecht: Kluwer.

Conference Board of Mathematical Sciences. (2001). The mathematical education of teachers: Part I. Washington, DC: Mathematical Association of America.

Kaput, J. (1999). Teaching and learning a new algebra. In E. Fennema & T. Romberg (Eds.), *Mathematics classrooms that promote understanding* (pp. 133-155). Mahwah, NJ: Lawrence Erlbaum.

Mathematical Association of America. (1991). *A call for change: Recommendations for the mathematical preparation of teachers of mathematics.* Washington, DC: MAA.

Moses, R. P., & Cobb, C. E. (2001). *Radical equations: Civil rights from Mississippi to the Algebra Project.* Boston: Beacon Press.

National Council of Teachers of Mathematics. (2000). *Principles and standards for school mathematics*. Reston, VA: NCTM.

National Council of Teachers of Mathematics. (1991). *Professional standards for teaching mathematics*. Reston, VA: NCTM.

UNIT ONE: LEARNING ALGEBRA THROUGH PROBLEM SOLVING

This unit contains:
Chapter 1: Introduction to Problem Solving
Chapter 2: Solving Equations

"Problem solving should be the central focus of the mathematics curriculum. As such, it is a primary tool of all mathematics instruction and an integral part of all mathematical activity. Problem solving is not a distinct topic but a process that should permeate the entire program and provide the context in which concepts and skills can be learned."
(National Council of Teachers of Mathematics, 1989, p. 23)

CHAPTER 1: INTRODUCTION TO PROBLEM SOLVING

The National Council of Teachers of Mathematics defines *problem solving* as, "engaging in a task for which the solution method is not known in advance" (NCTM, 2000, p. 52). Using this definition, not all mathematical activities involve problem solving. For example, using a set of rules to practice solving linear equations is *not* problem solving. Applying a memorized formula for determining the area of a rectangle is *not* problem solving, either. These are important mathematical activities, but they cannot be classified as problem solving because the solution methods are known in advance.

Problem solving in this textbook involves tackling problems for which specific strategies have not been taught. Readers examine the mathematical relationships in various situations, relating new discoveries to preexisting knowledge. They determine what strategies might be effective, adapting and refining as they proceed. Importantly, they reflect on the processes they use and articulate the meaning of their actions in discussions with classmates and their teacher. These problem-solving activities will thus lead readers to develop a solid ownership of the mathematics.

Problem solving is an important mathematical process, not only as a *goal* of learning mathematics but also as a *means* for learning mathematics (NCTM, 2000). In other words, mathematics is an important tool for problem solving, but problem solving is also an important tool for learning mathematics. It is possible to learn new mathematics by engaging in problem solving *before* learning the rules. Traditional mathematics instruction has emphasized problem solving as a goal for learning mathematics and not so much as a means for learning mathematics (Jacobs et al., 2006). Unfortunately, though, this view of learning mathematics through problem solving is not always reflected in mathematics classrooms (Jacobs et al., 2006).

A Shift from Traditional Methods of Mathematics Instruction

In many classrooms, mathematics instruction uses what may be called a show and tell approach. First, the teacher introduces a mathematical concept or skill. Then the teacher demonstrates how to solve example problems. Finally, the students practice solving similar problems on their own. Although this approach is commonly used, it is rarely successful in developing students' mathematical understanding. One difficulty with this approach is that it is teacher-centered rather than student-centered. Instead of encouraging students to develop their ideas, teachers show and tell their own ideas, leaving many students with the belief that mathematics is a static body of knowledge impossible to understand. Another difficulty with the show-and-tell approach is that students learn to expect teachers to show them the rules and then resist trying to solve problems for which solution methods have not been provided. This classroom culture fails to encourage students to persevere when the path to a solution is not obvious, so students miss the opportunity to *do* mathematics (NCTM, 2000).

We believe that effective mathematics instruction begins with students' *thinking* and that problem solving engages students in mathematical thinking. Students truly learn mathematics by solving problems and discussing solution strategies. In classrooms organized as communities of inquiry, students "pose their own questions, formulate conjectures, and assess the validity of various solutions" (Schifter, 1999). We designed this textbook to help provide opportunities for readers to develop strategies for solving *meaningful* problems set in contexts to help readers to make sense of mathematical relationships and symbols. We also provide opportunities for readers to discuss and reflect on mathematics and to construct solid mathematical knowledge.

Problem Solving in Elementary and Middle School

Well-chosen problems motivate students to build new mathematical knowledge as they work to solve the problems. Problems can be developed from the mathematics curriculum, from other content courses, and from situations in students' everyday lives. Problem solving need not be taught as a separate topic, but the strategies that students use can be highlighted and discussed to give students opportunities to add new problem-solving strategies to their personal strategy banks. Good problem-solving tasks encourage communication and reflection as students explain their thinking, justify their reasoning, and monitor the effectiveness of their strategies.

NCTM *Principles and Standards for School Mathematics*—Problem Solving (NCTM, 2000)

Instructional programs from prekindergarten through grade 12 should enable all students to—

- build new mathematical knowledge through problem solving;
- solve problems that arise in mathematics and in other contexts;
- apply and adapt a variety of appropriate strategies to solve problems;
- monitor and reflect on the process of mathematical problem solving. (p. 52)

Learning Algebra through Problem Solving in Elementary School

In the early elementary grades, children exercise their natural curiosity as they explore problems embedded in the mathematics content of their curriculum. Children can develop an understanding of the meaning of addition and subtraction and learn basic facts as they explore problems about everyday situations. The solution for a problem such as "How many feet do seven adults have?" seems obvious to older students, but provides a challenging problem for young children that can be solved with pictures or modeled with colorful manipulatives. When a problem is set in a meaningful context, very young students can successfully solve problems involving multiplication, division, fractions, and other more advanced functions.

As they create diagrams and model their solutions with manipulatives, elementary students begin to use symbols to represent their ideas. This representation of mathematical ideas with symbols is a fundamental aspect of algebra and leads to later work with variables. As they solve problems involving the basic mathematical operations, students investigate properties of the operations, and they begin to understand the structure of mathematics. Through problem solving, young children can lay the foundation on which they can build their knowledge and understanding of algebra.

NCTM *Principles and Standards for School Mathematics*—Algebra (NCTM, 2000)

In prekindergarten through grade 2 all students should—
  …
- use concrete, pictorial, and verbal representations to develop an understanding of invented and conventional symbolic notations;
- model situations that involve the addition and subtraction of whole numbers, using objects, pictures, and symbols;
  … (p. 90)

Good problem solving tasks in grades 3-5 continue to encourage reflection and communication about mathematical ideas and problem solving strategies. "They generally serve multiple purposes, such as challenging students to develop and apply strategies, introducing them to new concepts, and providing a context for using new skills" (NCTM, 2000, p. 183).

Students in grades 3-5 benefit from problem-solving tasks that encourage continuing exploration of properties such as commutativity, associativity, and distributivity of multiplication over addition. As they discover the wide applicability of these properties, they recognize the value of using variables to express general statements about relationships that are always true and thus increase their understanding of the structure of mathematics. Teachers of grades 3-5 whose students are investigating problems about patterns can help them understand that a pattern relationship expressed as an equation can be used to solve many problems. The appreciation of and ability to use variables and **formulate** equations will develop as students experience their usefulness in the context of engaging problem-solving tasks, but students need frequent opportunities to work on such tasks (NCTM, 2000).

NCTM *Principles and Standards for School Mathematics*—Algebra (NCTM, 2000)

In grades 3–5 all students should—
  …
- represent the idea of a variable as an unknown quantity using a letter or a symbol.
- express mathematical relationships using equations;

> - model problem situations with objects and use representations such as graphs, tables, and equations to draw conclusions;
>   ... (p. 158)

Learning Algebra through Problem Solving in Middle School

Problem solving affords middle school students opportunities to develop habits of mind such as planning effectively and monitoring their progress frequently. These habits not only help students become better problem solvers but also help them become better learners of mathematics. As they revisit their work in written reflections and class discussions, they solidify their understanding of the mathematics concepts. Problem solving with reflection encourages students to "use a variety of mathematical skills, develop a deeper insight into the structure of mathematics, and gain a disposition toward generalization" (NCTM, 2000, p. 261).

Carefully chosen problems can help middle school students develop an appreciation of the different uses of variables, which we will discuss in a later section. Middle school students' growing capacity for proportional reasoning is supported and extended by investigations of linear relationships. Students become more proficient with using symbolic algebra to capture the essence of a mathematical relationship. This ability to describe situations symbolically helps them recognize equivalent expressions and enriches their understanding of the structure of mathematics. Energized by their curiosity about the world outside their classroom, middle school students can investigate real world problems using a variety of technological tools to model situations with graphs, tables, and equations. Algebra provides both the necessary tools and a powerful way of thinking with which to tackle problems (NCTM, 2000).

> ### NCTM *Principles and Standards for School Mathematics*—Algebra (NCTM, 2000)
>
> **In grades 6–8 all students should—**
>
> ...
> - develop an initial conceptual understanding of different uses of variables;
>
> ...
> - use symbolic algebra to represent situations and to solve problems, especially those that involve linear relationships;
> - recognize and generate equivalent forms for simple algebraic expressions and solve linear equations;
> - model and solve contextualized problems using various representations, such as graphs, tables, and equations;
>   ... (p. 222)

Teachers Learning Algebra Through Problem Solving

Teachers who are skillful problem solvers themselves have a better chance of effectively helping their students to develop problem-solving abilities. The first chapter of this textbook helps you increase problem-solving proficiency as you explore various concepts and skills of algebra through problem solving. You will find a collection of complex mathematical tasks that require significant effort to solve. Many of the problems can be solved in a variety of ways, but all of them require some type of algebraic reasoning. We emphasize the writing of algebraic equations in this chapter.

We encourage you to first work individually and then in groups to solve these problems. Working individually will give you a chance to develop your own ideas and working in groups will give you the chance to verbalize your mathematical thinking and to hear the mathematical thinking and strategies of others. Subsequent class discussions led by your instructor will provide additional opportunities to share ideas and focus on important ideas.

The Problem-Solving Process

In his classic book on problem solving, George Polya (1945) outlined a four-phase process for solving problems. This model may be used flexibly; the phases can be practiced out of order and adapted to suit the needs of particular problem solvers.

1. Understanding the problem. Read the problem carefully, and ask various group members to discuss their interpretations. What is involved in the situation? What are you trying to find? What questions are you trying to answer? What do you already know? To gain a better understanding of the problem, you may want to restate the problem in your own words.

2. Devising a plan. This is usually the most challenging phase of the problem-solving process. The following list of problem-solving strategies should be helpful. Each problem may require the use of one or more of these strategies.

Problem-Solving Strategies

- Make a model
- Act it out
- Choose an operation
- Write an algebraic equation
- Draw a picture or diagram
- Guess-check-revise
- Simplify the problem
- Make a list
- Look for a pattern
- Make a table
- Use a specific case
- Work backward
- Use logical reasoning
- Think of a related problem

3. Carrying out the plan. As you implement your strategies, keep a written record of your work. You may need to retrace your steps. If you become stuck, you may have to revise your plan.

4. Looking back. When you find a solution, verify your answer by returning to the original problem. Is your answer reasonable? Does the answer fit the situation? Can you generalize or extend your findings? If your solution involves variables, can you state what each variable represents? Can you explain any algebraic expressions or equations that you wrote? Are there any alternate solutions?

Communication and Reflection

Communication is an essential part of learning mathematics through problem solving. Through oral and written communication, mathematical ideas become objects of reflection, which the learner can then analyze and describe. Conversations in which problems are explored from multiple perspectives can help learners sharpen their thinking and make connections. Writing about mathematical problems can help learners reflect on their work and clarify their thoughts about the ideas in the problems. "Students who have opportunities, encouragement, and support for speaking, writing, reading, and listening in mathematics classes reap dual benefits: they communicate to learn mathematics, and they learn to communicate mathematically" (NCTM, 2000, p. 60).

We recommend that at the end of each problem-solving session, each reader should complete an individual problem-solving report. This report should reflect both individual and group work. A suggested framework for problem-solving reports, adapted from Tsuruda (1994), appears below.

Framework for Problem-Solving Reports

For each problem, <u>label your paper with the title of the problem</u>, and provide the following:

I.   PROBLEM STATEMENT

Write a concise restatement of the problem in your own words. Provide enough detail so that someone reading your paper can understand what you were asked to do without referring to the original problem.

II.   SOLUTION STRATEGIES & ANSWERS

Present your solution in an organized format. Do *not* just turn in your scribbles or scratch work. Explain in detail, using complete sentences, what you did to solve the problem. Use pictures, diagrams, charts, or graphs where appropriate. If you used manipulatives to solve the problem, describe how you used them. Clearly state your answers to the questions posed in the problem, using complete sentences.

Identify and describe any patterns that you discovered in the problem. Include any graphs, tables, or diagrams that you used to solve the problem.

Provide a justification for your solution. That is, explain why your solution makes sense. If your solution strategies or answer(s) involve algebraic expressions or equations, explain how you derived these expressions or equations. Be sure to state what each variable represents.

III.   REFLECTION

Discuss what worked, what didn't work, and what you did when you got stuck. Did you get help from anyone? What kind of help? What relationships did you notice between the work you did for this problem and your work for other problems you have solved?

What did you learn from solving this problem? What mathematics did you find or learn in this problem? What did you learn about the process of problem solving? What did you learn that might help you be a better teacher of mathematics? What are you still working to understand better?

Goals of the Chapter

In this chapter, you will—

-• engage in problem solving as a means of exploring algebraic relationships,

• identify the role of pattern identification as a means of solving problems and understanding algebraic relationships,

- develop skills in writing equations to describe relationships between variables and writing equations where variables represent unknowns,

- connect algebraic expressions to problem situations,

- identify various uses of variables.

1.1. Silver Coins

When solving the following problem, pay attention to your thinking and to the strategies you are using.

Materials (optional): Cubes or some kind of counters

1) $\frac{x}{2} - 2$,   2) $\frac{x}{4} - 4$

EXPLORE

3) $\frac{x}{8} - 6$

One day a king left his castle with a bag of silver coins to wander his kingdom. To the first peasant he met, he gave one-half his coins plus two more. A little later, he met another peasant to whom he also gave half his coins plus two more. Walking on, he met a third peasant and again gave half his coins plus two more. Finally, the king went home with two coins left in his bag. How many coins did he have to begin with?

DISCUSS

$$x - \left(\frac{x}{2} - 2\right) - \left(\frac{x}{4} - 4\right) \left(\frac{x}{8} - 6\right) = 2$$

What strategies did you use to solve the Silver Coins problem? What strategies did your classmates use? Many students solve this problem by using a guess-check-revise strategy or by working backward. The structure of the story easily lends itself to those two types of strategies.

Focus on your own mathematical reasoning. If you used a guess-check-revise strategy, was your first guess correct? If not, what ideas helped you revise your guess? Was there anything special about the numbers you tried? What kinds of calculations did you make to check your guess? Did you notice a kind of rhythm, or pattern, developing in your calculations?

If you solved the problem by working backward, where did you start? And where did you end? What kinds of calculations did you make? Did you notice a kind of rhythm, or pattern, developing in your calculations? How would you describe this pattern in words?

By focusing attention on your mathematical thinking and processes, you are working toward *algebraic reasoning*, even though you may have not used any *algebraic symbols* to solve the problem.

An Algebraic Equation

Another strategy for solving the Silver Coins problem is to write an algebraic equation using a letter, or variable, to represent the starting number of coins. The equation is a symbolic way of representing the relationship between the starting number of coins (the input) and the number of coins left in the king's bag (the output).

If this was not the strategy you used, find someone in the class who did use this strategy or try writing an algebraic equation yourself. *Hint*: Let n equal the input, the number of starting coins.

How are the symbols in the equation related to the calculations that were made in the guess-check-revise solution or the work backward solution? Do you recognize a rhythm or pattern in the structure of the equation that is similar to the rhythm or pattern in the other two solutions?

If your goal is merely to find the answer to the problem, to determine the number of starting coins, then writing an algebraic equation is not necessarily the quickest strategy for accomplishing that goal. After all, first you have to write the equation, and then you have to solve the equation, both of which are fairly complicated processes for this problem!

In many of the remaining problems and investigations in this textbook, the goal will be to write equations to model various situations.

REFLECT

Write a problem-solving report. Refer to the Framework for Problem-Solving given earlier in this chapter. How and where did you use algebraic reasoning?

1.2. Crossing the River

The following problem is adapted from *MathScape: Seeing and Thinking Mathematically, Patterns in Numbers and Shapes* (Education Development Center, 1998).

Materials (optional): Cubes or other counters.

EXPLORE

Eight adults and two children need to cross a river. A boat is available that can hold one adult or one or two children (i.e., three possibilities: 1 adult in the boat, 1 child in the boat, or 2 children in the boat). Assume that every person can row the boat. How many one-way trips does it take for all of them to cross the river?

Can you describe how to work it out for 2 children and any number of adults? Write your rule as an equation. How does your rule work out for 2 children and 100 adults? What happens to the rule if there are different numbers of children? For example, what if there are 8 adults and 3 children? What if there are 8 adults and 4 children? Write a rule—an equation—for finding t, the number of trips across the river needed when a is the number of adults and c is the number of children.

DISCUSS

It is important to be able to recognize and explain the connections among various representations—words, pictures, tables, and equations—of mathematical ideas. Maybe you drew a picture or diagram to solve this problem. If so, how is your picture or diagram related to your rule? Is there a pattern in your picture? How is this reflected in your equation? Can you explain each part of your equation by referring to your picture? Perhaps you made a table. Are there patterns in your table? How are these patterns reflected in your equation? Compare the different equations written by you and your classmates. How do these different equations reflect different ways of looking at the problem situation?

Like the Silver Coins problem, the solution to the Crossing the River problem requires identification of a pattern. However, unlike the Silver Coins problem, the answer to the Crossing the River problem is not a particular number. Instead, the answer is a *rule* that expresses a generalization of the number of trips needed for specific numbers of adults and children—an equation. Writing equations is an especially important—and somewhat overlooked—aspect of algebra. An equation serves as a mathematical model of the problem situation. Writing an equation requires an ability (1) to recognize the structure of the problem situation and (2) to use mathematical symbols to express the structure.

Students often misuse the term "equation." Look back at the rule you wrote. Did you truly write an *equation*—a mathematical statement asserting the equality of two expressions? On the most basic level, does your mathematical statement contain an equal sign? If not, you wrote an *algebraic expression*—a combination of variables and other mathematical symbols—not an equation. For example, $x + 2$ is an algebraic expression whereas $x + 2 = 50$ is an equation. Similarly, "William and his dog" is a phrase, whereas "William and his 2-pound dog weigh 50 pounds together" is a sentence. Both the equation and the sentence make claims that allow us to draw conclusions. Our purpose for calling attention to the careful use of this mathematical terminology is not to be rigid but rather to acknowledge the importance of the concept of *equality* in the study of algebra. Later we will take a closer look at equality, but for now, be thoughtful with the word "equation."

One of the features that distinguish algebra from arithmetic is the use of letters. In arithmetic, letters often appear as *labels*. Some labels designate units of measurement. For example, "2 l" represents "2 liters," and "5 m" represents "5 meters." Other labels may occur more informally. For example, in a discussion about fruit, teachers or students may write "$5a + 3b$" as shorthand for "5 apples and 3 bananas," where a represents the word "apples" and b represents the word "bananas." Likewise, as you were working through this problem, did you perhaps write something like "$8a + 2c$" to represent "8 adults and 2 children?" If so, you were using the letters a and c as labels. If so, you were using the letters a and c as labels with a representing the *word* "adults" and c representing the *word* "child."

In algebra, letters are used as *variables*, symbols that represent values or quantities. Thus, a may represent the *number* of apples instead of the word "apples" and b may represent the *number* of bananas instead of the word "bananas." So if there are 5 apples and 3 bananas, then $a = 5$ and $b = 3$. The expression $a + b$ represents the sum of the *number* of apples and the *number* of bananas. In the Crossing the River problem, a represents the *number* of adults and c represents the *number* of children.

REFLECT

Write a problem-solving report.

1.3. Cutting Through the Layers

This problem is from the *Interactive Mathematics Program Year 1*, *Patterns* (Fendel, Resek, Alper, & Fraser, 1997).

Materials (optional): String and scissors

EXPLORE

Imagine a single piece of string that can be wound back and forth. In the illustration, the string is bent so that it has three "layers."

It is still one piece of string at this point. Imagine now that you take scissors and cut through the wound string, as indicated by the dotted line. The result will be four separate pieces of string, as shown in the next illustration.

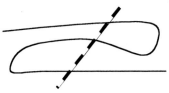

You can make more than one cut across the layers of string, creating more pieces. You can also start with more layers of bent string. Draw your own pictures of string with different numbers of layers and different numbers of cuts. Now suppose that the number of layers is l, the number of cuts is c, and the number of pieces is p. Find a rule, an equation, for describing the relationship between the number of layers, the number of cuts, and the number of pieces.

DISCUSS

Once again, it is important to be able to recognize and describe the connections between various representations of a problem. For Cutting Through the Layers, look again at the illustrations of the strings, and explain why the formula you have written makes sense.

This problem and the Crossing the River problem also provide an opportunity to examine some patterns in tables. Look back at the Crossing the River problem, and make a two-way table with the number of adults along the top and the number of children along the left-hand side. Record the corresponding numbers of trips in the cells of the table.

	Number of adults (*a*)							
Number of children (*c*)								

Problem Solving

Make a similar table for Cutting Through the Layers, with the number of layers along the top and the number of cuts along the left-hand side. For this table, record the corresponding number of pieces in the cells of the table.

	Number of Layers (l)							
Number of Cuts (c)								

Now compare and contrast the patterns you see in the two tables.

REFLECT

Write a problem-solving report. In your reflection, discuss how the tables for Crossing the River and Cutting Through the Layers are alike and how they are different. How are these similarities and differences reflected in the problems and in the subsequent equations?

1.4. Bossy the Cow

The following problem is adapted from *MathScape: Seeing and Thinking Mathematically, Patterns in Numbers and Shapes* (Education Development Center, 1998).

Materials (optional): Cubes or other counters.

EXPLORE

Bossy the cow is behind 50 other cows that are waiting to be milked. But being an impatient sort of cow, Bossy sneaks up the line two places every time the farmer takes a cow from the front to be milked. So, for example, while the first cow is being milked, Bossy moves ahead so that there are two cows behind her in line. If at some point it is possible for Bossy to move only one place, she does that instead of moving ahead two places.

How many cows get milked before Bossy? [Hint: Explore shorter lines of cows and use your results to discover a pattern that could help you solve the problem when there are 50 cows in front of Bossy.]

How many cows would get milked before Bossy if there were *n* cows in line? [Hint: Explore other numbers of cows in line and put the results in a table.] Formulate a rule using words.

Bossy gets more (and more) impatient! Explore how your rule changes if Bossy sneaks past 3 at a time, 4 at a time, or even 10 at a time. Describe how many cows, *c*, would get milked before Bossy if there are *n* cows in front of her and she sneaks past at most *k* cows at a time. Formulate a rule using words, and if possible, using an equation.

DISCUSS

Is it easier to describe the results of this problem using words or symbols? Why?

What do you need to describe the solution to this problem symbolically?

REFLECT

Write a problem-solving report. In your reflection, discuss how the structure or pattern for this problem is different from the three previous problems in this chapter. How did you discover this pattern or structure?

1.5. Painted Cubes

Use cubes to solve the following problem.

Materials: Cubes (plastic, wooden, or even sugar cubes).

EXPLORE

A large cube with edges of length 2 units is built from small unit cubes. If you paint the faces of this large cube and then break it back into small unit cubes, how many small unit cubes will be painted on exactly three faces? How many will be painted on exactly two faces? How many will be painted on exactly one face? How many will be unpainted on all faces? What is the total number of small unit cubes in the large cube?

What if the edge of the large cube has a length of 3 units? 50 units? n units?

DISCUSS

Like the Crossing the River problem, the goal in solving the Painted Cubes problem is to write equations that describe the relationships between various quantities. In the Painted Cubes problem, the quantities are (1) the length of the side of the large cube and (2) the number of small cubes with a given number of painted faces.

Describe how you arrived at your equations. Some readers may have constructed a table, examined patterns in the numbers, and then built their equations based on those patterns. Because of the geometric nature of this problem, though, it is also possible—and advisable—to look at the connections between the properties of the geometric model and the algebraic expressions that appear in the equations. In other words, can you demonstrate the meaning of your equations by using the cubes?

How are the concepts of surface area and volume related to the solution of this problem? How are the formulas for surface area and volume connected to the solution of the problem?

REFLECT

Write a problem-solving report. Be sure to describe the connections among various representations—equations, tables, and the geometric figures.

1.6. Chickens

This problem is from *Mathematics in Context, Comparing Quantities* (National Center for Research in Mathematical Sciences Education, & Freudenthal Institute, 1998). Try solving this problem alone. Later, after you have solved the problem, compare your solution strategies with those of your classmates.

EXPLORE

Three chickens weighed themselves in different groupings.

Also you can add all scales and divide by 2.

1. What should the scale read in the fourth picture?

2. Now you can find out how many kilograms each chicken weighs. Show how.

DISCUSS

Because the problem is presented in picture form, it is interesting to compare the various ways in which students use the pictures to solve the problem. Create a list of the methods your classmates used to solve this problem. How are these methods similar? How are they different? Describe the role of the pictures of the chickens in the various solution methods.

How is this problem different from previous problems in this chapter?

REFLECT

Write a problem-solving report. What did you learn from comparing the different solution methods described by your classmates?

1.7. Staircases

Use square tiles to solve the following problem.

Materials: Small square tiles.

EXPLORE

The figures below illustrate staircases with one step, two steps, and three steps.

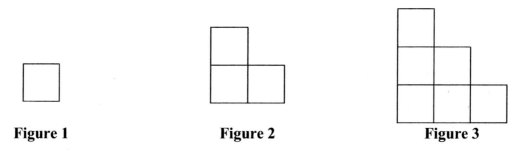

Figure 1   **Figure 2**   **Figure 3**

How many tiles are needed to make a staircase with 50 steps? 100 steps? *n* steps?

Try to find a way to predict the number of tiles needed for a given figure that does *not* depend on the number of tiles needed to build the previous figure.

DISCUSS

The relationship between the number of steps and the number of tiles can be *seen* in the tiles and *represented* in a rule, which is an algebraic equation. Different algebraic representations may arise from different ways of looking at the tiles. Compare your equation with those of your classmates. For each version of the equation, what connections can you make between the tiles and the symbolic expressions in the equation?

REFLECT

Write a problem-solving report. Be sure to describe the connections between the figure formed with the tiles and the symbolic expressions in your equation.

1.8. Counting Handshakes

In this problem, adapted from *Connected Mathematics: Frogs, Fleas, and Painted Cubes* (Lappan, Fey, Fitzgerald, Friel, & Phillips, 1998), you will explore three different versions of a situation.

EXPLORE

After a sporting event, the opposing teams often line up and shake hands. And to celebrate after their victory, members of the winning team may congratulate each other with a round of handshakes.

Case 1

Two teams with the same number of players shake hands with the opposing team members. How many handshakes will take place between two basketball teams with 10 players each? How many handshakes will take place between two soccer teams with 15 players each? Write an equation for the number of handshakes h between two teams with n players each.

Case 2

Two teams with different numbers of players shake hands with the opposing team members. How many handshakes will take place between a water polo team with 10 players and a water polo team with 9 players? How many handshakes will take place between a field hockey team with 15 players and a field hockey team with 14 players? Write an equation for number of handshakes h between a team with n players and a team with $n-1$ players.

Case 3

Members of the same team exchange handshakes. How many handshakes will take place among an academic quiz team with 4 members? How many handshakes will take place among a golf team with 12 members? Write an equation for the number of handshakes h that will take place among a team with n members.

DISCUSS

What kinds of strategies did you use to solve this problem? What kinds of representations did you use to record your thinking? In what ways is your equation for Case 3 different from your equations for Case 1 and Case 2? Why?

REFLECT

Write a problem-solving report. Why does it make a difference whether a team is shaking hands among themselves or with members of another team?

1.9. Variables

Variables are used in several different ways, depending on the context in which they are needed (Philipp, 1992; Usiskin, 1988). Here you explore different uses of variables that commonly appear in school mathematics.

EXPLORE

Consider the following six statements.

1. $I = p \times r \times t$ *Parameters*   *Vary in relationship*

2. $a \times b = b \times a$ (4) D.

3. $7 = 4x + 1$ (1) *Specific unknown*

4. $3x + 2y = 12$ (2) *Quantities that vary in relationship*

5. $y = ax^2 + bx + c$ (3) *Parameter*   /   *vary in relationship*

6. $A \in \{A,B,C,D\}$ (5) *Objects*

How does the use of letters differ in these statements? In particular, compare and contrast the use of the letters in statements 1 and 4, in statements 2 and 5, in statements 3 and 4, and in statements 2 and 6. What might the letters represent in each statement?

DISCUSS

Here are descriptions of five different uses of variables that commonly appear in school mathematics.

1. **Variables as specific unknowns**. In some problems, variables represent specific unknown values that do not change throughout the solution process. That is, the "variables" do not actually vary. In these situations, the goal is to find the correct value of one or more variables. In which of the above statements do the variables represent specific unknowns?

2. **Variables as quantities that vary in relationship**. In other problems, variables are used to represent values that vary in relationships to each other. That is, a change in one variable determines a change in another variable. In these situations, the values of the variables change throughout the solution process, and the goal is to find a way to describe the relationships among the values. In which of the above statements do the variables represent quantities that vary in relationship?

3. **Variables as parameters**. As we will discuss in Chapter 7, the relationship among the points on a line can be represented by an equation of the form $y = mx + b$. In this equation the variables x and y represent quantities that vary in relationship; the value of y changes

according to the value of x. The variables m and b are *parameters*; their values determine the particular relationship between x and y. That is, to identify a specific linear relationship, we need to know the particular values of m and b. For example, if $m = 3$ and $b = -5$, then we have the line $y = 3x - 5$. Likewise, if $m = \dfrac{1}{2}$ and $b = 6$, then we have the line $y = \dfrac{1}{2}x + 6$. These two lines have different values for the two parameters m and b. In which of the above statements do the variables represent parameters?

4. **Variables as generalized numbers**. In the number sentence, $a + b = b + a$, there are no specific values of a and b to be found. Nor is there a relationship between the values we are trying to describe. Instead, the letters stand for generalized numbers. That is, the statement is true no matter what values are substituted for the letters. You will explore more of this use of variables in later chapters. In which of the above statements do the variables represent generalized numbers?

5. **Variables as objects**. Sometimes variables do not represent numbers. Instead, the letters are objects in themselves and we are not concerned with finding numerical values them or with finding numerical relationships among them. In which of the above statements do the variables represent objects?

Common Misconceptions about Variables

Because the concept of variable is so complex, it is not surprising that students frequently have difficulties with the use of variables (Booth, 1988). As you work with children, you will probably encounter some common misconceptions.

First, it is important to recognize the distinction between letters used as labels and letters used as variables. The use of labels may actually lead students to develop misconceptions in algebra. For example, we know that there are 7 days in a week. So, consider the following problem.

Days of the Week: Let d represent the number of days, and w represent the number of weeks, which of the following equations correctly shows this relationship: $7d = w$ or $d = 7w$?

Many readers will choose the first equation. (Did you?) This seems to make sense if the letters "d" and "w" are being used as shorthand for the labels "days" and "weeks." But the variables d and w represent *quantities* of days and weeks, so let's replace the variables in the equation $d = 7w$ with specific numbers. If $w = 1$ then $d = 7$ because the number of days is 7 times the number of weeks. If $w = 2$ then $d = 14$, etc., so the correct equation must be $d = 7w$.

Another common misconception is that different variables must represent different values. For example, some students mistakenly believe that these two equations must have different solutions: $3 + m = 12$ and $3 + n = 12$. A similar misunderstanding is that $x + y + z$ can never represent the same thing as $x + p + z$.

When variables represent numbers, they can be combined with other numbers or variables through addition, subtraction, multiplication, division, etc. Operating on unknown values (variables), though, may be much more of a challenge for children who are accustomed to only operating on known values (numbers). One reason for this difficulty is that the focus of arithmetic is usually on finding numerical answers, whereas the focus of algebra is often on representing operations and their results with symbols. Thus students may feel uncomfortable accepting an expression like "$3n + 6$" as an answer to a problem. They may feel compelled to write "$9n$," "9," or "–2" instead. (Can you explain the misconception behind each of these wrong answers?)

The notation used for multiplication in algebra also presents a potential obstacle for student understanding. For instance, the algebraic expression, "ab," means "$a \times b$," but in arithmetic, the numerical expression, "$4\frac{1}{2}$," indicates addition, "$4 + \frac{1}{2}$." Furthermore, the juxtaposition of the variables has nothing to do with place value, so in algebra $ab = ba$ even though in arithmetic $35 \neq 53$.

It is important to keep in mind that, in general, misconceptions arise when students lack understanding of the concepts underlying mathematical symbols. In algebra, it is important for students to understand the meaning of variables, expressions, and equations. Students who have many opportunities to use variables to describe mathematical relationships are more likely to use variables effectively (Bishop, Otto, Lubinski, 2001). The introduction of variables through word problems provides students with important experience in connecting story situations to the algebraic syntax of formulas.

REFLECT

In this investigation you explored different uses of variables that commonly appear in school mathematics. These questions will help you summarize and extend what you learned.

1. Revisit the problems from this chapter. For each one, identify how variables are used in the problem.

2. Give the Days of the Week problem (from the Discuss section) to three people you know, and ask them to solve the problem and explain their reasoning. Record their responses.

Answer these questions and write a summary of what you learned from this investigation.

1.10. Additional Problems

1. **Silver coins revisited.** Here are some extensions to the Silver Coins problem.

    a) What if the king ended up with three coins in his bag? How many did he start with? What if he went home with four or five coins? Write a formula for the number of beginning coins if the king returned to the castle with k coins.

    b) Notice that the starting number of coins increases by 8 each time. Can you explain why there is an 8 in the formula?

    c) Change the king's gift to one-half his coins plus three more. Find the number of starting coins if the king ends with 2, 3, 4, or 5 coins. Write a formula to find the starting number of coins if the king ends with k coins.

    d) Change the king's gift to one-third of the coins plus two more. Find the starting number of coins if the king ends with 2, 3, 4, or 5 coins. Write a formula to find the starting number of coins if the king ends with k coins.

    e) How would the solution be different if the king gave coins to four peasants instead of three? What about five peasants? How is the number of peasants represented in your equation?

    These extensions to the Silver Coins problem were designed so that you may investigate various patterns. These patterns are then expressed as formulas. What connections do you observe between the patterns and the formulas? Explain the relationships between the formulas and the word problems.

2. **Diagonals of polygons**. A diagonal of a polygon is a line segment that connects two nonadjacent vertices. A triangle has no diagonals. A quadrilateral has two diagonals. How many diagonals are in a pentagon? How many are in a hexagon? Write an equation to represent the number of diagonals, d, in polygon with n sides.

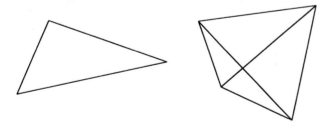

3. **Towers of Hanoi.** The classic game of the Towers of Hanoi begins with seven graduated discs on one of three pegs. The goal is to transfer all the discs from the peg to another peg. Only one disc may be moved at a time. A disc can be placed either on an empty peg or on top of a larger disc. Try to transfer all the discs using the smallest number of moves possible.

What is the minimum number of moves required if there are only four discs? What if there are seven discs? What is the minimum number of moves required if there are *n* discs?

Repetition is an important factor in both the Crossing the River and the Towers of Hanoi problems. How is this problem similar to Crossing the River? How is it different?

4. **Using variables.** Below are several brief descriptions of situations, followed by an algebraic representation of the situation. For each, identify what the variable(s) stand for and which of the five uses of variable described in 1.9 is being represented.

   a) For every three lemons used for lemonade, you need 1/2 cup of sugar.
   $$\frac{x}{6} = y$$

   b) Tom has 12 coins in nickels and quarters, for a total of $2.00 in change.
   $$25x + 5(12 - x) = 200$$

   c) When you square the sum of two numbers, you square both terms and add twice the product of the terms.
   $$(f + g)^2 = f^2 + g^2 + 2fg$$

   d) The length of a rectangle with area 28 cm^2 is 3 cm more than its width.
   $$\begin{cases} a \times b = 28 \\ a = b + 3 \end{cases}$$

   e) It doesn't matter how you pair up three integers when you add them.
   $$(x + y) + z = x + (y + z)$$

   f) The fine for a speeding violation is $35 plus $5 for each mile over the speed limit.
   $$T = 35 + 5(N - R)$$

1.11. Pedagogical Explorations

1. **Problem-solving interview**. Choose one of the problems from Chapter 1.

   a) Predict how an elementary or middle school student would solve the problem. What types of mistakes do you think a student might make?

   b) Actually pose the same problem to an elementary or middle school student. Ask questions to elicit as much information as you can about the student's reasoning.

   c) Using the information gathered in part b), begin with the student's name (use a pseudonym), age, and grade. Briefly describe the setting for the interview. Also note any general observations you made about the student's personality or behavior.

   d) Describe the student's work with the problem. Note the problem you posed, the questions you or the student asked, the strategies the student attempted, and the student's explanation of his or her answer. If the student is not completely successful, report any partial answers that he or she found.

   e) Based on observations of the student's work with this problem, what patterns do you see in his or her algebraic thinking? Are there recurrent strengths or struggles?

   f) Reflect on the notion of problem solving. Do you believe that the student you interviewed was engaged in problem solving as it was described in the introduction to this chapter? Explain why or why not. Was there evidence that the child was building new mathematical knowledge? Discuss.

   g) Reflect on the interview. Is there anything else you wish you had asked the student or anything you might do differently if you did the interview again? Describe what you learned about teaching and learning mathematics from conducting this interview

2. **Textbook analysis I**. Locate an elementary or middle school mathematics textbook. Using the categories of variables described in section 1.9, describe how the variables are used in the textbook. How many different categories for uses of variables can you find? Include examples. Do you think the way the book uses variables helps or confuses the students' understanding of algebra?

3. **Textbook analysis II**. Examine an elementary or middle school textbook to locate examples of activities that incorporate problem solving. Refer to a copy of the *Principles and Standards for School Mathematics* (NCTM, 2000) and read the sections on problem solving at the preK-2, grades 3-5, and grades 6-8 levels. Discuss ways in which the examples you found fit the meaning of problem solving as it is described in the *Principles and Standards for School Mathematics*. If you feel that the textbook you examined does not incorporate problem solving as described by the NCTM, give at least two examples that support your opinion.

4. **Two-Problem Comparison Report**. Select one of the problems from this chapter. Then locate an elementary or middle school textbook and select a problem that you believe incorporates mathematical concepts similar to the ones from this chapter. Make a photocopy of the textbook page and attach it to your paper, indicating the grade level of the textbook. Show your complete solutions to both problems. Write a paragraph in which you explain the mathematics involved in both problems and describe the common ideas that the two problems share.

5. **Classroom vignette**. The following vignette is adapted from Carpenter et al. (1999). First read the vignette to appreciate the children's reasoning. Then reread to focus on teacher actions that promote problem solving. Identify at least three of the teachers' comments or actions and explain how each one promotes problem solving and understanding in her classroom.

A first grade class was preparing for a field trip to a restaurant. As they compared prices of items on the menu, Ms. K, their teacher, posed the following problem:

> *At Bucky's Burger Barn a hamburger costs $3.65, and a steak sandwich costs $4.92. How much more does a steak sandwich cost than a hamburger?*

While the children worked, Ms. K. talked with individual children about their strategies to solve this problem. Here are some of the conversations:

Ms. K: Kurt, can you tell me what you are doing?

Kurt: I'm trying to find out how much more four dollars and ninety-two is than three dollars and sixty-five cents.

Ms. K: OK, how are you going to do that?

Kurt: Umm. I'd make three sixty-five.

Ms. K: OK, go ahead.
    [Kurt uses base-10 blocks to make 365. He puts out 3 hundred-flats, 6 ten-bars, and 5 unit cubes.]

Ms. K: Then what would you do?
    [Kurt uses the base-10 blocks to make 492, putting out 4 hundred-flats, 9 ten-bars, and 2 single units.]

Ms. K: OK, what are you going to do next?
    [Kurt does not respond.]

Ms. K: What are you trying to find?

Kurt: How much bigger four ninety-two is than three sixty-five.

Ms. K: Can what you did here [indicating the two sets of base-10 blocks Kurt has put out] help you?

Kurt: Ummm. I want to find out how much more there is here [pointing first to the set of 492] than here. [He points to the set of 365, then proceeds to match the two sets, pairing off the hundreds, tens, and ones. When there are not enough ones in the 492 group to go with the 5 ones in the 365 group, he trades a ten for 10 ones.] There's one twenty-seven more. That's $1.27.

Becky had solved the problem for herself.

Ms. K: Can you tell me what you did, Becky?

Becky: Well, I know that 5 more than 65 would be 70, and then it would be 20 more to 90, and then 2 more would be 92. So that's 5 and 20 and 2, and that's 27. Then I knew that I needed a dollar more to make it $4. So it's $1.27. [Becky has written in her math journal "65 + 5 + 20 + 2 = 92. 5 + 20 + 2 = 27. The extra dollar from the 4 makes it $1.27."]

Ms. K: That's good, Becky. Can you solve it another way?
           [Becky goes to work on a second solution.]

Kisha shared her solution with the entire class.

Kisha: [Puts 2 translucent plastic quarters, 4 dimes, and 2 pennies on the overhead projector] That's the 92 cents. [She takes away the two quarters.] That's 50. [She takes away one dime]. That's 60. [She takes away one of the dimes and starts to replace it with 10 pennies.]

Ms. K: Can you tell us what you are doing now?

Kisha: I can't take away the 5, so I need more pennies.

Ms. K: Why can you do that?

Kisha: Because a dime is the same as 10 pennies.

Ms. K: I see; you are trading a dime for 10 pennies so you can take away 5 pennies.

Kisha: Yeah. [She continues to count out 10 pennies, and then removes 5 pennies from the group of 12 pennies. She counts the pennies.] It's 27.

Ms. K: So the steak sandwich costs 27 cents more than the hamburger?

Kisha: [After a moment's pause] No! A dollar and 27.

Ms. K: OK. Where did the dollar come from?

Kisha: I knew that $4 was one more than $3.

Ms. K: Can someone tell me how Kisha's solution is like Kurt's?

1.12. Summary

Terminology

Equation: A mathematical statement asserting the equality of two expressions on either side of an equal sign.

Expression: A combination of variables and other mathematical symbols. An expression may or may not contain an equal sign.

Problem solving: Engaging in a task for which the solution method is not known in advance.

Big Ideas

Problem solving is an important mathematical process, not only as a *goal* of learning mathematics but also as a *means* for learning mathematics.

Five different uses of variables commonly appear in school mathematics: specific unknowns, quantities that vary in relationship, parameters, generalized numbers, and objects.

References

Bishop, J. W., Otto, A. D., & Lubinski, C. A. (2001). Promoting algebraic reasoning using students' thinking. *Mathematics Teaching in the Middle School, 6*, 508-514.

Booth, L. R. (1988). Children's difficulties in beginning algebra. In A. F. Coxford & A. P. Shulte (Eds.), *The ideas of algebra, K-12* (pp. 20-32). Reston, VA: National Council of Teachers of Mathematics.

Carpenter, T. P., Fennema, E., Fuson, K., Hiebert, J. Human, P., Murray, H., Olivier, A., & Wearne, D. (1999). Learning basic number concepts and skills as problem solving. In E. Fennema & T. Romberg (Eds.), *Mathematics classrooms that promote understanding* (pp. 45-61). Mahwah, NJ: Lawrence Erlbaum.

Education Development Center. (1998). *Patterns in Numbers and Shapes*. Mathscape: Seeing and Thinking Mathematically series. Mountain View, CA: Creative Publications.

Fendel, D., Resek, D., Alper, L., & Fraser, S. (1997). *Patterns*. Interactive mathematics Program series. Emeryville, CA: Key Curriculum Press.

Jacobs, J. K., Hiebert, J., Givvin, K. B., Hollingsworth, H., Garnier, H., & Wearne, D. (2006). Does eighth-grade mathematics teaching in the United States align with the NCTM standards? Results from the TIMSS 1995 and 1999 video studies. *Journal for Research in Mathematics Education, 37*, 5-32.

Lappan, G., Fey, J. T., Fitzgerald, W. M., Friel, S. N., & Phillips, E. D. (1998a). *Frogs, fleas, and painted cubes: Quadratic relationships.* Connected Mathematics series. Glenview, IL: Prentice Hall.

National Center for Research in Mathematical Sciences Education, & Freudenthal Institute. (1998). *Comparing quantities.* Mathematics in Context series. Chicago, Illinois: Encyclopaedia Britannica Educational Corporation.

National Council of Teachers of Mathematics. (1989). *Curriculum and evaluation standards for school mathematics.* Reston, VA: Author.

National Council of Teachers of Mathematics. (2000). *Principles and standards for school mathematics.* Reston, VA: Author.

Philipp, R. A. (1992). The many uses of algebraic variables. *Mathematics Teacher, 85*, 557-561.

Polya, G. (1945). *How to solve it.* Princeton, N.J.: Princeton University Press.

Schifter, D. (1999). Reasoning about operations: Early algebraic thinking in grades K-6. In L. V. Stiff & F. R. Curcio (Eds.), *Developing mathematical reasoning in grades K-12* (pp. 62-81). Reston, VA: National Council of Teachers of Mathematics.

Tsuruda, G. (1994). *Putting it together: Middle school math in transition.* Portsmouth, NH: Heinemann.

Usiskin, Z. (1988). Conceptions of school algebra and uses of variables. In A. F. Coxford & A. P. Shulte (Eds.), *The ideas of algebra, K-12* (pp. 8-19). Reston, VA: National Council of Teachers of Mathematics.

CHAPTER 2: SOLVING EQUATIONS

To *solve an equation* for a given variable means to find the value(s) of the variable that makes the equation a true statement. The process of solving various types of equations often involves a series of rules for symbolic manipulation. But many traditional algebra classes focus on the rules for symbolic manipulation without developing students' understanding of the mathematical relationships that the symbols represent.

Such manipulative skills are obviously important, but we have chosen to place the study of equations in the context of problem-solving situations. According to Lesh, Post, and Behr (1987), algebraic problem solving involves two important activities: (1) describing the problem and (2) calculating the solution. In Chapter 1 we focused on the first activity, describing problem situations by *writing* equations. Writing equations required a careful examination of the relationships among various quantities in problem situations and an ability to express those relationships using algebraic symbols. In this chapter we focus on calculating the solutions to problems by *solving* equations. We encourage readers to focus not merely on symbolic manipulation but on the relationships among quantities in the problem situations.

Instruction in elementary and middle schools should also focus on helping students understand the concepts underlying symbolic manipulation. In particular, two important ideas are associated with students successfully solving equations: an understanding of the equal sign (Knuth, Stephens, McNeil, & Alibali, 2006) and relational thinking (Falkner, Levi, & Carpenter, 1999), both of which we address in this chapter.

Common Misconceptions about Equality

Children often develop misconceptions about the meaning of the equal sign. To illustrate, the following question was posed to a large group of elementary children.

What number would you put in the box to make this number sentence true?
$$8 + 4 = \boxed{} + 5$$

Of the 145 sixth-grade children interviewed, each said that either 12 or 17 should go in the box (Falkner, Levi, & Carpenter, 1999). Further consideration reveals that putting 12 in the box would result in a statement that 12 equals 17. Putting 17 in the box would result in the statement that 12 equals 22. Why are children misled about this number sentence? One answer to this question is that many students have the misconception that the equals sign should be read as, "The answer is coming next."

Why do children develop this misconception about the equal sign? A possible explanation is that many elementary school children only see examples of number sentences such as the following, with two numbers and an operation to the left of the equal sign and the answer to the right:

$$2 + 3 = \qquad 10 - 7 = \qquad 6 \times 8 = \qquad 18 \div 3 =$$

They rarely see other types of number sentences such as the following, where the unknown is not isolated on the right side of the equal sign:

$$+ 3 = 7 \qquad = 13 - 9 \qquad 3 \times = 24 \qquad 15 \div = 20 \div 4$$

Children generally fail to think of equality as a *relation*; in other words, they fail to see the equal sign as a symbol that should be read, "Is the same as." Instead, they interpret the equal sign as a command to operate or compute. Rather than seeing the equal sign as a symbol of balance, they mistakenly see it as a symbol indicating direction from left to right. This misconception may arise from students' and sometime teachers' *inappropriate* use of the equal sign to connect a string of calculations:

$$20 + 40 = 60 + 5 = 65 + 3 = 68$$

As written, the statement incorrectly indicates that $60 = 65 = 68$. An accurate way to represent the same string of calculations would be with three separate equations:

$$20 + 40 = 60$$
$$60 + 5 = 65$$
$$65 + 3 = 68$$

Relational Thinking

Children whose mathematical experiences have been limited to carrying out procedural steps, such as those used in standard algorithms for subtraction of multi-digit numbers or multiplication of fractions, to find answers are more likely to make errors than children who have had plenty of experiences examining relationships among quantities. It is possible for children to learn arithmetic in a way that fosters mathematical thinking. In particular, it is important for children to engage in *relational thinking*—the search for relationships between expressions to simplify calculations instead of merely carrying out the indicated calculations. For example, Robin, a first grader, used relational thinking to solve the open sentence: $18 + 27 = + 29$. She said, "Twenty-nine is two more than 27, so the number in the box has to be two less than 18 to make the two sides equal. So it's 16" (Carpenter, Franke, & Levi, 2003, p. 4). Robin demonstrated the kind of thinking that is found in a classroom where students are encouraged to engage in relational thinking to make sense of mathematical relationships and symbols.

Children can be encouraged to engage in relational thinking through the use of open number sentences, like the one in the previous paragraph, and true/false number sentences, like the ones shown below. For both types of problems, it is essential that children have the opportunity to explain their reasoning. In the following examples, Ms. F., a fourth-grade teacher, introduces true/false number sentences to her students. She has encouraged her students to think about how the changes in the numbers being added or subtracted are reflected in the answer to the calculation.

Ms. F.:   Is this number sentence true or false? $12 - 9 = 3$
Jamie: True.
Ms. F.:   How do you know this is true?
Jamie: Because 12 minus 10 is 2, and 9 is one less, so the answer has to be one more.
Ms. F: Did anybody figure it out a different way?

Students provide several different explanations for how they know that 12 – 9 is 3.

Ms. F: How about this one? 34 – 19 = 15
Celia: True, because 34 take away 10 is 24, and take away 9 more is like take away 4 more and then 5 more, so it's 15.
Carrie: I think it's true, too. I did 34 take away 20. That's 14, but we only had to take away 19, so it's one more, 15, and that's what it says.

Students provide several more explanations for how they know it's a true number sentence.

Ms. F: How about this one? 5 + 7 = 11
James: False. Five and 7 is 12, not 11.
Ms. F.:   OK, how about this one? 58 + 76 = 354
Sarah: That's false.
Ms. F.:   How did you get that so quickly? You didn't have time to figure out 58 plus 76.
Sarah: I didn't have to. Fifty-eight and 78 are both less than 100, so the answer has to be less than 200.

(Carpenter, Franke, & Levi, 2003, pp. 31-32). As a pedagogical tool, the use of true/false number sentences shifts the focus away from finding the numerical answer that is coming after the equal sign. Instead, students focus on the relationships between quantities on either side of the equal sign.

Teachers' Knowledge of Equations

It is important for elementary and middle school teachers to value inquiry into students' thinking about mathematical ideas. Teachers can get some insights into students' mathematical thinking by reading about common student difficulties or misconceptions. By doing so, teachers gain appreciation for the actual complexity of seemingly simple mathematical ideas and they gain insights on how to address these misconceptions when they occur in their classrooms. Teachers can also develop some appreciation for students' mathematical thinking by engaging in mathematical tasks in the same ways that thoughtful children might. The investigations in this chapter provide opportunities for teachers to think about equations in new ways and examine various ways to solve equations, sometimes as students might. These explorations will shed light on children's mathematical thinking and they will also help teachers develop flexibility in their own mathematical thinking.

Goals of the Chapter

In this chapter, you will—

- develop a relational understanding of equality,

- use relational thinking to solve equations,

- work backward to solve problem situations and equations,

- use arithmetic thinking and algebraic thinking to solve equations,

- describe connections between solving problems with equations and solving problems with pictures, charts, tables, and so forth.

2.1. Relational Thinking

In this investigation, adapted from Carpenter, Franke, and Levi (2003), you will examine number sentences that are designed to encourage children's relational thinking. The goal is to analyze the *relationships* among the numbers, not to compute the sums, differences, products, or quotients.

EXPLORE

Consider the following number sentences. Without calculating, determine whether each number sentence is true or false and explain your reasoning.

1. $53 + 86 = 51 + 88$ *True*

2. $65 + 41 = 68 + 44$ *False*

3. $95 - 52 = 93 - 54$ *False*

4. $76 - 37 = 78 - 39$ *True*

5. $53 \times 34 = 51 \times 36$ *False*

6. $48 \times 36 = 16 \times 72$ *False*

7. $48 \times 36 = 24 \times 72$ *True*

8. $16 \times 27 = 32 \times 54$ *False*

9. $42 \div 14 = 21 \div 7$ *True*

10. $24 \div 8 = 48 \div 4$ *False*

DISCUSS

Compare your reasoning about the above number sentences with the reasoning of your classmates. For each number sentence, describe how the two numbers on the left of the equal sign are different from the two numbers on the right. Next separate the sentences into those that are true and those that are false. For each of the false number sentences, change one of the numbers on the right side of the equal sign to make a true statement. How can the addends of an addition statement be changed to produce the same sum? How is altering the factors of a multiplication statement similar to altering the addends of an addition statement? How can the minuend (the number from which another is subtracted) and the subtrahend (the number that is subtracted) of a subtraction statement be altered to produce the same difference? How can the dividend (the number being divided) and the divisor (the number doing the dividing) of a division statement be altered to produce the same quotient? Is the relationship of parts of a division statement more closely related to a multiplication or subtraction statement?

Some people may actually visualize objects or pictures when they think about these true/false number sentences. What kinds of pictures might you draw to visualize the relationships? Share some examples with your classmates.

REFLECT

In this investigation you explored ways to alter addition, subtraction, multiplication, and division statements to create true number sentences. These questions will help you summarize what you learned.

1. For each unfinished number sentence below, write a brief description of at least one way you can change the expression that is given so that the new numbers you write on the right side of the equal sign will make a true number sentence. Then complete each number sentence using numbers that illustrate the relationship you have described.

    a) $75 + 43 =$ _____ + _____   b) $165 - 97 =$ _____ - _____

    c) $56 \times 15 =$ _____ × _____   d) $96 \div 16 =$ _____ ÷ _____

2. Create a true and a false numbers sentence for each operation—addition, subtraction, multiplication, and division—and draw a picture to illustrate the relationships in each number sentence.

Answer these questions and write a summary of what you learned from this investigation.

2.2. Using Relational Thinking to Solve Equations

In this investigation, adapted from Carpenter, Franke, and Levi (2003), you will explore further how relational thinking can be used to solve equations.

EXPLORE

Relational thinking can be used to solve equations as well as to determine whether or not they are true. Use relationships like those you identified in Section 2.1 to solve the following equations without calculating. For each equation, explain the relationship you used to solve the equation.

1. $143 + 572 = 149 +$

2. $24 \times 42 = 48 \times$

3. $\div 9 = 360 \div 45$

4. $- 172 = 275 - 182$

5. $845 - 720 = - 735$

6. $144 \times = 20 \times 288$

DISCUSS

Discuss your thinking processes for solving the equations. How do the techniques you used to solve these equations differ from "traditional" approaches to solving linear equations? How are they the same?

REFLECT

The following questions will help you summarize what you have learned about solving equations using relational thinking.

1. Write an equation with similar addends on both sides that could be solved using relational thinking. Describe how the of use relational thinking to solve your equation is different from a traditional approach.

2. Write an equation with similar factors on both sides that could be solved using relational thinking. Describe how the of use relational thinking to solve your equation is different from a traditional approach.

Answer these questions and write a summary of what you learned from this investigation.

Solving Equations

2.3. Working Backward to Solve Equations

In this investigation, you will explore the connections between working backward to solve a problem and writing and solving a linear equation to solve the same problem.

EXPLORE

Solve the following problem two different ways. First, work backward, recording all the steps you take. Second, write a linear equation and then solve it.

> **Gizmos.** The Gizmo electronic device was first sold in 2000. In 2001, the price was raised $8. In 2002, the price was lowered $14 because of lower demand. In 2003, a competing device was introduced and the price of the Gizmo was cut in half to $18. Find the original price of the Gizmo.

DISCUSS

Describe the relationship between the steps you took when working backward and your solution process for solving the equation you wrote. In the Silver Coins problem we observed that working backward and writing an equation could both be used to obtain a solution. Describe the relationship between the steps you took working backward for the Silver Coins problem with writing an equation for the same problem.

Each operation used in the working backward process "un-does" the last operation performed in the problem situation. Here, the last thing done to the price of the Gizmo was to cut it in half, so the first step in working backward is to double the $18. In Silver Coins, the last thing the Prince did was to give away two more coins, so the first step in working backward was to add two coins to the two the Prince returned home with.

In Section 1.9, we discussed five different uses for variables. Which of the five uses for variables are used in this investigation?

REFLECT

In this investigation, you explored the connections between working backward to solve a problem and writing and solving a linear equation to solve the same problem. Answer these questions to help you summarize and extend what you learned.

1. Explain how you can work backward to solve each of these equations for x.

    a) $\dfrac{1}{3}\left(\dfrac{1}{3}\left(\dfrac{1}{3}x+2\right)+2\right)+2=4$

    b) $\dfrac{2}{3}\left(4x+2\right)-5=7$

2. For the two equations above, write a word problem for which the equation would be appropriate.

Answer these questions and write a summary of what you learned from this investigation.

2.4. Operating with the Unknown

In this investigation, you will compare solution processes to a problem that cannot be solved by working backward but can be represented by a single equation.

EXPLORE

Find a solution for the problem below without writing an equation. Then solve the problem by writing and solving a single equation. (It is also possible to solve the problem using a system of equations, which we will discuss in the next section.)

> **Cell Phones**. Sal's Cells offers a phone package that charges a $20 monthly fee plus 5¢ per minute. Phones-to-Go charges 7¢ per minute, but only a $10 monthly fee. At how many minutes per month do the two plans cost the same?

DISCUSS

What approaches did you and others use to solve this problem? Was it easier to solve the problem with or without an equation?

Solving the equation for the Cell Phones problem is different from solving the equation for the Gizmo problem in the previous investigation. Some researchers make the distinction between *arithmetic thinking* and *algebraic thinking* (Stacey & MacGregor, 1999). Solving the equation for the Gizmo problem requires arithmetic thinking rather than algebraic thinking even though a variable appears in the equation. Arithmetic thinking involves operating on known values to find an unknown. Because the variable appears on only one side, the equation can be solved using logical reasoning and operating with numbers. The solution does not require a systematic procedure involving operations with unknowns.

Solving the equation for the cell phone problem, however, requires algebraic thinking, which requires operating with an unknown as if it were known. Algebraic thinking is cognitively more demanding (Filloy & Rojano, 1984), and it occurs when a variable appears on both sides of an equation. The systematic procedure for solving this type of equation is "do the same thing to both sides." The result is a chain of logically linked equations, with the last equation having the unknown by itself on one side of the equal sign (Stacey & MacGregor, 1999).

REFLECT

These questions will help you summarize and extend what you learned.

For problems 1-2, write two solutions for the following problem, (a) first using arithmetic and (b) then using algebra to write and solve an equation.

1. Renting a car from Alamo costs $100 per day and 20 cents per mile. How far can you drive if the most you can afford to pay is $240?

2. Renting a car from Alamo costs $100 per day and 20 cents per mile. Renting a car from Budget costs $120 per day and 15 cents per mile. For what distance is each company cheaper?

3. Although you used algebra to write and solve an equation in problems 1 and 2, only one of the solutions required *algebraic thinking*. Which solution required arithmetic thinking and which one required algebraic thinking? Explain.

4. What does it mean to operate with an unknown as if it were known?

Answer these questions and write a summary of what you learned from this investigation.

2.5. Farmer Brown

In this investigation, you will compare various methods of solving a problem, some using equations and some not.

EXPLORE

Solve the following problem in two different ways: (1) *without* writing equations and (2) *with* writing equations.

> **Farmer Brown**. Farmer Brown has 25 animals in the barnyard. Goats and chickens are the only animals Farmer Brown raises. Altogether there are 80 legs in the barnyard. How many goats and how many chickens does Farmer Brown have?

DISCUSS

Compare the various methods that you and your classmates used to solve this problem *without* writing equations. No matter what approach is used—guess, check and revise, make a table, draw a picture, etc.—two numeric relationships were used and/or verified to successfully solve the problem. What are those two relationships?

Now examine your methods for solving the problem by writing equations. How do the same numerical relationships appear in your equations?

How many equations did you write? What variables did you use? What do the variables represent? In Section 1.9, we discussed five uses of variables. Which of the five uses for variables are used in this problem? What techniques did you use to solve the equations?

In solving this problem, did you use a system of equations?

A *system of equations* is a set of two or more equations using the same variables. For example, here is a system of two equations relating two variables s and p:

$$\begin{cases} s - 4p = 0 \\ 0.5s + 12p = 56 \end{cases}$$

The solution to a system of equations is a collection of values for the variables that makes all the equations true at the same time. Traditional methods for solving systems of equations include substitution and elimination. The *substitution* method involves solving an equation for one variable and substituting instances of the variable in the other equation(s) with this expression to reduce the number of variables in the system. This process may be repeated until you are left with one equation using one variable. Here is a solution to our example using the substitution method:

> Step 1: Solve the first equation for s.
> $$s = 4p$$

Step 2: Substitute this new expression for s in the second equation.
$$0.5(4p) + 12p = 56$$

Step 3: Solve this equation for p.
$$2p + 12p = 56$$
$$14p = 56$$
$$p = \frac{56}{14} = 4$$

Step 4: Substitute this value of p in the first equation to find the value of s.
$$s = 4(4) = 16$$

Step 5: Check to be sure these values of p and s make both of the original equations true.
$$\begin{cases} 16 - 4(4) = 0 \\ 0.5(16) + 12(4) = 56 \end{cases}$$

The *elimination* method involves multiplying the terms of one or more equations by a constant, so that when corresponding terms of the equations are added together one variable is eliminated from the system. Here is a solution to the same example using the elimination method:

$$\begin{cases} s - 4p = 0 \\ 0.5s + 12p = 56 \end{cases}$$

Step 1: Multiply the first equation by 3.
$$3(s) - 3(4p) = 3(0)$$
The resulting system of equations is
$$\begin{cases} 3s - 12p = 0 \\ 0.5s + 12p = 56 \end{cases}$$

Step 2: Add together the corresponding terms of these two equations.
$$(3s + 0.5s) + (-12p + 12p) = (0 + 56)$$
After simplifying, the result is one equation and one variable. Notice that the terms involving the variable p have been eliminated.
$$3.5s = 56$$

Step 3: Solve this equation for s.
$$s = \frac{56}{3.5} = 16$$

Step 4: Replace this value of s in one of the original equations to find the value of p.

$$s - 4p = 0$$
$$16 - 4p = 0$$
$$16 = 4p$$
$$p = \frac{16}{4} = 4$$

Step 5: Check to be sure these values of p and s make both of the original equations true.

$$\begin{cases} 16 - 4(4) = 0 \\ 0.5(16) + 12(4) = 56 \end{cases}$$

REFLECT

In this investigation, you compared methods of solving a problem, some with and some without using a system of equations. These questions will help you summarize and extend what you learned:

1. How did your solution process without using equations use the numerical relationships that later appeared in the equations?

2. Describe other connections between your solution process without using equations and the methods used to write and solve a system of equations.

3. Solve the following problem using two different methods: (1) by drawing a picture, and (2) by writing and solving a system of equations.

    Bicycles and Tricycles: A bicycle store has many disassembled bicycles and tricycles. Altogether, there are 43 wheels and 17 frames. If all of the wheels are put on all of the frames, how many bicycles and how many tricycles will there be?

4. Which method—substitution or elimination—did you use to solve your system of equations? How did you decide which method to use?

Answer these questions and write a summary of what you learned from this investigation.

2.6. Additional Problems

1. **Relational thinking**. Use relational thinking to solve the following equations.

   a) $75 + 58 = 73 + 61 + x$
   b) $90 - 55 = 92 - 54 + t$
   c) $69 + 76 = 76 + 66 + w$
   d) $74 - 36 = 72 - 38 + s$
   e) $105 \times 20 = 21 \times 4 \times y$

2. **Compare two processes**. Solve the problem below both by working backward and by writing an equation. Compare the processes.

   Jordan and Kerry inherited a collection of paintings from their grandmother. As the older, Jordan first selected three paintings to keep. Kerry then took one-fourth the remaining paintings. The remaining six paintings were to be kept until Jordan and Kerry were older and then handed down to them. How many paintings did they inherit altogether?

3. **With and without using equations**. Solve the following problem with and without using equations and compare your processes. Be sure to define the variables you use.

   Chen had 12 coins, some nickels and some dimes. If the total value of the coins was 70¢, how many nickels and how many dimes did Chen have?

4. **Write word problems**. Write a word problem that would be appropriate for each of the following equations.

   a) $x - 12 = 40$

   b) $3x = 24$

   c) $3x + 13 = 4x + 4$

5. **System of equations**. Solve each of the following problems using two different methods: (1) *without* writing equations and (2) *with* writing a system of equations.

   a) Larry and Louise are siblings. Louise has twice as many brothers as she has sisters. Larry has the same number of brothers as sisters. How many boys and how many girls are in the family?

   b) At a flower shop, Betsy paid $33 for 3 roses and 9 tulips. Bert paid $48 for 12 roses and 8 tulips. Find the cost of one rose and find the cost of one tulip.

c) At a movie theater, tickets for two adults, two seniors, and two children cost $46. Tickets for one senior and two children cost $19.50. Tickets for one adult, one senior, and three children cost $36.00. What is the cost of each ticket?

6. **Systems of equations**. Solve each of the following systems of equations. Then write a word problem that would be appropriate for each system.

a) $\begin{cases} 4x + 3y = 96 \\ x + y = 27 \end{cases}$

b) $\begin{cases} x + y + z = 7.00 \\ 2x + 2y + z = 12.00 \\ 4x + 3y + 2z = 20.50 \end{cases}$

2.7. Pedagogical Explorations

1. **Textbook analysis**. Locate an elementary or middle school mathematics textbook.

   a) Reread the discussion of equality at the beginning of this chapter. Examine your elementary or middle school textbook to identify examples that show how students might be influenced to think that an equal sign indicates that an answer is coming next or that an equal sign identifies the relationship between two quantities. Include both kinds of examples if you can.

   b) Find an example of a problem or an activity in the textbook that promotes relational thinking. Explain how this activity would promote relational thinking. If you can't find a good example, describe the kinds of problems and activities that are typical for your text. Describe why these do not lend themselves to relational thinking.

2. **Equality, equations, and variables.** Locate a copy of the *Principles and Standards for School Mathematics* (NCTM, 2000), or find the electronic version on the NCTM website at www.nctm.org. Examine the sections on Algebra at the PreK-2, Grades 3-5, and Grades 6-8 levels. Describe the big ideas that NCTM recommends be developed for equality (or equations) and variables at each of these levels (exception: variables are not discussed at the PreK-2 level).

3. **Relational thinking interview.** Interview a student in grades 2-6. Ask the student to determine whether each number sentence from Section 2.1 is true or false and to explain his or her reasoning. No calculators allowed! Write an analysis of the interview that describes the reasoning the student used. Do you notice any general patterns of reasoning? Were some problems more difficult than others? Why?

4. **Posing effective questions.** Consider the following equations:

$$24 \times 7 = \underline{} \times 42$$
$$12 \times \underline{} = 168$$
$$\underline{} \times 56 = 6 \times 28$$
$$28 \times 6 = 84 \times \underline{}$$

   Assume that you chose these equations to help your students in grades 3 to 5 develop a richer understanding of the idea that an equation represents the equality of two quantities. Write at least 3 questions that would encourage students to think about this essential concept.

2.8. Summary

Terminology

Arithmetic thinking: Operating on known values to find an unknown.

Algebraic thinking: Operate with an unknown as if it were known.

Equation: A mathematical statement asserting the equality of two expressions on either side of an equal sign.

Relational thinking: The search for relationships between expressions to simplify calculations instead of merely carrying out the indicated calculations.

System of equations: A set of two or more equations using the same variables.

Big Ideas

An equation indicates that the quantities on either side of the equal sign have equal value. Misconceptions about the equal sign create obstacles to learning algebra.

Equations can be solved in a variety of ways—relational thinking, working backward, traditional methods of doing a sequence of operations to both sides. Some situations require a system of equations.

Solving some equations requires arithmetic thinking whereas others require algebraic thinking.

References

Carpenter, T. P., Franke, M. L, & Levi, L. (2003). *Thinking mathematically: Integrating arithmetic and algebra in elementary school.* Portsmouth, NH: Heinemann.

Crauder, B., Evans, B., & Noell, A. (1999). *Functions and change: A modeling alternative to college algebra* (preliminary edition). Boston: Houghton Mifflin.

Falkner, Karen P., Linda Levi, and Thomas P. Carpenter. (1999). Children's understanding of equality: A foundation for algebra. *Teaching Children Mathematics, 6,* 232-236.

Filloy, E., & Rojano, T. (1984). From an arithmetical to an algebraic thought. In J. M. Moser (Ed.), *Proceedings of the Sixth Annual Meeting of PME-NA* (pp. 51-56). Madison: University of Wisconsin.

Knuth, E. J., Stephens, A. C., McNeil, N. M., & Alibali, M. W. (2006). Does understanding the equal sign matter? Evidence from solving equations. *Journal for Research in Mathematics Education, 37*, 297-312.

Lesh, R., Post, T., & Behr, M. (1987). Dienes revisited: Multiple embodiments in computer environments. In I. Wirszup & R. Streit (Eds.), *Developments in school mathematics education around the world* (pp. 647-680). Reston, VA: National Council of Teachers of Mathematics.

Stacey, K., & MacGregor, M. (1999). Taking the algebraic thinking out of algebra. *Mathematics Education Research Journal, 11*, 25-38.

Unit Two LEARNING ALGEBRA THROUGH PATTERNS AND SEQUENCES

THIS UNIT CONTAINS:
Chapter 3: Introduction to Patterns
Chapter 4: Growing Patterns
Chapter 5: Sequences

"Patterns are everywhere. Children who are encouraged to look for patterns and to express them mathematically begin to understand how mathematics applies to the world in which they live."
--(National Council of Teachers of Mathematics [NCTM], 1989, p. 260)

CHAPTER 3: INTRODUCTION TO PATTERNS

Mathematics has been called the "science of patterns." Patterns are associated with repetition, which may be observed in real-world situations, geometric figures, numbers, symbols, and relationships among quantities. Patterns play a prominent role in algebra, especially when the notion of algebra is extended beyond the study of symbolic manipulation. According to Chambers (1994), algebraic thinking "embodies the construction and representation of patterns and regularities, deliberate generalization, and most important, active exploration and conjecture" (p. 85).

In the first unit of this textbook, the solutions to many of the problems required identification and description of patterns in numbers and relationships between quantities. This second unit is devoted to exploring patterns in symbols, geometric figures, numbers, and, again, relationships between quantities. The third unit focuses on functions as an extension of the study of patterns in relationships between quantities. And finally, the fourth unit focuses on generalization of patterns in numbers and operations and the notion of proof.

The *Principles and Standards for School Mathematics* (NCTM, 2000) repeatedly emphasizes recognition and extension of patterns in its discussions of algebra for prekindergarten through 12th-grade. The NCTM recommends that students engage in concrete activities in which they investigate patterns in shape and number, formulate verbal rules to describe these patterns, and then represent these rules symbolically. Work with patterns provides opportunities to experience the power of generalization in mathematics, as students discover that once a critical relationship is identified, it can be used to solve many problems about the pattern.

Exploring Patterns in Elementary School

As early as pre-Kindergarten children learn to extend and create patterns. Given an opportunity to explore diverse materials, young children use a variety of attributes to structure their pattern-making, including shape, size, orientation, color, and position. They create patterns using objects, colors, words, musical tones, and physical movements. Children link different forms of patterns by relating hand motions to songs and by coloring different shapes different colors on paper. Later they recognize that the same pattern sequence may be shown in different ways and they learn to translate patterns from one form to another--for example translating a red-blue-red-blue-red-blue plastic cube chain to writing R B R B R B on a sheet of paper. Children develop important reasoning skills when they make conjectures about patterns, for example when they predict the color of the tenth figure, and then verify their conjectures.

A *repeating pattern*, such as a chain of alternating red and blue plastic cubes, has a continuously recurring unit sequence (red, blue) within a longer sequence. The ability to identify the unit sequence and to express what is repeating lies at the heart of using patterns to solve problems. For example, in the Crossing the River problem in Chapter 1, you identified a sequence of steps that resulted in moving one adult across the river. Once this essential unit sequence was identified, it was possible to predict how many trips were needed to move a specified number of adults across the river, and eventually, to determine the number of trips needed to move any number of adults and children across the river. As children learn to distinguish the critical relationship within the larger sequence of a repeating pattern, they take first steps toward mathematical generalization.

Children also encounter *growing* patterns, where each element of the pattern is an extension of previous elements. The following is an example of a growing pattern.

| Figure 1 | Figure 2 | Figure 3 |

Geometric growing patterns can often be translated into number relationships, and thus be used to introduce ideas that lead to work with algebraic expressions and functions.

Numerical sequences form a special category of number patterns. Children consider different types of sequences, figure out ways to find the next number in a sequence, and later write a rule to determine any specified term in the sequence.

NCTM *Principles and Standards for School Mathematics*—Algebra (NCTM, 2000)

In prekindergarten through grade 2 all students should—

- recognize, describe, and extend patterns such as sequences of sounds and shapes or simple numeric patterns and translate from one representation to another;
- analyze how both repeating and growing patterns are generated;
  …
- describe quantitative change, such as a student's growing two inches in one year. (p. 90)

In grades 3–5 all students should—
- describe, extend, and make generalizations about geometric and numeric patterns;
- represent and analyze patterns and functions, using words, tables, and graphs;
  …
- investigate how a change in one variable relates to a change in a second variable. (p. 158)

Exploring Patterns in Middle School

The study of patterns in middle school focuses on the use of multiple representations for quantitative relationships. Students use tables, graphs, words, and symbolic expressions to represent and examine functions and patterns of change, working more frequently with algebraic symbols than elementary school students (NCTM, 2000). Middle school students should become increasingly adept at moving back and forth among representations as they relate symbolic expressions containing variables to verbal, tabular, and graphical representations of quantitative relationships.

The various representations allow students to examine patterns from numerous perspectives, as each representation may highlight different aspects of the pattern. For instance, a table may illustrate the regular increases in the numbers of two linear patterns, but the graphs of those patterns will contrast the rates at which the numbers increase. In middle school, students explore numerical and geometric patterns that relate to linear functions—those that involve a constant rate of change—as well as nonlinear functions. Middle school students' quest to make sense of the world around them feeds their natural appetite for increasingly complex patterns.

NCTM *Principles and Standards for School Mathematics*—Algebra (NCTM, 2000)

In grades 6–8 all students should—
- represent, analyze, and generalize a variety of patterns with tables, graphs, words, and, when possible, symbolic rules;
- relate and compare different forms of representation for a relationship;
  … (p. 222)

Teachers' Knowledge of Patterns

Elementary and middle school teachers can also develop algebraic reasoning through exploration of patterns. The problems and investigations in this chapter will introduce you to the notion of repeating patterns. You will analyze patterns and make predictions.

Goals of the Chapter

In this chapter, you will—

- make predictions about repeating patterns,

- use the division algorithm to analyze repeating patterns,

- use quotients and remainders to answer questions about repeating patterns.

3.1. Four Repeating Patterns

The following problems are all found in resources created for students in early elementary grades. They go beyond recognizing or continuing patterns, asking students to analyze repeating patterns and make predictions based on the relationships they see. In this investigation, you examine the similarities and differences among the four patterns.

Materials: Colored Pattern Blocks.

EXPLORE

1. Work through each of the following activities. As you work, think about the patterns, the questions you are asked, and the type of thinking they require.

   a) **Pattern Block Walls** (Hirschhorn, 2000, p.55)

   Can you figure out what Pattern Blocks you will need to make a wall with a pattern that repeats 10 times?

   - Look at the 5 pictures below. In each picture, a set of Pattern Blocks is repeated twice. Decide what the pattern is in each picture.

   - Work with a partner. Choose the pattern in one of the pictures to use in a Pattern Block wall. Use Pattern Blocks to copy what you see. Make your wall stand like a real wall.

   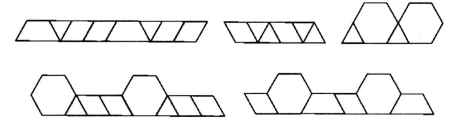

   - Continue building your wall, repeating the pattern 5 times.

   - Trace your work on a paper strip and color it in. Count and write down how many blocks of each kind you used, and how many blocks you used altogether.

   - Try to think of ways to know how many blocks of each kind and how many total blocks you will need to make the wall pattern repeat a total 10 times.

   - Now complete the wall and count the blocks to check whether your numbers were close.

   - Be ready to talk about what you did and what you found out.

   b) **What Color Would the Twentieth Block Be?** (Stewart, Walker, & Reak, 1995)

"Make this pattern with your Pattern Blocks: red, red, green, red, red, green. Suppose this pattern continued. What color would the twentieth block be? Make a recording. Write how you know what color the block would be" (p. 22).

c) **How many blocks will be blue?** (Stewart, Walker, & Reak, 1995)

"Make this pattern with your Pattern Blocks: red, green, blue, red, green, blue. Suppose there are 20 blocks in the pattern. How many blocks would be blue? Make a recording of your work. Write how you know what the number of blue blocks would be" (p. 34).

d) **How many green blocks will there be?** (Stewart, Walker, & Reak, 1995)

"Make this pattern using your Pattern Blocks: yellow, green, green, yellow, green, green. When there are 8 yellow blocks in the pattern, how many green blocks will there be? Make a recording. Explain how you figured out how many green blocks there will be" (p. 42).

2. What is alike about the patterns in parts a through d? What is different? What makes these patterns repeating patterns? How are the questions for part a and part d alike? How did the questions asked in parts b and c differ from those asked in parts a and d? What features of the patterns did you think about when you answered the questions?

DISCUSS

Discuss the various group responses with the class. In general, what types of questions are asked about repeating patterns? What mathematical concepts and skills are related to the types of questions asked about repeating patterns?

How many times does a sequence of blocks have to repeat in order to determine the pattern? What is the difference between recognizing a pattern and describing a pattern? How were you engaged in algebraic reasoning as you explored these repeating patterns?

REFLECT

In this investigation, you explored repeating patterns. These questions will help you summarize and extend what you learned.

1. Create a repeating pattern and write three questions that you could ask children to promote their algebraic reasoning.

2. Describe how your questions promote algebraic reasoning.

Answer these questions and write a summary of what you learned from this investigation.

3.2. Predicting with Patterns

In this investigation, you will use repeating patterns to make predictions.

Materials: Colored Pattern Blocks (optional)

EXPLORE

The following pattern questions build on the work you did in section 3.1. Notice that the questions asked about each pattern are similar to the questions asked about the patterns in section 3.1.

1. Make the following pattern block pattern: yellow, green, green, red, yellow, green, green, red.
   a) What color will the 287th block be? Explain how you arrived at your answer.
   b) How many of each color block will there be when there are 254 blocks altogether? Explain how you arrived at your answer.
   c) How many green blocks will you have used when you place the 35th yellow block in the pattern? Explain how you arrived at your answer.

2. Make the following pattern block pattern: green, blue, green, green, red, green, blue, green, green, red.
   a) What color will the 386th block be? Explain how you arrived at your answer.
   b) How many of each color block will there be when there are 739 blocks altogether? Explain how you arrived at your answer.
   c) If you have extended the pattern until you used exactly 56 green blocks, how many blocks total are there? Explain how you arrived at your answer.

DISCUSS

Share solutions with the class. Listen carefully to how your classmates arrived at their answers.

As you solved the problems, you probably noticed that each repeating pattern has a core that appears over and over. We call this core a *unit sequence*. What is the unit sequence for each of the above problems? How many times was the unit sequence repeated in each problem? How many pieces were left over?

In the yellow, green, green, red pattern, the unit sequence is four pieces long. When you were deciding what color the 287th block would be, you may have asked yourself, "How many complete groups of 4 can we make from 287?" and "How many are left over when we make all possible complete groups of 4 from 287?" These questions should remind us of the operation of division. When we divide 287 by 4, we report the number of groups that can be made as the *quotient* and the number of pieces left over after forming these groups as the *remainder*. Dividing 287 by 4, we see that the core repeats 71 times with 3 blocks left over. So the quotient is 71 and the remainder r is 3.

The Division Algorithm for Whole Numbers

An *algorithm* is a step-by-step procedure for accomplishing a task.
The procedure for determining the relationships among the values in a repeating pattern is formally stated as *The Division Algorithm for Whole Numbers*: For all whole numbers n and $d \neq 0$, where d is the length of the unit sequence, there exist two whole numbers q and r, with $0 \leq r < d$, such that $n = qd + r$. That is, when we divide n by the divisor d we get the quotient q and a remainder r. For example, the pattern below is 26 shapes long and the core consists of 4 blocks. If we assume that the pattern continues indefinitely and we wish to predict what a specific shape will be, we can use the division algorithm to determine how many times the core has been repeated and how many pieces are left over. Then we can count off the pattern against the remaining pieces to determine what the last piece is. For instance, if we wished to determine the 75th shape in the pattern below, then $n = 75$. Because the core is 4, that means $d = 4$. So we divide 75 by 4 to yield a quotient of 18, that is $q = 18$, and we get a remainder of 3, with $r = 3$. If the third shape in the unit sequence is a triangle, the 75th shape in the pattern would be a triangle.

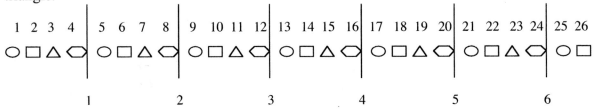

Explain the connection between the Division Algorithm and these three questions: What is the unit sequence? How many times is it repeated? What is the remainder? The Division Algorithm provides a general method for working with repeating patterns and a common language for communicating about them. Although most of the previous examples have involved patterns of geometric figures or colors, repeating patterns of other types such as patterns made with numbers or symbols can also be analyzed with the same three questions that were asked above.

REFLECT

In this investigation, you explored the use of the division algorithm in analyzing repeating patterns. These questions will help you summarize what you learned:

1. Create a repeating pattern of pattern block shapes, and write three questions about the pattern that are similar to the first three questions of each problem in the Explore section.

2. Using the Division Algorithm, write an equation using values for n, q, d, and r that could be used to answer each of your questions.

3. What information does the quotient tell you about the pattern?

4. What information does the remainder tell you about the pattern?

5. How can you decide whether to use the quotient or the remainder or both to answer a given question?

Answer these questions and write a summary of what you learned from this investigation.

3.3. Number Array

The number pattern in the following problem (adapted from Zazkis & Liljedahl, 2002) is not a conventional repeating pattern, but you may find it helpful to identify aspects of the array that repeat.

EXPLORE

$8K+1$

$+8$ $+6, +8$ $+4$ $+2, +6$ $+8$

Number Array

1	2	3	4	
	8	7	6	5
9	10	11	12	
	16	15	14	13
17	18	19	20	
	24	23	22	21
25	26	27	28	
	32	31	30	29
33	34	35	36	

1. Continue the pattern into the ninth row.

2. Suppose you continue it indefinitely. Do you see any patterns that would help you predict where a particular number will be placed? What patterns do you see?

3. In what row and column will the number 32 be? 40? 50? 150? And how about 86? 87? 187? 392? 546? 7386?

4. Describe how you could use the Division Algorithm to predict where any whole number will appear in this pattern. Explain why your strategy works.

DISCUSS

What patterns did you see in the array? How did these patterns help you solve the problem? How is this problem like and unlike the previous problems in 3.1 and 3.2 with repeating patterns? What could be considered a unit sequence in this problem? Did you use the Division Algorithm in your solution? If so, how?

REFLECT

Write a problem-solving report using the framework provided in Chapter 1. Describe how you used the Division Algorithm in your solution to this problem.

3.4. Additional Problems

1. **License plate**. You get a 90-day temporary license plate for your new car. If you got the license on a Friday, on what day will it expire?

2. **Odometer**. The odometer on your car shows the total number of miles traveled up to 99,999 miles, after which the odometer turns over and begins again from 0. If the odometer shows 98,654 miles, what will it show after a coast-to-coast trip of 3,782 miles?

3. **Predicting the value of the ones place**. Use a repeating pattern to find the numeral that will be in the ones place of 2^{387}.

4. **Patterns with the imaginary number *i*.** As you may recall from previous mathematics classes, the letter *i* is used to represent the imaginary number $\sqrt{-1}$. Note that $i^1 = i$, $i^2 = -1$, $i^3 = -i$, $i^4 = 1$, $i^5 = i$, ... Use patterns to simplify i^{2987}.

5. **Clockwise**. The hand on a dial rotates clockwise 45° every 10 seconds. If it points straight up, or 0°, at 3:15 p.m., what will the angle be at 40 seconds past 3:26 p.m.?

6. **Design stencil**. A stencil of Pennsylvania Dutch designs consists of a tulip, a wheel of fortune, a pomegranate, a peacock, and a heart. Each figure on the stencil is 4 centimeters wide. You are decorating a day care center and you wish to stencil the designs near the top edge of a wall in a hallway that measures 1468 centimeters long. If you stencil the figures in the order indicated until you run out of room, what will be the last figure you stencil?

7. **Clock faces**. In a drawing of a series of clock faces, the minute hand rotates 45° from one clock to the next. If the hand begins pointing straight down, what will be its position on the 11th clock? On the 29th?

8. **Even numbers**. Beginning with 2, the digits in the ones place of even numbers are 2, 4, 6, 8, 10, etc. What digit is in the ones place of the 357th even number?

9. **Pattern block patterns**. Picture a pattern block pattern consisting of red, red, red, green, green, yellow, green, green, red, red, red. If this pattern were continued, what color would the 586th piece be? How many of each color would be used when the 586th piece was added?

3.5. Pedagogical Explorations

1. **Primary student's thinking about repeating patterns**. Select three repeating pattern problems from section 3.1. Predict how a child in grades 1-3 would solve the problems and discuss the types of mistakes that might be made. Then actually pose the problems to a child in one of those grades and observe carefully as the child works with the problems. Ask questions until you understand how the child reasoned about the problems. Write a report about the interview that includes the problems you used, a description of the child's solution to the problem and the information you gathered about the child's thinking. Reflect on the interview. Describe your reactions to the interview, including how the outcome matched your expectations or how it was different. Indicate anything you learned from the experience. Based on what you observed, describe what you would do to help this particular child extend his or her thinking about patterns.

2. **Intermediate student's thinking about repeating patterns.** Select two repeating pattern problems from section 3.1, one or two from section 3.2, and one or two from section 3.4. Predict how a student in grades 3-5 would solve the problems and discuss the types of mistakes that might be made. Then pose the problems to a student in one of those grades and observe carefully as the student works the problems. Ask questions to probe the student's thinking until you understand how the student thought about solving the problems. Prepare a report on the interview that includes the problems you used, a description of the student's solution to the problem, and the information you gathered about his or her thinking. Reflect on the interview. Describe your reactions to the interview, including how the outcome matched your expectations or how it was different. Indicate anything you learned from the experience. Based on what you observed, describe what you would do to help this particular child extend his or her thinking about patterns.

3. **Middle school students' thinking about repeating patterns.** Select three to five repeating pattern problems with a wide range of level of difficulty. Select at least one each from sections 3.1, 3.2, and 3.4. Predict how a student in grades 5-8 would solve the problems and discuss the types of mistakes that might be made. Then pose the problems to a student in one of those grades and observe carefully as the student works the problems. Ask questions to probe the student's thinking until you understand how the student thought about the problems. Prepare a report on the interview that includes the problems you used, a description of the student's solution to the problem, and the information you gathered about his or her thinking. Reflect on the interview. Describe your reactions to the interview, including how the outcome matched your expectations or how it was different. Indicate anything you learned from the experience. Based on what you observed, describe what you would do to help this particular child extend his or her thinking about patterns.

4. **Comparing children's thinking about repeating patterns.** Imagine that you gave problem 4 from section 3.1 to a student in grade 2 and a student in grade 5. How do you think their approaches to the problem would be alike, and how do you think they would be different?

3.6. Summary

Terminology

Division Algorithm for Whole Numbers: For all whole numbers n and $d \neq 0$, there exist two additional whole numbers q and r, with $0 \leq r < d$, such that $n = qd + r$.

Remainder: In a division problem the remainder is the number left over when dividing two numbers if a whole-number quotient cannot be found.

Repeating pattern: A pattern with a continuously recurring unit sequence within a longer sequence.

Quotient: The quotient is the result of dividing two numbers. This may or may not be a whole number.

Unit Sequence: The core of a repeating pattern, a recurring sequence within a longer sequence.

Big Ideas

The ability to identify the unit sequence of a repeating pattern lies at the heart of solving problems involving repeating patterns. The Division Algorithm for Whole Numbers provides a general method for working with repeating patterns and a common language for communicating about them.

References

Chambers, D. L. (1994). The *right* algebra for all. *Educational Leadership, 51,* 82-84.

Hirschhorn, D. (Ed.) (2000). *The super source: Pattern blocks, grades K-2.* Vernon Hills, IL: ETA Cuisenaire.

National Council of Teachers of Mathematics. (1989). *Curriculum and evaluation standards for school mathematics.* Reston, VA: Author.

National Council of Teachers of Mathematics. (2000). *Principles and standards for school mathematics.* Reston, VA: Author.

Stewart, K., Walker, K., & Reak, C. (1995). *20 thinking questions for pattern blocks: Grades 1-3.* Mountain View, CA: Creative Publications.

Zazkis, R., & Liljedahl, P. (2002). Generalization of patterns: The tension between algebraic thinking and algebraic notation. *Educational Studies in Mathematics, 49*, 379-402.

CHAPTER 4: GROWING PATTERNS

A growing pattern does not have a continuously repeating unit sequence within a longer sequence, as does a repeating pattern. Instead, a growing pattern methodically changes from step to step according to a mathematical rule. Also, growing patterns are always geometric figures, unlike repeating patterns, which may appear in various forms. The growing patterns in this chapter are similar to those found in elementary and middle school curriculum materials, and they set the stage for the study of functions in Unit 3.

Explorations of growing patterns provide opportunities for elementary and middle school students to develop two important aspects of algebraic reasoning: generalization and representation of mathematical relationships (Ferrini-Mundy, Lappan, & Phillips, 1997). These explorations should be guided by questions that prompt students to focus on important aspects of the mathematical relationships within the patterns.

Growing Patterns in Elementary School

In the early grades, work with growing patterns often involves modeling with pattern blocks or other manipulatives and counting the pieces used. In the intermediate grades, students can begin to use variables to describe the relationships and look for rules that explain the pattern of growth.

One growing pattern activity for primary grade children asks students to use pattern blocks to build a series of apartments like those shown below (where first one apartment is shown, then two, and then three) and to determine the number of blocks required to build 10 apartments (Ward, 1995).

          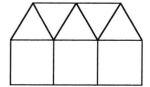

Figure 1   **Figure 2**   **Figure 3**

Take a few minutes to solve the problem. How was it different from the pattern block problems you solved in section 3.1? You may have noticed that this is not a repeating pattern because there is no unit sequence that repeats as the pattern continues. Instead, each figure in the series is larger than the one before it, increasing by the same amount each time.

In this problem, children are asked to extend the pattern to a specific number of apartments. Although school children will not have sufficient numbers of pattern blocks to actually build the requested figure and count blocks, they may use any one of a variety of numeric strategies to find the answer. Some children will skip count, 2, 5, 8, 11, 14..., the total number of blocks. Others will identify a relationship between the number of apartments and the number of blocks needed, and use this relationship to calculate the number of blocks required to build 10 apartments.

The apartment problem can be extended by asking the following: "Think of a way to predict how many blocks you would need to make any number of apartments." Moving from the number of blocks needed to build a specific number of apartments toward a rule for building any number of apartments is an important step toward thinking algebraically. A statement that describes how many blocks are needed for any number of apartments is an example of a generalization, a powerful tool of mathematics. In grades 1-3, the statement will probably use everyday language instead of mathematical symbols, but if a student can describe a rule or relationship for the pattern, then she is thinking algebraically.

Growing Patterns in Middle School

In middle school, growing patterns provide a context in which students can develop an appreciation for the precision of algebraic expressions or equations that describe patterns of change. Students learn to recognize the particular aspects of a pattern that signal a linear or quadratic relationship, building a foundation for work with functions. By middle school, students may use the language of functions to describe the relationships in growing patterns.

For example, in this lesson from *Mathematics In Context, Patterns and Figures* (National Center for Research in Mathematical Sciences Education, & Freudenthal Institute, 1998), seventh graders examine a growing pattern, complete a table, and write equations to represent the number of dots in the W-pattern.

Patterns and Figures

Squadrons of airplanes sometimes fly in a W-formation.

Look at the following sequence of W-patterns.

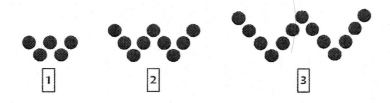

12. a. Copy and complete this chart for the W-patterns.

Number of Dots	5	___	___	___	___	___
Pattern Number	1	2	3	4	5	6

b. Write a step-by-step formula for the number of dots in the W-pattern sequence.

c. How many dots are in pattern number 16?

d. Find a direct formula to describe the number of dots in any W-pattern. Then use your formula to find the number of dots in pattern number 25.

Teacher's Knowledge of Growing Patterns

Elementary and middle school teachers need to be able to recognize growing patterns and identify places in the mathematics curriculum where growing patterns can be used to develop and extend student's mathematical thinking. In this chapter, you will explore a variety of growing patterns and write equations for describing pattern relationships. You will often be looking for an equation that tells how to find the nth term of a pattern or sequence. That is, the equation that you write will describe the specific mathematical relationship no matter what value is substituted for the letters. You will use variables to represent the relationships among varying quantities when the change in one variable determines the change in another variable.

Goals of the Chapter

In this chapter, you will—

- determine recursive rules for growing patterns,

- determine explicit rules for growing patterns,

- describe how the numbers in recursive and explicit rules are related to visual features of growing patterns,

- create growing patterns that corresponds to given rules.

4.1. Tile Patios

In this problem you will explore growing patterns in two colors and examine the connections between patterns in the tiles and patterns in tables.

Materials: Small square tiles of two different colors.

EXPLORE

Patricia is building square patios with dark colored tiles, and surrounding them with borders of a single layer of light-colored tiles. What is the smallest patio she can build? Use square tiles to build this patio and its border. What is the next larger patio she can build? Build this patio and its border. And the next larger patio she can build? Build this patio and its border. How do you know there are no patios in between the three you have built?

Use square tiles to build the fourth and fifth patios in the pattern. Make a table listing the patio number, the number of dark patio tiles, the number of light border tiles, and the total number of tiles for the first five patios. Then determine the values in the table for the nth patio.

DISCUSS

What patterns did you see in the table? What patterns did you see in the figures? How are the patterns in the table related to the patterns in the figures? What rules did you find for predicting the values in the table for the nth patio? How did you determine these rules?

There are multiple ways to *see* the number of border tiles in the nth patio. How many different ways can you visualize this amount? Write as many different expressions as you can. For each expression, describe how it *shows* the number of border tiles needed.

REFLECT

Write a problem-solving report using the framework from Chapter 1.

4.2 Multiple Ways of Seeing

In this investigation, you will explore multiple ways of seeing patterns. You will explain why various expressions make sense as descriptions for a growing pattern.

EXPLORE

A group of 7th and 8th grade students participated in individual interviews in which they were asked questions about the perimeters of the following sequence of pattern block figures (Bishop, 2000). Note that the side length of each square and each equilateral triangle is one unit.

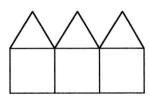

Figure 1   **Figure 2**   **Figure 3**

1) First study the figures and write your own expression for the perimeter of the nth figure. You may want to use pattern blocks.

2) Then study the expressions below that the students wrote to represent the perimeter of nth figure in the sequence. Describe how a student might have counted the sides of the figure to arrive at each expression.

   a) $(n+1)2 + n$

   b) $5 + (n-1) \times 3$

   c) $5n - 2 - 2(n-2)$

   d) $n \times 2 + 2 + n$

   e) $n + n + n + 2$

DISCUSS

Compare the various strategies found by you and your classmates for counting the sides of the figures. What does it mean for algebraic expressions to be equivalent? One definition says that equivalent expressions are expressions that simplify to an equal value when numbers are substituted for the variables in the expression. Another definition says that equivalent expressions are expressions that represent the same value but are presented in a different format using the properties of numbers. Which of these definitions most closely supports your method for verifying the equivalence of the expressions above? How can we verify that all of the expressions written by the students are equivalent?

REFLECT

In this investigation, you explored multiple ways of seeing a growing perimeter pattern. These questions will help you summarize and extend what you learned.

1. Here's another sequence of pattern block figures investigated by 7th and 8th graders (Bishop, 2000). Note that the side length of each square and each equilateral triangle is one unit.

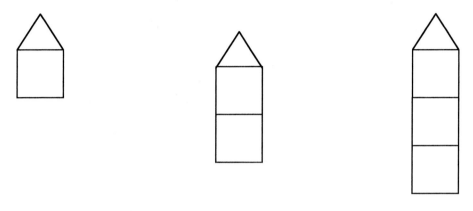

Figure 1   **Figure 2**   **Figure 3**

Study the figures and write your own expression for the perimeter of the *n*th figure. Describe how each student might have counted the sides of the figures to arrive at these expressions for the perimeter of the *n*th figure.

   a) $(n+3)+n$

   b) $2(n-1)+2+3$

   c) $n \times 2 + 1 + 1 + 1$

   d) $n \times 3 - (n-3)$

2. Verify that all of the expressions in #1 are equivalent.

Answer these questions and write a summary of what you learned from this investigation.

4.3. Rows and Columns

This problem was adapted from Mason (1996).

Materials: Toothpicks

EXPLORE

The picture below shows a rectangle made up of two rows and four columns of squares outlined by toothpicks. How many toothpicks would be needed to make a rectangle with r rows and c columns?

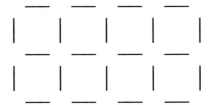

Try to find at least three different ways to *see* how to determine the number of toothpicks, and write these as general rules.

DISCUSS

Compare the various rules found by you and your classmates and the corresponding methods for determining the number of toothpicks. What strategies did you use to solve this problem? How can we verify that the expressions are equivalent?

REFLECT

Write a problem-solving report using the framework from Chapter 1. Choose three different rules and discuss the connections between the different rules and the methods for determining the number of toothpicks. Be sure to illustrate the various rules with pictures of the toothpicks.

4.4. Toothpick Patterns

In this problem, you will use two types of reasoning to explore growing toothpick patterns.

Materials: Toothpicks

EXPLORE

For each of the patterns started below, use toothpicks to copy the given figures. Extend the pattern by building the next three figures. Count the number of toothpicks for each figure and record the numbers in a table, extending the table to Figure 10. Then find a rule, an equation, for finding the number of toothpicks in the nth figure of each pattern.

1. **Toothpick Triangles**

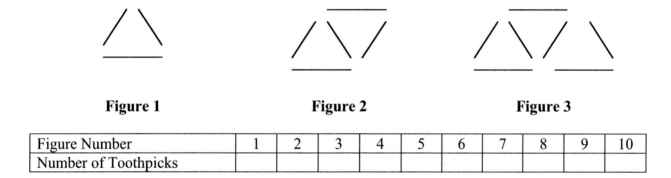

Figure 1	**Figure 2**	**Figure 3**

Figure Number	1	2	3	4	5	6	7	8	9	10
Number of Toothpicks										

2. **Toothpick Squares**

Figure 1	**Figure 2**	**Figure 3**

Figure Number	1	2	3	4	5	6	7	8	9	10
Number of Toothpicks										

3. Toothpick Pentagons

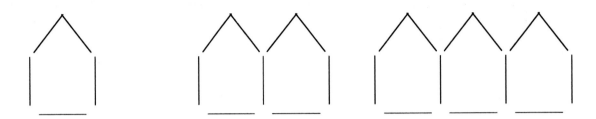

| **Figure 1** | **Figure 2** | **Figure 3** |

Figure Number	1	2	3	4	5	6	7	8	9	10
Number of Toothpicks										

DISCUSS

While exploring growing patterns and creating expressions to describe them, two types of reasoning are typically used: recursive and explicit. *Recursive* reasoning involves the mathematical relationship between consecutive terms in a growing pattern or sequence. While extending the growing toothpick patterns, did you find yourself noticing how many toothpicks were added to each new figure? If so, you were engaging in recursive reasoning. The recursive strategy, though, is not so helpful if you need to find, say, the 53rd figure of a pattern. Then the recursive strategy becomes tiresome, with many more opportunities to make an error. *Explicit reasoning* does not require knowledge of the previous terms in a sequence. When you found a rule for finding the *n*th figure of each growing toothpick pattern, you were engaged in explicit reasoning.

An *explicit rule* describes how two variables are related. What explicit rules did you write for the growing toothpick patterns? Compare the various rules developed in the class.

A *recursive rule* describes how a pattern changes from term to term. For example, consider the toothpick triangle pattern and the corresponding table. A recursive rule for a growing pattern has two parts. First, it identifies the starting value. The starting value of a growing pattern corresponds to Figure 1. For the toothpick triangle pattern, the starting value is 3. The second part of a recursive rule is a *NOW-NEXT* equation that expresses the recursive relationship, in this case an additive relationship. That is, add 2 toothpicks to the current figure to build the next figure in the pattern. We can represent this recursive rule using the following system of equations:
$$\begin{cases} \text{START} = 3 \\ \text{NEXT} = \text{NOW} + 2 \end{cases}$$

Write recursive rules for the toothpick squares and the toothpick pentagons.

What do you suppose would be the explicit and recursive rules for a growing pattern of toothpick octagons? What would be the explicit and recursive rules for a growing pattern of toothpick polygons with p sides? Explain your reasoning.

REFLECT

Write a problem-solving report using the framework from Chapter 1. Discuss both recursive and explicit rules for each of the patterns.

4.5. More Tile Patterns

Tile patterns can provide a visual context for illustrating the difference between recursive and explicit reasoning (Roebuck, 2005). In this investigation, you will explore several growing tile patterns.

Materials: Square tiles, crayons or colored pencils, square grid paper (optional)

EXPLORE

For each of the patterns started below, use tiles to copy the given figures. Extend the pattern by building the next two figures. Count the number of tiles for each figure and record the numbers in a table, extending the table to Figure 10. Write a recursive rule for finding the number of tiles needed to build the figures. Then draw the first five figures and use crayons or colored pencils to shade the squares that were added to each new figure. Next write an explicit rule for finding the number of tiles in the nth figure of each pattern. Then draw the first five figures and use crayons or colored pencils to shade the figures to illustrate the relationship between each figure number and the way the figure was created.

1. **Growing T's**

Figure 1   Figure 2   Figure 3

Figure Number	1	2	3	4	5	6	7	8	9	10
Number of Tiles										

2. Growing Crosses

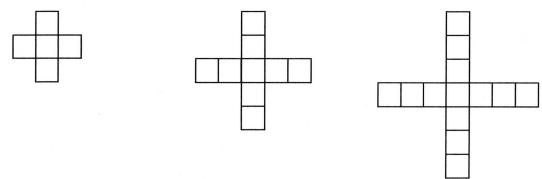

Figure Number	1	2	3	4	5	6	7	8	9	10
Number of Tiles										

3. Growing H's

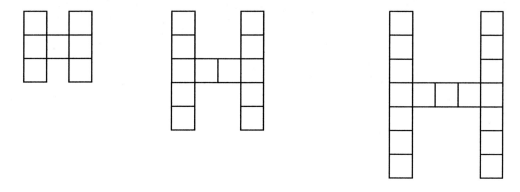

Figure Number	1	2	3	4	5	6	7	8	9	10
Number of Tiles										

Growing Patterns

4. **Growing Rectangles**

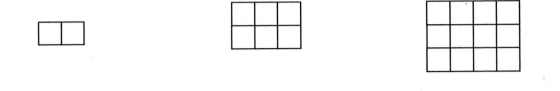

Figure 1	Figure 2	Figure 3

Explicit
Recursive

Figure Number		1	2	3	4	5	6	7	8	9	10
Number of Tiles											

(Hint: For the recursive rule, you will need to use the terms PREVIOUS, NOW, and NEXT.)

DISCUSS

Compare the methods of shading used by you and your classmates to illustrate recursive and explicit reasoning for each tile pattern. How does the shading help us to understand the rules? In the Growing T's, Growing Crosses, and Growing H's, how do the numbers in the recursive rules relate to the shapes of the figures? What is changing in each figure? What is staying the same? How is this information reflected in the explicit rules?

How is the pattern in Growing Rectangles different from the others? How are the recursive and explicit rules for this pattern different from the others?

REFLECT

Write a problem-solving report using the framework from Chapter 1. Discuss both recursive and explicit rules for each of the patterns.

4.6. Matching Rules to Patterns

In this investigation, you will match rules to growing tile patterns. Then you will work backward—beginning with algebraic representations and building growing patterns to match.

Materials: Square tiles

EXPLORE

Here are six explicit rules for finding the *n*th figure of six different growing patterns illustrated with tiles. In each rule, *n* is the figure number and *T* is the number of tiles. Three of the growing patterns are pictured. Match each of the three patterns with one of the rules. Then design growing patterns to illustrate the remaining rules. Also, write a recursive rule for each pattern.

Rule 1: $T = 3n + 2$ **Rule 2:** $T = 3n + 1$ **Rule 3:** $T = 2n + 3$

Rule 4: $T = 2n + 4$ **Rule 5:** $T = 4n + 2$ **Rule 6:** $T = 4n + 1$

Pattern A

        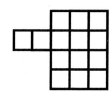

Figure 1   Figure 2   Figure 3

Pattern B

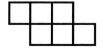   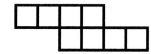   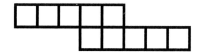

Figure 1   Figure 2   Figure 3

Pattern C

        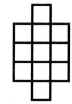

Figure 1   Figure 2   Figure 3

DISCUSS

How did you determine which rules matched the three growing patterns? Compare with your classmates the patterns you created for the three remaining rules. How are the explicit rules reflected in the shapes of the figures? While your figures may look different, they may match the same rule.

What connections do you see between the explicit rules and the recursive rules for these patterns?

REFLECT

Write a problem-solving report using the framework from Chapter 1. Describe how the numbers in the explicit rules are related to the visual features of the figures.

4.7. Pattern Block Patterns

In this investigation, you will explore several different growing patterns created with pattern blocks.

Materials: Colored pattern blocks

EXPLORE

Here are the first three figures in a growing pattern. Notice that Figure 1 is a single square pattern block, and Figure 2 is the result of surrounding the square block with blocks of the same kind. By "surrounding" we mean that tiles are attached to all of the exposed edges of the figure. Figure 3 is then the result of surrounding Figure 2 with blocks of the same kind, and Figure 4 is the result of surrounding Figure 3 with blocks of the same kind. Similar growing patterns can be created with other pattern blocks.

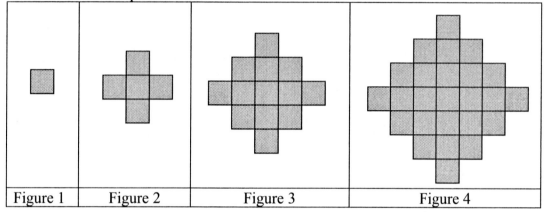

| Figure 1 | Figure 2 | Figure 3 | Figure 4 |

Use orange pattern block squares, blue rhombuses, or white rhombuses to build the first, second, third, fourth, and fifth figures in the growing pattern. (Different groups may be simultaneously assigned to investigate the patterns with each of these three different pattern blocks.) Remember, to "surround" a figure means to attach tiles to all of the exposed edges of the figure. Make a table listing the figure number, the number of blocks, and the perimeter of the figure for the first five figures. Find an explicit rule to determine the number of blocks in the nth figure. Then find a recursive rule for the number of blocks in each figure. Also, find an explicit rule to determine the perimeter of the nth figure. Then find a recursive rule for the perimeter of each figure.

Repeat the activity using green triangles and yellow hexagons. (Different groups may be simultaneously assigned to investigate patterns with each of these two different Pattern blocks.)

DISCUSS

What patterns did you see in the table for each pattern block? How are the patterns in the tables related to the patterns in the figures? How are the explicit and recursive rules related to these patterns? How did you determine your explicit and recursive rules?

Growing Patterns

How do the patterns in the table for the square pattern block compare to the patterns in the tables for the green triangles, the blue rhombuses, and the yellow hexagons? What similarities and differences do you see in the explicit rules for these different pattern blocks? What similarities and difference do you see in the recursive rules?

REFLECT

Write a problem-solving report using the framework from Chapter 1.

4.8. Additional Problems

1. **Dots**. The drawing below represents a set of overlapping rectangles.

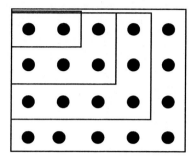

The first (top) rectangle contains 2 dots.
The second rectangle contains 6 dots.
The third rectangle contains 12 dots.
The fourth rectangle contains 20 dots.

a) How many dots in the fifth rectangle?
b) How many dots in the hundredth rectangle? How do you know?
c) How many dots in the nth rectangle? How do you know?

2. **Create two different patterns**. Create two different growing patterns for which the given figure is the second figure (see below). Sketch the first, third, and fourth figures of each pattern. Write a recursive rule for each pattern. Use words to describe how you would build the 50th figure in each pattern. Write an explicit rule for the total number of dots T in the nth figure for each pattern.

Pattern 1

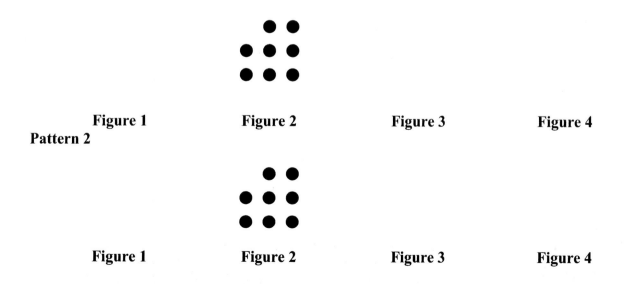

| Figure 1 | Figure 2 | Figure 3 | Figure 4 |

Pattern 2

| Figure 1 | Figure 2 | Figure 3 | Figure 4 |

Growing Patterns

3. **Area and Perimeter**. Here are the first three figures in a growing pattern.

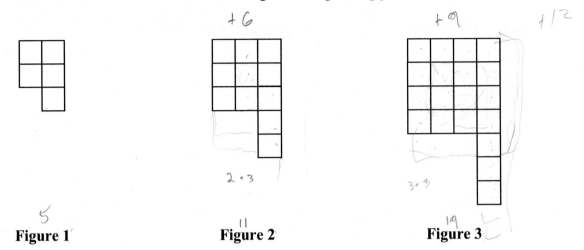

Figure 1   Figure 2   Figure 3

a) Write a recursive rule for finding the area of the *n*th figure in the pattern.
b) Write a recursive rule for finding the perimeter of the *n*th figure in the pattern.
c) Write an explicit rule for finding the area of the *n*th figure in the pattern.
d) Write an explicit rule for finding the perimeter of the *n*th figure in the pattern.

4. **Black and White**. Here are the first three figures in a growing pattern.

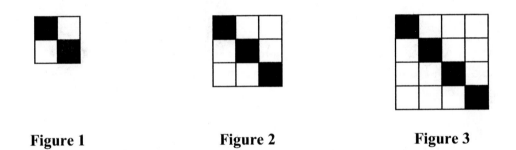

Figure 1   Figure 2   Figure 3

a) Write an explicit rule for finding the number of black tiles needed to build the *n*th figure in the pattern.
b) Write an explicit rule for finding the number of white tiles needed to build the *n*th figure in the pattern.

5. **Laying Bricks**. A bricklayer is building a large base for a sign. She uses 6 blocks for the top layer and each layer requires 8 more blocks than the layer above it. The bottom layer has 102 bricks. How many layers are there in the sign base?

6. **House of Cards**. Below is a house of cards that is four stories high.

    a) Find the number of cards needed to build a house that is eight stories high.

    b) Write an explicit rule for finding the number of cards needed to build a house that is *n* stories high.

7. **Skeleton Tower**. In the Skeleton Tower below, find a rule that describes the total number of cubes at each stage of the tower's growth. Find two more ways of "seeing" that generate two different ways of writing the rule.

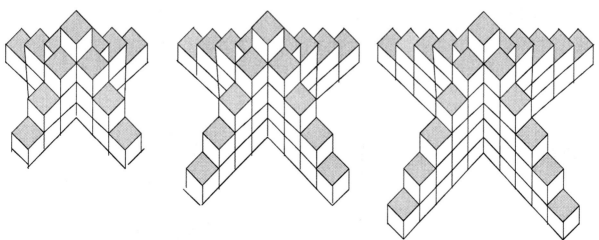

| Figure 4 | Figure 5 | Figure 6 |

8. **Multiple Ways of Seeing: Rectangle Border Problem** (Orton, Orton, & Roper, 1999). The figure below shows a rectangle 2 squares wide and 3 squares long. How many squares are needed to build a border one square thick all the way around the rectangle?

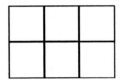

Investigate how many squares will be needed for other rectangles. In general, let *l* represent the length of a rectangle and *w* represent the width. How many squares will be needed to build a border one square thick all the way around the rectangle?

For each expression listed below, draw a figure to show how the squares are counted. Check to see whether or not the expressions are equivalent.

a) $2l + 2w + 4$

b) $2(l + 2) + 2(w + 2) - 4$ $2(l+2)+2w$

c) $(l + 2)(w + 2) - lw$

4.9. Pedagogical Explorations

1. **Children's thinking about the container problem.** The following figures are the first three in a sequence of toothpick containers (Orton, Orton, & Roper, 1999).

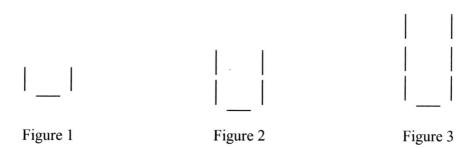

Figure 1   Figure 2   Figure 3

a) Determine how many toothpicks there would be in the fourth figure, the 10th figure, the 37th figure, and the nth figure. Find more than one way to count the toothpicks so that you have more than one way to represent the pattern.

b) Discuss your expressions with a partner, making sure that each of you understands and agrees with the other's work.

c) Examine the following three examples of children's thinking (ages 9-13) about the container problem. For each example, write a paragraph describing what the child is noticing about the pattern, describing the child's strategy or strategies, and your assessment of the accuracy of the strategy.

   i.) **Emma**

   Emma: 3 in the first, 5 in the next, 7, . . . all you have to do is add 2 on. Next is 9, . . . next is 11.

   Interviewer: So how many for number 20? Number 1 is 3, number 2 is 5, number 3 is 7, number 4 is 9, number 5 is 11 (pointing at a systematic written record of these results). How many for number 20?

   Emma: . . . 23. There's 3 at number 1, and then if you just had one (indicating the bottom toothpick in each shape) and you added up all the ones up to 20, you'd get 20. And then if you added 3 you'd get 23.

   (Orton, Orton, & Roper, 1999. p. 130)

   ii.) **Paul**

   Paul: 3, 4, 7, 9, . . . gives 11, . . . up by 2.

Interviewer:	So what would the twentieth be?
Paul:	44, . . . just multiply by 4.
Interviewer:	And for the hundredth?
Paul:	It will be 11 times 20, . . . or 44 times 5.
Interviewer:	And for any number n?
Paul:	(Long pause) . . . It will be n multiplied by 2 and add 1. I've just remembered doing something like this before. I know what you mean now . . . what you were asking for.

(Orton, Orton, & Roper, 1999. p. 132).

iii.) **Katie** (thinking about the 20th term)

Katie:	It's 2 times 20, then . . . hang on, . . . 2 times 19 add 3, . . . add 4, . . . hang on, . . . mm, . . .
Interviewer:	Keep going.
Katie:	Yes, 19 times 2, . . . 19 times 2 add 3.
Interviewer:	Can you explain how you got that?
Katie:	Because if you forget about that (pointing at the bottom three matches forming a sort of U-shape) for the moment, and then you add, . . . you always add 2, and there's 19 of them, . . . and then you add that (pointing again at the initial U-shape). It could be 20 times 2, and then it would just be add 1.
Interviewer:	Now do you think you could get the hundredth?
Katie:	99 times 2 add 3, . . . or 100 times 2 add 3, . . . sorry, add 1.

(Orton, Orton, & Roper, 1999, p. 132).

2. **A sequence for developing pattern concepts**. The following three problems are part of a sequence of problems designed to help students learn to generalize pattern relationships (Gibbs, 1999). For each sequence, find an expression that you could use to find the *n*th term. Think about the kind of reasoning required by each problem. Then list the order that you would use the problems with a 5th or 6th grade class and explain why you put them in that order.

a) **Hidden rectangles**

Investigate the relationship between the number of rectangles that can be found in a row of squares and the length of the row by filling in the table. Remember that a square is a special kind of rectangle. For example, in the second figure, count each square and the rectangle formed from two squares, so there are three rectangles in the second figure.

Length of row	1	2	3	4	n
Number rectangles					

b) **Herringbone patterns**

Shown below are the first three patterns in a sequence of herringbone designs. Investigate the relationship between the width of the pattern and the total number of line segments in the design by filling in the table.

Width of pattern	1	2	3	n
Number of segments				

c) **How many squares?**

Investigate the number of squares in each of the rectangles (including the hidden squares) by filling in the table and find if there is a connection between the width of the rectangle and the total number of squares. For example, in the second figure, there are four 1×1 squares and one 2×2 square for a total of five squares.

Width of rectangle	1	2	3	4	n
Number of squares					

3. **Writing questions to promote algebraic reasoning**. Ferrini-Mundy, Lappan, and Phillips (1997, p. 288) offer the following general questions for organizing a class discussion to promote algebraic reasoning:

- What are the variables in this situation? What quantities are changing?
- How are the variables related?
- As one variable increases, what happens to the other variable?
- How can you represent this relationship using words, concrete objects, pictures, tables, graphs, or symbols?
- How can you build connections among representations?
- How can you use this relationship to predict information about the variables?

First, complete the investigation shown in the reproduced textbook page involving W-patterns in the introduction to Chapter 4. Note that a "step-by-step formula" is the same as a recursive rule and a "direct formula" is the same as an explicit rule. Then, write six specific questions a teacher could ask about this investigation that would promote algebraic reasoning in a class discussion. Answer your own questions. Also, for each question, explain how it promotes algebraic reasoning, that is, how it promotes generalization and representation of mathematical relationships or how it addresses the NCTM Algebra standard for middle school students.

4.10. Summary

Terminology

Explicit Rule: A rule that tells directly how to find any term in the pattern.

Growing Pattern: A pattern that changes consistently from step to step.

Recursive Rule: A rule that describes how a pattern changes from term to term.

Big Ideas

Growing patterns can be described using either recursive or explicit reasoning and rules. Recursive rules focus on the change between consecutive figures in a pattern. Explicit rules focus on the relationship between the figure number and the figure itself.

References

Bishop, J. (2000). Linear geometric number patterns: Middle school students' strategies. *Mathematics Education Research Journal, 12*(2). 107-126.

Ferrini-Mundy, J., Lappan, G., & Phillips, E. (1997) Experiences with patterning. *Teaching Children Mathematics, 3*, 282-288.

Gibbs, W. (1999). Pattern in the classroom. In A. Orton (Ed.), *Pattern in the teaching and learning of mathematics* (pp. 207-220). New York: Cassell.

Lee, L. (1996). An initiation into algebraic culture through generalization activities. In *Approaches to algebra: Perspectives for research and teaching* (pp. 87-106). Dordrecht: Kluwer.

Mason, J. (1996). Expressing generality and roots of algebra. In N. Bednarz, C. Kieran, & L. Lee (Eds.), *Approaches to algebra: Perspectives for research and teaching* (pp. 65-86). Dordrecht: Kluwer.

National Center for Research in Mathematical Sciences Education, & Freudenthal Institute. (1998). *Patterns and Figures.* Mathematics in Context series. Chicago, Illinois: Encyclopaedia Britannica Educational Corporation.

Orton, J., Orton, A., & Roper, T. (1999). Pictorial and practical contexts and the perception of pattern. In A. Orton, (Ed.), *Pattern in the teaching and learning of mathematics* (pp. 121-136). New York: Cassell.

Roebuck, K. I. M. (2005). Coloring formulas for growing patterns. *Mathematics Teacher*, 7, 472-475.

Ward, S. (1995), *Constructing ideas about patterns: Grades 1-3.* Creative Publications.

CHAPTER 5: SEQUENCES

In the previous two chapters, we explored repeating patterns and growing patterns, most of them involving geometric figures. In this chapter, we explore sequences, which are *number* patterns. A sequence is an ordered list of numbers; it is often just the set of numbers associated with a growing pattern. Some familiar sequences are:

Whole numbers: 0, 1, 2, 3, …
Even numbers: 0, 2, 4, 6, 8, …
Odd numbers: 1, 3, 5, 7, 9, …
Multiples of 3: 0, 3, 6, 9, 12, …
Square numbers: 0, 1, 4, 9, 16, 25, …

The study of sequences often involves special vocabulary and symbolism. This textbook addresses these aspects of sequences through investigations and problem solving. Readers will learn that the exploration of sequences may involve recursive or explicit reasoning. That is, the terms of a sequence can be found by applying a recursive rule such as "Add 2 to the previous term" or by using an explicit rule such as, "Square the whole numbers."

Sequences play an important role in elementary and middle school mathematics. They provide a link between the familiar focus on numbers and the not-so-familiar focus on relationships between numbers. To help them feel confident in their understanding of sequences, elementary and middle school students should have opportunities to examine and describe the relationships, first with words and then with symbols.

Sequences in Elementary School

The set of counting numbers is likely to be the earliest number sequence elementary school children encounter. Soon after mastering basic counting, children begin counting by 2s, by 5s, and by 10s. They may be asked to begin at 4 and count by 5s, or to begin at 3 and count by 2s.

With a calculator, young children can explore skip-count patterns forward and back from larger numbers and with larger intervals than they could do easily with mental mathematics, providing additional opportunities to recognize patterns in the numbers. Many visual patterns can be described with numerical sequences. For example, the following growing dot pattern can be described with the sequence of *triangular* numbers 1, 3, 6, 10, ….

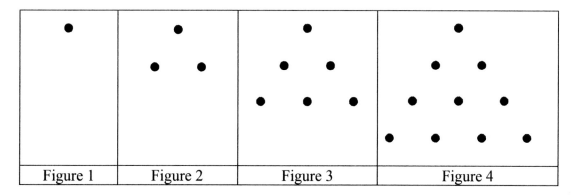

| Figure 1 | Figure 2 | Figure 3 | Figure 4 |

Sequences

In the upper elementary grades, the sequences encountered by students become more challenging. The sequence problems below are from *Scott Foresman-Addison Wesley Math for Grade 5* (2002):

Look for patterns. Copy and write the next three numbers.

1. $3\frac{11}{12}$, $3\frac{7}{12}$, $3\frac{1}{4}$, $2\frac{11}{12}$, $2\frac{7}{12}$, ...

2. $\frac{1}{3}$, $\frac{1}{6}$, $\frac{1}{12}$, ...

3. 1, $\frac{2}{3}$, $\frac{4}{9}$, ...

4. $\frac{1}{4}$, $\frac{3}{4}$, $1\frac{1}{4}$, ...

Although sequences with fractional numbers require more complex calculations, subsequent terms for each sequence can still be found by applying the appropriate rule.

Sequences in Middle School

In the middle grades, sequences may express real-world relationships, providing a link between number patterns and the notion of function. For example, in this somewhat traditional lesson from *Glencoe Mathematics: Applications and Connections, Course 1* (1999) for middle school students, one sequence describes the speed of a falling object at one-second intervals. Students are also asked to recognize, extend, and describe sequences.

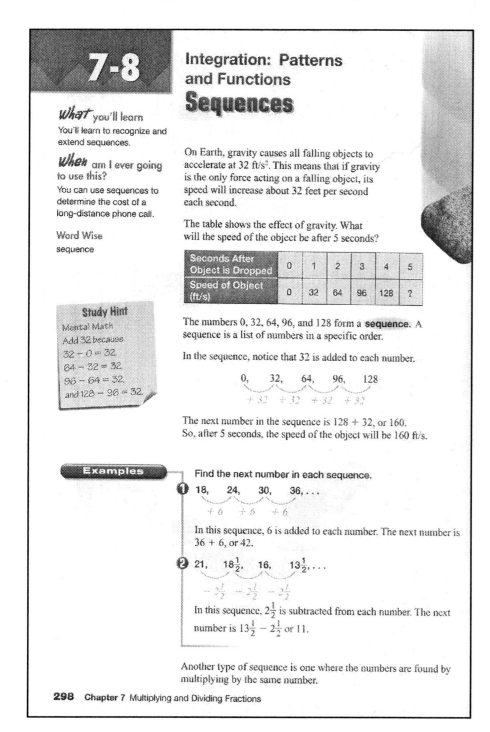

7-8

Integration: Patterns and Functions
Sequences

What you'll learn
You'll learn to recognize and extend sequences.

When am I ever going to use this?
You can use sequences to determine the cost of a long-distance phone call.

Word Wise
sequence

Study Hint
Mental Math
Add 32 because
$32 - 0 = 32$,
$64 - 32 = 32$,
$96 - 64 = 32$,
and $128 - 96 = 32$.

On Earth, gravity causes all falling objects to accelerate at 32 ft/s². This means that if gravity is the only force acting on a falling object, its speed will increase about 32 feet per second each second.

The table shows the effect of gravity. What will the speed of the object be after 5 seconds?

Seconds After Object is Dropped	0	1	2	3	4	5
Speed of Object (ft/s)	0	32	64	96	128	?

The numbers 0, 32, 64, 96, and 128 form a **sequence**. A sequence is a list of numbers in a specific order.

In the sequence, notice that 32 is added to each number.

$$0, \quad 32, \quad 64, \quad 96, \quad 128$$
$$+32 \quad +32 \quad +32 \quad +32$$

The next number in the sequence is $128 + 32$, or 160.
So, after 5 seconds, the speed of the object will be 160 ft/s.

Examples

Find the next number in each sequence.

1 $18, \quad 24, \quad 30, \quad 36, \ldots$
$+6 \quad +6 \quad +6$

In this sequence, 6 is added to each number. The next number is $36 + 6$, or 42.

2 $21, \quad 18\frac{1}{2}, \quad 16, \quad 13\frac{1}{2}, \ldots$
$-2\frac{1}{2} \quad -2\frac{1}{2} \quad -2\frac{1}{2}$

In this sequence, $2\frac{1}{2}$ is subtracted from each number. The next number is $13\frac{1}{2} - 2\frac{1}{2}$ or 11.

Another type of sequence is one where the numbers are found by multiplying by the same number.

298 Chapter 7 Multiplying and Dividing Fractions

Sequences

Examples

Study Hint

Problem Solving
You may want to use
the look for a pattern
strategy to help you
with these sequences.

Find the next number in each sequence.

3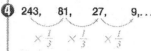
2,   8,   32,   128,...

$\times 4 \quad \times 4 \quad \times 4$

Each number in the sequence is multiplied by 4. The next number is 128×4, or 512.

4 243,   81,   27,   9,...

$\times \frac{1}{3} \quad \times \frac{1}{3} \quad \times \frac{1}{3}$

Each number in the sequence is multiplied by $\frac{1}{3}$. The next number is $9 \times \frac{1}{3}$, or 3.

APPLICATION **5** Carpentry A roof rafter of a building is to be braced as shown. The length of braces *A*, *B*, and *C* are $10\frac{1}{2}$ inches, 21 inches, and $31\frac{1}{2}$ inches, respectively. Find the lengths of braces *D* and *E*.

$10\frac{1}{2}$,   21, $31\frac{1}{2}$,...

$+ 10\frac{1}{2} + 10\frac{1}{2}$

In the sequence, $10\frac{1}{2}$ is added to each number.
The length of brace *D* is $31\frac{1}{2} + 10\frac{1}{2}$, or 42 inches.
The length of brace *E* is $42 + 10\frac{1}{2}$, or $52\frac{1}{2}$ inches.

CHECK FOR UNDERSTANDING

Communicating Mathematics

Read and study the lesson to answer each question.

1. *Write*, in your own words, a definition for sequence.

2. *Tell* how the numbers are related in the sequence $16, 4, 1, \frac{1}{4}$.

3. *You Decide* Janet says that the next number in the sequence $5, 7\frac{1}{2}, 10, 12\frac{1}{2}$, is 14. Joshua says the next number is 15. Who is correct? Explain your reasoning.

Guided Practice

Find the next two numbers in each sequence.

4. 6, 18, 54, 162, ...

5. 45, 38, 31, 24, ...

Find the missing number in each sequence.

6. 2, _2_, 9, $12\frac{1}{2}$, ...

7. _2_, 25, 5, 1, ...

8. *Geometry* Draw the next two figures in the sequence.

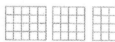

Teachers' Knowledge of Sequences

Elementary and middle school teachers need to be able to recognize and describe sequences and identify places in the mathematics curriculum where sequences can be used to develop and extend students' algebraic reasoning. In this chapter you will examine various types of sequences and use algebraic notation to describe these sequences with recursive and explicit rules. The investigations and problems are designed to challenge you to think more deeply about sequences.

Goals of the Chapter

In this chapter, you will—

- practice skip counting aloud and use a calculator and a hundred chart to skip count and describe resulting patterns,

- identify and describe arithmetic sequences,

- identify and describe geometric sequences,

- identify and describe the Fibonacci sequence.

Sequences

5.1. Skip Counting

Skip counting is counting by values other than one—that is, counting by twos, threes, fives, tens, and so forth. The starting point and the direction (forward or backward) are optional. A calculator with an automatic constant for addition or subtraction can be used to help find the terms in a skip-counting sequence. For example, the keystroke sequence for counting forward by fives beginning at 3 would be $3 + 5 =====$. Likewise, the keystroke sequence for counting backward by twos starting at 20 would be $20 - 2 =====$. In this investigation, you explore skip-counting sequences.

Materials: Calculator with an automatic constant for addition or subtraction, several copies of a hundred chart, crayons

EXPLORE

1. In your group, practice skip counting aloud together by twos, threes, and fives. Try starting at different numbers. Also, try counting forward and counting backward.

2. Practice using a calculator to skip count. Record the resulting sequences. Try these:

   $4 + 4$:   __4__ , _____, _____, _____, _____, _____, _____, _____, $\cdots$
   $2 + 6$:   __2__ , _____, _____, _____, _____, _____, _____, _____, $\cdots$
   $12 - 3$:   __12__ , _____, _____, _____, _____, _____, _____, _____, $\cdots$
   $15 - 4$:   __15__ , _____, _____, _____, _____, _____, _____, _____, $\cdots$

3. Record several skip-counting sequences by coloring in the numbers of the sequences on hundred charts like the one below. Record each sequence on a separate chart and describe the patterns you see in each chart.

1	2	3	4	5	6	7	8	9	10
11	12	13	14	15	16	17	18	19	20
21	22	23	24	25	26	27	28	29	30
31	32	33	34	35	36	37	38	39	40
41	42	43	44	45	46	47	48	49	50
51	52	53	54	55	56	57	58	59	60
61	62	63	64	65	66	67	68	69	70
71	72	73	74	75	76	77	78	79	80
81	82	83	84	85	86	87	88	89	90
91	92	93	94	95	96	97	98	99	100

DISCUSS

What kinds of things did you observe or learn from practicing skip counting aloud with your group? What kinds of things could elementary or middle school students learn?

What kinds of things did you observe or learn from using a calculator to skip count? What kinds of things could elementary or middle school students learn?

What kinds of patterns did you see in the hundred charts? What kinds of skip-counting sequences resulted in vertical stripes? What do you notice about the numbers in the vertical stripes? What kinds skip-counting sequences resulted in diagonal stripes? What do you notice about the numbers in the diagonal stripes? What other kinds of patterns did you create? What skip-counting sequences produced these patterns?

REFLECT

In this investigation, you explored skip-counting sequences. These questions will help you summarize and extend what you learned.

1. What different things did you learn from skip counting aloud, using a calculator to skip count, and coloring skip-counting sequences on hundred charts?

2. What can elementary or middle school students learn from practicing skip counting aloud, using a calculator to skip count, and coloring skip-counting sequences on a hundred chart?

Answer these questions and write a summary of what you learned from this investigation.

Sequences

5.2. Describe the Rule

In this investigation, you will examine and describe various sequences.

EXPLORE

For each of the following sequences, (a) find the next three terms in the sequence, and (b) use words to describe the rule you used to determine the new terms.

1. 4, 6.5, 9, 11.5, …

2. 5, 10, 20, 40, …

3. 20, 17, 14, 11, …

4. 1, 3, 6, 10, 15, …

5. $\dfrac{1}{12}, \dfrac{1}{6}, \dfrac{1}{4}, \dfrac{1}{3}, \ldots$

6. 12, 6, 3, $\dfrac{3}{2}$, …

7. −12, 36, −108, 324…

8. 1, 3, 8, 16, 27, …

DISCUSS

Some of the sequences you explored have special names. An *arithmetic* (a rith met′ ic) *sequence* is one in which the same number is added to or subtracted from each term to get the next term in the sequence. A *geometric sequence* is one in which the same number is multiplied by or divided by each term to get the next term in the sequence.

Which of the above sequences are arithmetic sequences? Which ones are geometric sequences? Which sequences are neither arithmetic nor geometric?

These definitions of arithmetic and geometric sequences are *recursive* descriptions. That is, they describe the mathematical relationship between consecutive terms of the sequences. We can express these recursive rules using mathematical symbols. We can also write *explicit* rules for these sequences, rules that do not depend on previous terms. For both types of rules, though, we will use the symbolism that is typically used with sequences.

We denote the terms of a sequence using subscripts that indicate their position in the sequence. We call this *subscript notation*. In the first sequence above, $a_1 = 4$, $a_2 = 6.5$, $a_3 = 9$, $a_4 = 11.5$, and so on. We use a_1 to represent the *initial* term and a_n to indicate the *n*th term in the sequence. The *n*th term represents the *n*th time the rule that defines the sequence has been applied. Notice the similarities to the notation we used in Chapter 4, where Figure 1 represented the initial value of a growing pattern and Figure *n* would represent the *n*th figure. With sequences, the subscripts 1, 2, 3, … correspond to the sequence of counting numbers. Similarly, with growing patterns, the figure numbers correspond to the sequence of counting numbers.

Rules for Arithmetic Sequences
The value that is added to or subtracted from each term of an arithmetic sequence is called the *common difference* between consecutive terms, and we label this amount *d*. Note that the value of *d* may be positive or negative.

Consider the following arithmetic sequence: 2, 5, 8, 11, ... The initial term is $a_1 = 2$ and the common difference is $d = 3$. The recursive rule for describing this arithmetic sequence is
$$\begin{cases} a_1 = 2 \\ a_{n+1} = a_n + 3 \end{cases}$$. How is this notation similar to the NOW-NEXT equations we saw in Chapter 4?
Verify that the explicit rule for finding the *n*th term in this arithmetic sequence is
$a_n = 2 + 3(n-1)$.

Rules for Geometric Sequences
The value that is multiplied by or divided by each term of a geometric sequence is called the *common ratio* between consecutive terms, and we label this amount *r*.

Consider the following geometric sequence: 1, 3, 9, 27, ... The initial term is $a_1 = 1$ and the common ratio is $r = 3$. The recursive rule for describing this geometric sequence is
$$\begin{cases} a_1 = 1 \\ a_{n+1} = a_n \times 3 \end{cases}$$
Verify that the explicit rule for finding the *n*th term in this geometric sequence is $a_n = 1 \times 3^{n-1}$.

Use subscript notation to write a recursive rule for each of the sequences in the EXPLORE section. Then use the NOW-NEXT notation described in section 4.4 to represent the same relationships. What similarities and differences do you see between these two types of notation?

Also, for each sequence, write an explicit rule for finding the *n*th term of the sequence. Then use each explicit rule to find the 20th term of the sequence.

REFLECT

In this investigation you examined and described various sequences. Answer these questions to help you summarize and extend what you learned.

1. For each of the following sequences, indicate whether it is arithmetic, geometric, or neither. Then use subscript notation to write a recursive rule for each sequence. Also, write an

Sequences

explicit rule to find the *n*th term of each sequence. Then use the explicit rule to find the 20th term of the sequence.

a) $\dfrac{1}{12}, \dfrac{1}{6}, \dfrac{1}{3}, \dfrac{2}{3}, \ldots$

b) -10, -20, -30, -40, …

c) 0.2, 3.0, 5.8, 8.6, …

d) 1, 3, 6, 10, 15, …

e) 5, -15, 45, -135, …

2. Using the expressions a_1 and d, what is a *general* explicit rule for determining a_n, the *n*th term of *any* arithmetic sequence?

3. Using the expressions a_1 and r, what is a *general* explicit rule for determining a_n, the *n*th term of *any* geometric sequence?

Answer these questions and write a summary of what you learned from this investigation.

5.3. Arithmetic and Geometric Sequences

The following problem combines the notions of arithmetic and geometric sequences. You may find it helpful to use explicit rules for these sequences.

EXPLORE

Four distinct positive integers a, b, c, and d form an arithmetic sequence. Also, the integers a, b, and d form a geometric sequence. If the sum of the four integers is a perfect cube, what is the smallest possible value of a? Explain how you know this is the smallest possible value of a.

DISCUSS

How did you find your solution? Compare with others in your class. How can you solve this problem using algebraic equations?

If you removed the condition on the sum of the integers, would 1, 3, 6, and 9 work for the integers a, b, c, and d? Without the condition on the sum of the integers, what values (other than the ones you found above) would work?

REFLECT

Write a problem-solving report using the format from Chapter 1.

5.4. Honeybees

In this investigation, you find a rule to describe the number of honeybees in a given generation.

EXPLORE

Honeybees have a peculiar family structure. Because male honeybees develop from unfertilized eggs, they have only one parent, a "mother." Female honeybees, on the other hand, develop from fertilized eggs and so have two parents, a "mother" and a "father."

1. Use this fact to draw the family tree of a male honeybee. Trace his ancestry for seven generations. (You may find it easier to work "upside down" from a traditional family tree – that is, to start at the top with our subject bee and show parents and grandparents below in successive layers.) The first five generations are shown below (M stands for a male bee and F stands for a female bee).

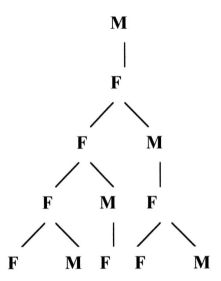

2. Make a table showing the generation, starting with our subject male bee as generation 1, the number of male bees, the number of female bees, and the total number of bees in the generation. From the table, predict the number of bees in the tenth generation. How many bees would be in the fifteenth generation?

3. Use words to describe how to find the number of bees in a given generation.

DISCUSS

You probably noted that the number of bees in any generation followed a pattern that although is easy to describe in words, is difficult to express with an explicit rule. A recursive rule, though, can be written that tells the first two values of the sequence and then tells how to find any term from the two preceding terms. Can you write this recursive rule using subscript notation?

This sequence is called the *Fibonacci Sequence*. Fibonacci, who was born in the 1170s and died in the 1240s, is recognized as the greatest European mathematician of the middle ages. Although his full name was Leonardo of Pisa, he called himself Fibonacci, standing for "son of Bonacci," which was his father's name. The sequence developed as a result of a problem posed by Fibonacci about how fast rabbits could breed in ideal circumstances. According to the problem, we start with a pair of newborn rabbits, one male and one female. Assume the rabbits can mate at the end of one month so that a new pair, again one male and one female, is born at the end of the second month. Suppose our rabbits never die and that every female produces one new pair of rabbits per month, starting at the end of the second month. The original problem asked how many pairs of rabbits there would be in one year. You should check to see that this produces the same sequence of numbers as the honeybee problem.

The numbers from the sequence occur frequently in nature, in the number of petals on a flower, the number of spirals on a pinecone, the pattern of leaves on a stem, and many other instances.

REFLECT

In this investigation, you explored the Fibonacci sequence. These questions will help you summarize and extend what you learned:

1. Use subscript notation to write a recursive rule for this sequence.

2. Why is it necessary to give the first two terms of the Fibonacci sequence in the recursive rule?

3. If the first two terms of the sequence were changed to 2, what would the next six terms be?

4. If the first two terms of the sequence were changed to 3, what would the next six terms be?

Answer these questions and write a summary of what you learned from this investigation.

5.5. Additional Problems

1. **Bacteria**. Two bacteria were placed in a dish. The number of bacteria quadruples every hour. There are now 131,072 bacteria in the dish. How many hours have passed since the original two bacteria were placed in the dish?

2. **Extend**. Find the next 3 terms of the sequence below.

    4, 5, 9, 14, 23, 37, . . .

3. **Predict**. For each sequence find the 40th term and the nth term:

    a) 10, 13, 16, 19, 22, 25, . . .
    b) 3, 6, 12, 24, 48, 96, . . .

4. **Arithmetic sequence**. In an arithmetic sequence with the 2nd term 8 and the 6th term 20, find the 100th term.

5. **Population**. The population of Wrigleyville is predicted to increase by 1100 each year for the next 10 years. If the population is 43,000 now, how much will it be in 7 years?

6. **Stamps**. A full stamp dispenser holds 12, 288 stamps. At the end of each day half the stamps have been removed and not replaced. How many stamps will be left in the machine after 6 days? Assume that the machine was filled at the end of the first day.

7. **Increasing income**. Michelle's annual income has been increasing by the same amount every year. The first year her income was $28,000. In the 6th year it will be $37,000. In what year will it be $46,000?

8. **Dominos**. We want to create rectangles created with dominos. Each rectangle will have a height of 2 and a width of n. The dominoes may be placed horizontally or vertically to create the rectangle.

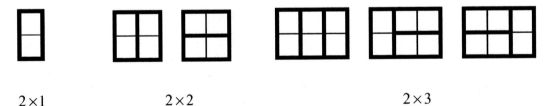

    2×1 2×2 2×3

    Continue creating all the $2 \times n$ rectangles for $n = 1$ to 8. Predict the number of ways to make a 2×12 rectangle.

5.6. Pedagogical Explorations

1. **Children's thinking about sequences**. Examine the examples of two children's thinking about an arithmetic sequence. Compare and contrast them and, for each example, describe how you think the child would respond to a request for the 40th term.

$$2 \quad 7 \quad 12 \quad 17 \quad 22$$

Caroline (age 8): $2 + 5 = 7$ and $7 + 5 = 12$. If $2 + 5 = 7$, then $12 + 5 = 17$. And like $7 + 5 = 12$, $17 + 5 = 22$. The pattern is it keeps adding 5. (Hargreaves, Threlfall, Frobisher, & Shorrocks-Taylor, 1999, p. 72)

$$2 \quad 5 \quad 8 \quad 11 \quad 14$$

Sarah (age 8): Well it goes up in 3s, but instead of starting with 3 there it's 1 below all the 3 times table. (Hargreaves, Threlfall, Frobisher, & Shorrocks-Taylor, 1999, p. 74)

2. **Textbook analysis**. Locate an elementary or middle school mathematics textbook. Look for problems or activities that involve mathematical patterns. Determine whether each pattern is a repeating pattern or a growing pattern. Try to find at least three examples of each. Which of the patterns you identified could be described by an arithmetic sequence? Which of the patterns you identified could be described by a geometric sequence? Explain.

3. **Student's reasoning about sequences**. Consider the sequences below. For each sequence, describe how a student might use recursive reasoning to answer the questions, and describe how a student might use explicit reasoning to answer the questions.

   For each sequence below, write the next three numbers in the sequence and write the 25th number in the sequence.

   a) 2, 6, 10, 14, 18, …
   b) 9, 12, 15, 18, 21…
   c) 6, 12, 24, 48, 96…

   Interview: After you have written your descriptions, ask a student in grades 3-8 to answer the questions. Then write an analysis describing the interview. Be sure to discuss any evidence of recursive and/or explicit reasoning. A student may use either form of reasoning or a combination of the two.

5.7. Summary

Terminology

Skip Counting: Counting by values other than one—that is, by twos, threes, fives, tens, etc.

Arithmetic Sequence: A sequence formed by identifying an initial term and a constant difference between terms.

Fibonacci Sequence: The sequence that begins with 1, 1 and each successive term is the sum of the two preceding terms.

Geometric Sequence: A sequence formed by identifying an initial term and a constant ratio between terms.

Big Ideas

Skip counting may serve as an introduction to sequences.

Arithmetic and geometric sequences have specific structures, determined by their initial term and a change value. These structures allow us to write recursive rules for describing the patterns and explicit rules for finding the *n*th term of the sequence.

The Fibonacci sequence is an example of a sequence that is best described using a recursive rule.

References

Glencoe Mathematics: Applications and Connections, Course 1. (1999). Westerville, OH: The McGraw-Hill Companies.

Hargreaves, M., Threlfall, J., Frobisher, L., & Shorrocks-Taylor, D. (1999). Children's Strategies with Linear and Quadratic Sequences. In A. Orton (Ed.), *Pattern in the teaching and learning of mathematics* (pp. 67-83). New York: Cassell.

Scott Foresman-Addison Wesley Math, Millennium Edition, Grade 5, (2002), Glenview, IL: Pearson Education.

UNIT THREE: LEARNING ALGEBRA THROUGH FUNCTIONS AND MODELING

This unit contains:
Chapter 6: Representing Functional Relationships
Chapter 7: Linear Functions
Chapter 8: Quadratic Functions
Chapter 9: Exponential Functions

"Functional relationships offer fertile ground for making mathematical connections. As a unifying idea in mathematics, the function concept helps students connect different mathematical ideas and procedures. Functional relationships also provide connections to other content areas and a perspective from which to view real-world phenomena."
(Day, 1995, p. 54)

CHAPTER SIX: REPRESENTING FUNCTIONAL RELATIONSHIPS

A function is a relationship between two or more varying quantities in which one quantity depends on the other(s). We have already seen several examples of functional relationships in this textbook. For example, in Crossing the River in Chapter 1, the number of trips depended on the number of adults and the number of children. The growing patterns in Chapter 4 were also examples of functional relationships in which the number of toothpicks or tiles depended on the figure number.

Functional relationships often appear in real-world quantities, and they may be represented using words, tables, graphs, and equations. This process of constructing these representations is called modeling. An understanding of functions includes the ability to construct, interpret, and translate among the various representations. This textbook focuses on developing those abilities.

The study of functions in elementary and middle school allows students to explore a variety of representations for mathematical relationships. These relationships offer interesting contexts for using variables. When variables represent meaningful quantities, it is more likely that students will develop a real understanding for them in graphs, tables, and equations.

Functions in Elementary School

Functions appear in elementary school mathematics as an extension of the study of patterns. An understanding of functions requires the ability to recognize and describe the pattern that exists between two varying quantities, an *input* and an *output*. This pattern is often expressed as a rule.

Activities involving function machines provide opportunities for children to explore functional relationships (Willoughby, 1997). A large box, big enough for a child to comfortably sit inside, is decorated to look like a machine with two slots labeled "input" and "output." Initially, the input and output may be concrete objects such as wooden sticks or plastic straws. A number of objects are put into the machine, and according to a specified rule, a second number of objects come out of the machine. The process is repeated several times for the same rule, using different input values. Input and output values may also be written on slips of paper. The goal is for children to guess the rule.

After children have actually used the large box, pictures of function machines may serve the same purpose. Tables may be used to record the input and output numbers for a given rule.

To illustrate, in this lesson from *Everyday Mathematics* (University of Chicago School Mathematics Project, 1995), first-graders solve "What's My Rule?" problems. The aim is to figure out what rule a function machine uses to do something to the numbers that are put in. Children are encouraged to describe the rule in different ways. For example, in the first problem, expected responses from children include the following:

- The "out" number is always 3 less than the "in" number.
- The function machine is subtracting 3 from the "in" number.
- The "in" number gets smaller by 3.

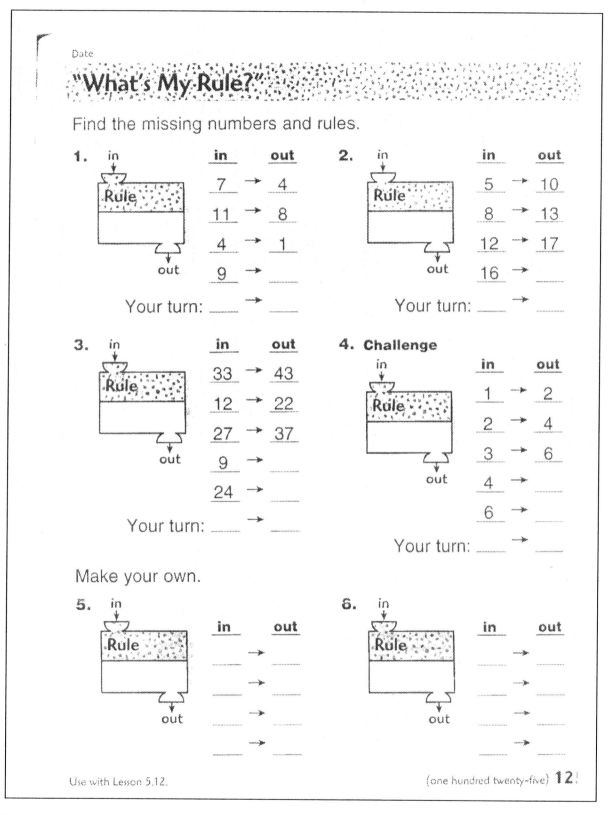

This lesson is an example of an activity that requires young children to think about the relationship among two varying quantities, input and output. Not only do they identify the given relationships, but they also create their own relationships.

Representing Functions

In another lesson from Everyday Mathematics (University of Chicago School Mathematics Project, 1995), fifth-graders also solve "What's My Rule?" problems. First, they are expected to write the rules using words. Then they identify the number sentences, or equations, that match the rules.

What's My Rule?

1. a. State in words the rule for the "What's My Rule?" table at the right.

   _____

   _____

   _____

   _____

X	Y
5	1
4	0
−1	−5
1	−3
2	−2

   b. Circle the number sentence that describes the rule.

   $Y = X / 5$ $Y = X - 4$ $Y = 4 - X$

2. a. State in words the rule for the "What's My Rule?" table at the right.

   _____

   _____

   _____

   _____

Q	Z
1	3
3	5
−4	−2
−3	−1
−2.5	−0.5

   b. Circle the number sentence that describes the rule.

   $Z = Q + 2$ $Z = 2 * Q$ $Z = \frac{1}{2}Q * 1$

3. a. State in words the rule for the "What's My Rule?" table at the right.

   _____

   _____

   _____

   _____

g	t
$\frac{1}{2}$	2
0	0
2.5	10
$\frac{1}{4}$	1
5	20

   b. Circle the number sentence that describes the rule.

   $g = 2 * t$ $t = 2 * g$ $t = 4 * g$

- 110 -

Experiences like these help students understand that one input value generates exactly one output value. As they learn to determine the input when they are given the output for a specific function, they explore inverse relationships, eventually constructing inverse operation rules that undo what other operations did. These notions provide a foundation for the formal study of functions.

Students in grades 3-5 should have opportunities to represent functional relationships using words and using numbers and symbols. They should also have opportunities to discover different models may represent the same situation. They need to develop flexibility in using a variety of techniques for organizing and expressing ideas about functional relationships.

NCTM *Principles and Standards for School Mathematics*—Algebra (NCTM, 2000)

In prekindergarten through grade 2 all students should—

- recognize, describe, and extend patterns such as sequences of sounds and shapes or simple numeric patterns and translate from one representation to another;
  …
- describe qualitative change, such as a student's growing taller;
  … (p. 90)

In grades 3–5 all students should—

- represent and analyze patterns and functions, using words, tables, and graphs;
  …
- investigate how a change in one variable relates to a change in a second variable;
  … (p. 158)

Functions in Middle School

Middle school students explore functional relationships and study patterns of change in the real world by conducting experiments, gathering data, and constructing tables and graphs. They analyze and compare the information contained in the tables and graphs, use words to describe the patterns and features they see, and eventually write equations to model functional relationships.

For example, four sixth graders watch intently as a matchbox car rolls down a ramp and across the floor of a multi-purpose room. When the car stops, two of them carefully measure the distance traveled, a third student records in a table the measurement of the cars, and the fourth student adds a book to increase the height of the ramp for a subsequent trial. In an animated discussion, the students predict the effect raising the ramp will have on the distance traveled by the car. Later the students will prepare a graph that shows the relationship between the height of the ramp and the distance traveled. This engaging activity provides a context for the students to investigate how change in the input value, the height of the ramp, is related to change in the output value, the distance traveled by the matchbox car.

> **NCTM *Principles and Standards for School Mathematics*—Algebra (NCTM, 2000)**
>
> **In grades 6–8 all students should—**
> - represent, analyze, and generalize a variety of patterns with tables, graphs, words, and, when possible, symbolic rules;
> - relate and compare different forms of representation for a relationship;
>   …
> - model and solve contextualized problems using various representations, such as graphs, tables, and equations;
>   … (p. 222)

Teachers' Knowledge of Functions

Because of the emphasis on multiple representations of patterns and functions in elementary and middle school mathematics, it is important for elementary and middle school teachers to understand the relationships among these multiple representations. This chapter provides an introduction to multiple representations of functional relationships. You explore function machines, record data in tables and graphs, and examine connections between real-world situations and their graphs. This helps you develop a deeper understanding of the notion of function. Subsequent chapters focus on particular types of functions—linear, quadratic, and exponential.

Goals of the Chapter

In this chapter, you will—

- write function rules using words and using equations,

- identify the independent and dependent variables in functional relationships,

- describe situations for graphs that show relationships between two variables,

- sketch graphs to represent situations that involve relationships between two variables,

- interpret features of graphs that illustrate increasing and decreasing functions, rates of change, concavity, and intercepts.

6.1. Function Machine

The following investigation is designed to let you experience the fun of a function machine to solve some "What's My Rule?" problems. If possible, use a very large box (big enough for someone to fit inside). If a large box is not available, a presentation board (big enough for someone to sit behind) can be transformed into a function machine. If neither of these large structures is available, a smaller box such as a shoebox can be used (but it is *not* as much fun). The function machine should include an input slot, an output slot, and a slot for rule cards, and these should be clearly labeled. A reset button, to set the machine to accept a new rule card, is also a nice feature to include on a function machine.

Function machines are used to investigate relationships between input and output values. The input and output may be concrete objects or they may be numbers (or other symbols) written on slips of paper.

Materials: Index cards, a large collection of concrete objects such as craft sticks or drinking straws (anything small enough to fit in the function machine slots), and slips of paper.

EXPLORE

First, the instructor will prepare a set of rule cards. A function rule describes the relationship between input and output. Some examples of simple function rules are:
- Add 3 to the input to get the output.
- Subtract 2 from the input to the output.
- Subtract the input from 5 to get the output.
- Multiply the input by 2 to get the output.

The function machine requires at least three people to operate it—someone we will call a machine operator to manage the rule cards and oversee the input and output and someone we will call the internal mechanism to sit inside the machine and perform the operations. A third person—someone we will call the recorder—is responsible for recording the input and output values for each function in a table on the chalkboard.

To operate the function machine, the machine operator presses the reset button to prepare the machine to accept a new rule card, and inserts the rule card into the rule slot. Then he or she inserts the input through the input slot. The internal mechanism then uses the rule to compute the output and sends it to the machine operator through the output slot. If the input is a collection of concrete objects, then the output will also be a collection of concrete objects. For example, if the function is "Add 3 to the input to get the output," then if two objects—say, straws—are inserted into the input slot, then the internal mechanism will send out a total of five straws via the output slot. If the input is written on a slip of paper, then the internal mechanism will write the output on a slip of paper. Use several input values for each rule. Also, try several rules with each format, actual objects and slips of paper.

For each function, the recorder records the input-output pairs in a table on the board. The class must then use the table to guess the function rule. For each function, class members should first use words to describe the rule. Then, if possible, they should write an algebraic equation for the rule, using the variable x to represent the input and y to represent the output. Some functions, though, may not be represented by an equation. An example of this type of function is the following: Input values are students' names, and output values are 0 for female names and 1 for male names.

DISCUSS

Young children are likely to use only words to express function rules. Older elementary and middle school students, though, can be encouraged to write algebraic equations to express the rules. It is important, then, to examine the connections between the words and the symbols in the function machine. As readers of this textbook, what connections do you see in the rules found by your own classmates?

In Section 1.9, we discussed five uses of variables. How are variables used in these rules?

What is a function?

In elementary and middle school, it is sufficient to think of a function as a dependence relationship between input and output values. As teachers, however, it is important to be aware of a more formal definition along with more formal terminology and symbolism.

A *function* is a relationship between two sets, the domain and the range, such that each value in the domain corresponds to exactly one value in the range.

The *domain* is the set of input values of the function, and the *range* is the set of output values. The symbol that represents an arbitrary value in the domain of the function is called the *independent variable*. The symbol that represents a value in the range of the function is called the *dependent variable*. In other words, the independent variable represents the input and the dependent variable represents the output. We often use the symbol f to represent a function, the variable x to represent the independent variable, and the variable y or the symbol $f(x)$ to represent the dependent variable, but other symbols and variables may also be used.

Identify the domain and range for some of the functions you encountered in this investigation. Some of the functions involved input in the form of concrete objects and others had input in the form of numbers or other symbols written on slips of paper. How might the domains for these functions be different?

The symbol $f(x)$ is read "f of x" and describes *the value of the function f at x*. The symbol $f(x)$ does not typically appear in elementary or middle school curriculum materials, perhaps to avoid confusion with multiplication. [Note that $f(x)$ does not mean "f times x" because, in this symbol, the letter f is not being used as a variable and the parentheses do not indicate multiplication.] The equation $y = f(x)$ tells us that y and $f(x)$ are different names for the same values. Thus the symbols y and $f(x)$ are often used interchangeably in higher level mathematics.

Practice using the function symbol $f(x)$ to write some of the function rules from this investigation.

Examples and Non-examples

As stated in the definition of a function, each value in the domain corresponds to exactly one value in the range. The examples and non-examples shown below emphasize this important aspect of functions.

Examples	Non-examples
If the independent variable is x and the dependent variable is y, the table below represents a function.	The following table, though, does *not* represent a function. Can you explain why it does not?

x	y
-3	9
-2	4
-1	1
0	0
1	1
2	4
3	9

x	y
3	-9
2	-4
1	-1
0	0
1	1
2	4
3	9

Likewise, the graph below represents a function.	But the following graph does *not* represent a function. Why not?

Output

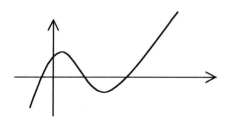

Input

Output

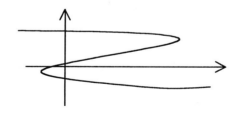

Input

If the independent variable is x and the dependent variable is y, this equation represents a function.	If the independent variable is x and the dependent variable is y, why does this equation *not* represent a function?

$$y = x^2 + 3$$

$$y^2 = x$$

The following verbal description of a real-world situation represents a function.

In order to divide his students into groups, Mr. Thomas assigned a number between 1 and 6 to each of the 24 students in his fourth-grade class. The input is each student's name, and the output is each student's number.

The following verbal description does *not* represent a function. Can you explain the difference between the two situations?

In order to divide her students into groups, Ms. Jones assigned a number between 1 and 5 to each of the 20 students in her third-grade class. The input is the number, and the output is each student's name.

Why is it important that there is no more than one corresponding output value for each input value? Is it possible to have more than one input value for a given output value?

In Section 1.9, we discussed five uses of variables. How are variables used in this investigation?

REFLECT

In this investigation, you explored relationships between values of input and output using a classroom tool—a function machine. You then discussed some definitions and examined some examples and non-examples of functions. These questions will help you summarize and extend what you learned:

Use the definition of a function to determine whether each of the following mathematical relationships is a function. If the relationship is a function, explain how you know it is a function. If the relationship is not a function, explain why it is not. For each relationship, assume x is the independent variable and y is the dependent variable.

Tables

1.

x	0	1	2	3	4	5	6
y	1	1	3	3	5	5	7

2.

x	0	0	2	2	4	4	6
y	1	2	3	4	5	6	7

3.

x	1	3	5	7	9	11	13
y	1	2	3	1	2	3	1

Graphs

4.

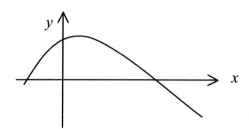

5.

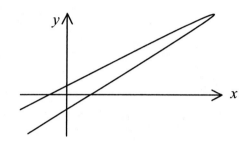

6.

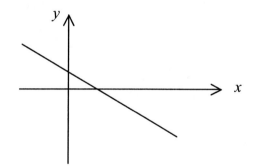

Equations

7. $y = \sqrt{x-2}$

8. $y = \pm\sqrt{x+4}$

9. $y^3 = x$

10. $y = |x-2|$

Words

Determine whether each of the following mathematical relationships is a function. If the relationship is a function, explain how you know it is a function. If the relationship is not a function, explain why it is not. For each relationship that is a function, state the independent and dependent variables. Also describe the domain and range of each function.

11. Belle earns $1.00 for each magazine she sells for her school's fundraiser. What kind of relationship is there between the number of magazines she sells and her total earnings?

12. Mr. Frisbee has his students use string and rulers to measure the diameter and the circumference of several circular jar lids. What kind of relationship is there between diameter and circumference?

13. Mrs. Block has her students build as many rectangles as they can with 12 square tiles. What kind of relationship is there between area and perimeter of the rectangles?

14. A 75-gallon bathtub takes 10 minutes to empty after the drain is opened. What kind of relationship is there between elapsed time and the number of gallons left in the tub?

Answer these questions and write a summary of what you learned from this investigation.

6.2. Jumping Jacks and Crackers

In this investigation, you will explore two real-world functional relationships by collecting data, recording the data in tables, and using the data to construct graphs. Groups may be assigned to one of two experiments conducted simultaneously. The groups will then compare the two experiments and the two representations of these experiments by tables and graphs.

Materials for Experiment 1: A clock or a watch with a second hand (one for each group), graph paper, transparencies for graphs.

Materials for Experiment 2: Oyster crackers (63 per group), drinking water, graph paper, transparencies for graphs.

EXPLORE

Experiment 1: Jumping Jacks

This experiment is adapted from *Connected Mathematics, Variables and Patterns: Introducing Algebra* (Lappan, Fey, Fitzgerald, Friel, & Phillips, 1998).

This experiment requires four people:
- a jumper (to do jumping jacks)
- a timer (to keep track of the time)
- a counter (to count jumping jacks)
- a recorder (to write down the number of jumping jacks)

As a group, decide who will do each task. When the timer says, "Go," the jumper begins doing jumping jacks. The counter counts the jumping jacks out loud. Every 10 seconds, the timer says "time" and the recorder writes down the cumulative total number of jumping jacks the Jumper has done to this point. Record the total number of jumping jacks after every 10 seconds, up to a total time of 2 minutes (120 seconds).

Collect the Data. Construct a table like the following for recording the total number of jumping jacks after every 10 seconds, up to a total time of 2 minutes (120 seconds).

Time (seconds)	0	10	20	30	40	50	...
Total Number of Jumping Jacks							...

Graph the Data. Make a coordinate graph of your jumping jack data. The horizontal axis should correspond to the independent variable and the vertical axis should correspond to the dependent variable. Be prepared to share your graph with the class on a transparency.

Experiment 2: Crackers

This experiment requires three people:

- a muncher (to eat the oyster crackers; make sure this person knows how to whistle)
- a timer (to keep track of the time)
- a recorder (to write down the number of seconds)

As a group, decide who will do each task. When the timer says "go," the muncher pops three oyster crackers into his or her mouth and begins chewing. After swallowing the crackers, the muncher tries to whistle. As soon as the muncher whistles successfully, the timer announces the number of seconds that have elapsed from the beginning of chewing to the whistle, and the recorder writes down the number of seconds. The muncher takes a drink of water, and then repeats the cycle five more times, first with six oyster crackers, then with nine, and so forth, up to 18 crackers.

Collect the Data. Construct a table like the following for recording the number of seconds it takes to whistle after eating a given number of oyster crackers.

Number of crackers	0	3	6	9	12	15	18
Time (in seconds)							

Graph the Data. Make a coordinate graph of your data. The horizontal axis should correspond to the independent variable and the vertical axis should correspond to the dependent variable. Be prepared to share your graph with the class on a transparency.

DISCUSS

Examine graphs from both experiments. What is the independent variable in the Jumping Jacks experiment? What is the dependent variable? What is the independent variable in the Crackers experiment? What is the dependent variable? How did you choose the independent and dependent variables as you did? How did you select a scale for each axis? What is the domain for each experiment? What is the range?

Did you and your classmates connect the points on your graphs? Connecting the points on a graph may help you see the functional relationship more clearly. In general, it is appropriate to connect the points in situations in which it makes sense to consider what is happening *between* the points. This is true when both the independent and dependent variables are *continuous* variables. That is, within the limits of the domain and the range, all values of x and y are possible. If either one of the variables is *discrete*—that is, not continuous—then the points should not be connected. Is it appropriate to connect the points in the graph of the Jumping Jacks data? Why or why not? Is it appropriate to connect the points in the graph of the Crackers data? Why or why not?

Rate of change is a measure of how fast one variable changes in relation to another.

For a function $y = f(x)$, the average rate of change over a particular interval of values, $a \le x \le b$, can be calculated with the formula,

$$\text{Average rate of change} = \frac{\text{change in } y}{\text{change in } x} = \frac{f(b) - f(a)}{b - a}.$$

What was the average rate of change for each of the various time intervals in the jumping jack experiment? What was the average rate of change over the entire experiment? How should you label the units? How did this value change as you increased the number of seconds? How is this shown in your table? How is this shown in your graph?

What were the corresponding rates of change for the crackers experiment? How should you label these units? What similarities or differences do you see between rate of change in the Crackers experiment and rate of change in the jumping jacks experiment?

In each experiment, is the relationship between the two variables easier to see in the table or the graph? Explain.

REFLECT

In this investigation, you explored two situations, each involving two variables. You constructed tables and graphs to show the relationships between the variables. These questions will help you summarize what you learned:

1. What was the independent variable and what was the dependent variable in each situation?

2. How were the tables and graphs for the two situations similar? How were they different?

3. What are the advantages of seeing the relationship between two variables in a table? What are the advantages of seeing the relationship in a graph?

Answer these questions and write a summary of what you learned from this investigation.

6.3. From Graphs to Situations

Graphs are a useful source of information about mathematical relationships. Typically, labels that indicate which axes relate to independent and dependent variables and appropriate scales for the axes help the reader understand the meaning of a graph. Qualitative graphs, those that tell a story without using numbers, provide opportunities for students to focus on functional relationships without getting lost in the numbers. These graphs without numbers help students think about what the shape of the graph is telling about change in a quantity. For example, in this lesson from *Everyday Mathematics*, fifth-graders match the descriptions of real-world events with their graphs. Take a moment to match each event with its graph.

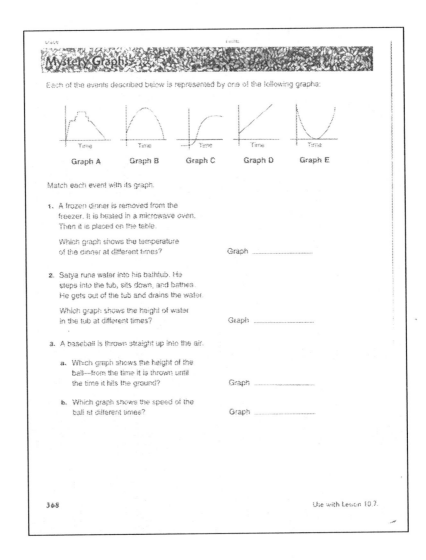

In this investigation, you will interpret graphs and write stories to describe situations involving relationships between two variables.

EXPLORE

In groups, examine one or more of the following graphs. For each graph given, write a story to describe a situation that would produce the graph for the relationship shown between the two variables. For simplicity, all of the graphs are continuous even though some of the variables may not be continuous.

Graph #1: Attendance at a Water Park

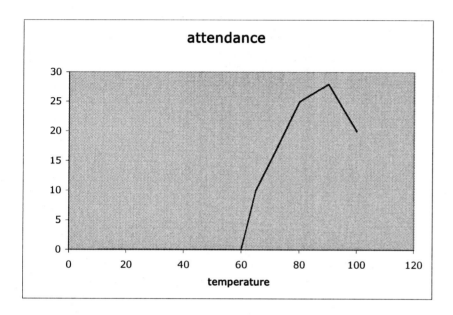

Graph #2: Portion of a House Painted over Time

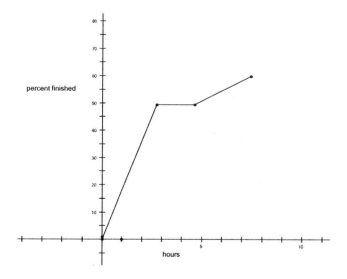

Representing Functions

Graph #3: Profit Earned from the Sale of Scarves

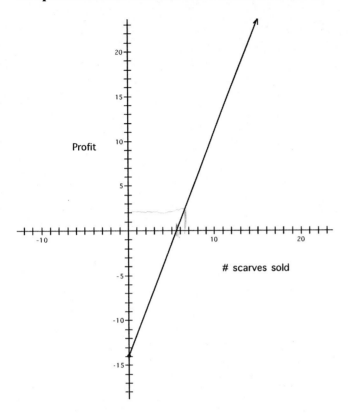

Profit

scarves sold

Graph #4: Distance from Home of a Person on a Bicycle

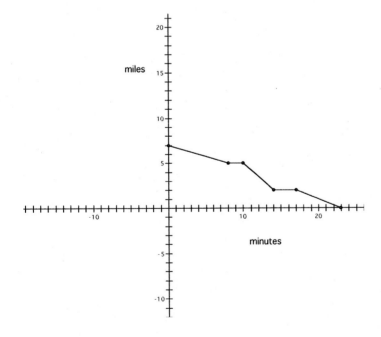

miles

minutes

Graph #5: Water Level in a Small Pond over the Course of Several Months

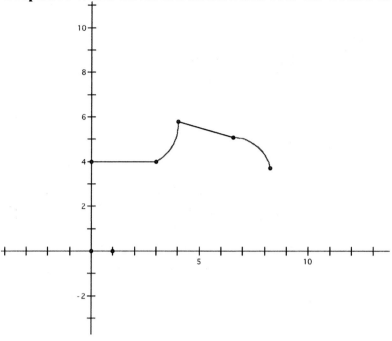

Graph #6: Speed during a Drive Home from Work

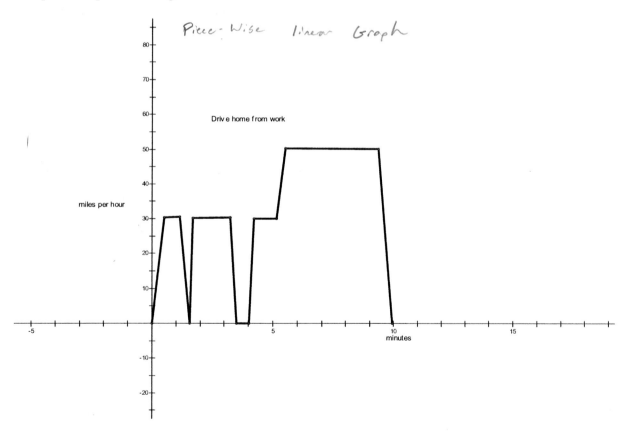

DISCUSS

Share your stories with the class.

The appearance of a graph provides several clues about the relationship between the two variables represented by the graph. Let us introduce some terminology that is often used to describe important features of a graph.

Increasing, Decreasing, and Constant Functions
When a graph is sloping upward from left to right, the function is *increasing*. That is, as the values of the independent variable are increasing, the values of the dependent variable are also increasing.

Similarly, when a graph is sloping downward from left to right, the function is *decreasing*. That is, as the values of the independent variable are increasing, the values of the dependent variable are decreasing.

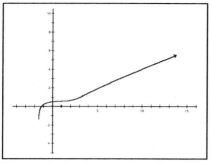

Figure 1. An increasing function

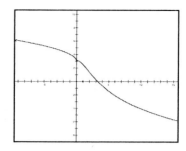

Figure 2. A decreasing function

A function is *constant* when it is neither increasing nor decreasing. That is, as the values of the independent variable are increasing, the values of the dependent variable are all the same (see Figure 3).

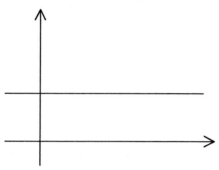

Figure 3. A constant function

Compare Graph #2 and Graph #4. Which one is never increasing and which one is never decreasing? What does that tell you about each of the situations? What does the constant portion of each graph tell you?

Rate of Change

In the previous section, we discussed the notion of rate of change. Rate of change can also be described as a measure of how fast a function is increasing or decreasing. It is the change in one variable in relation to the change in another variable.

Consider Graph #2. Over what time intervals were the painters working the fastest? What is the rate of change in Graph #3? What does this tell you about the profit earned from the sale of a single scarf? In Graph #4, how did the cyclist's speed change over the trip? In contrast, what was the average speed over the entire trip?

Concavity

Concavity is another important feature of the graph of a function. A graph that is *concave up* has the shape of a wire whose ends are bent upward (see Figure 4). A graph that is *concave down* has the shape of a wire whose ends are bent downward (see Figure 5).

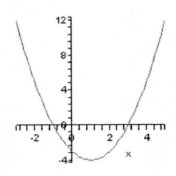

Figure 4. A graph that is concave up.

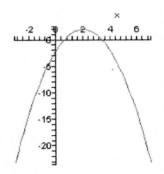

Figure 5. A graph that is concave down.

A function may include intervals where the graph is concave up and other intervals where the function is concave down. Concavity does not determine whether a function is increasing or decreasing, but it reveals the *rate* at which a function is increasing or decreasing. When a graph is concave up, the function is either increasing or decreasing at an increasing rate. When a graph is concave down, the function is either increasing or decreasing at a decreasing rate.

Describe the concavity in Graph #1. What does this say about attendance at the water park? Where is Graph #5 concave up and where is it concave down? What does this tell you about the water level during those time intervals?

Intercepts

Two other important types of points on a graph are the *intercepts*, the points where the graph intersects the horizontal and vertical axes. A graph intersects the horizontal axis at the points where the value of the dependent variable is zero. This point is called the horizontal intercept or the *x*-intercept. A graph intersects the vertical axis at the point where the value of the independent variable is zero. This point is called the vertical intercept or the *y*-intercept. A function may have more than one *x*-intercept, but a function can have only one *y*-intercept. (Why?)

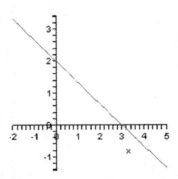

Figure 6. A graph with *x*-intercept at (3,0) and *y*-intercept at (0,2).

What do the *x*- and *y*-intercepts indicate about the situations represented by Graph #1, Graph #3, Graph #4, and Graph #6?

Maximum and Minimum Values

A *local maximum* of a function occurs when the graph changes from increasing to decreasing. Similarly, a *local minimum* of a function occurs when the graph changes from decreasing to increasing. *Absolute* maximum and minimum values for a function may occur at a local maximum/minimum or at the endpoints of a particular interval; that is, at the highest or lowest values of the domain.

In Graph #1, what was the maximum attendance at the water park? In Graph #2, was the paint job completed? How do you know? In Graph #6, what conjectures can you make about speed limits? Explain.

REFLECT

In this investigation, you interpreted graphs and described situations involving relationships between two variables. These questions will help you summarize what you learned:

1. How did important features of the graphs (intervals of increase, decrease, and constancy; rate of change; concavity; intercepts; and maximum and minimum values) appear in your original descriptions?

2. Write revised stories for Graph #5 and Graph #6 to include these important features.

3. In Graph 6, approximately how far does the driver live from work? Explain how you determined your answer.

Answer these questions and write a summary of what you learned from this investigation.

6.4. From Situations to Graphs

In this investigation, you will sketch graphs to represent various situations, each involving two variables.

EXPLORE

In groups, study one or more of the following situations. For each situation, identify the independent and dependent variables and sketch a graph of the relationship described. Label your axes with the names of the variables. For some of the situations, you may decide to put numbers on the axes.

Situation #1: Rachel is taking her dog Spunky on a walk. They walk slowly at a constant rate for the first two blocks. Then Spunky sees a squirrel. He races after the squirrel, chasing it for a block until the squirrel runs up a tree. Spunky stands at the base of the tree barking for two minutes. Finally, Rachel pulls him away and they jog back home. Sketch a graph of distance versus time. Sketch another graph of rate versus time.

Situation #2: A plane is circling an airport waiting for clearance to land. Sketch a graph of distance from the airport versus time.

Situation #3: A concession stand at a swim meet opens 90 minutes before the first race for parents to buy breakfast while swimmers are warming up. Snack sales continue during the morning sessions while most spectators are in the bleachers. Lunch is sold between morning and afternoon sessions and snacks are sold again during the afternoon races. Sketch a graph of concession stand income versus time.

Situation #4: Juanita is opening a lemonade stand. She spends $12 on supplies to make her lemonade. She opens her stand on a busy street just as workers are taking their lunch break and sells lots of lemonade for $1.50 per cup. Over the afternoon sales taper off until another peak in sales at 5:00 p.m. Sketch a graph of profit versus the number of cups of lemonade sold.

DISCUSS

Share your graphs with the class. For each one, relate features of the story to the appearance of the graph. Include intervals of increasing, decreasing, and constant; rate of change; concavity; intercepts; and maximum and minimum. For example, where were the graphs you drew for the four situations increasing or decreasing? What did this mean in the situation described?

Describe the average rate of change for Situation #2. When would you expect the graph of Situation #3 to show the greatest rate of change? Why?

When would you expect the graph for Juanita's lemonade profits in Situation #4 to be concave down? Why?

REFLECT

In this investigation, you sketched graphs to represent situations involving two variables. These questions will help you summarize what you learned:

1. In general, what is happening in a real-world situation when the corresponding function is increasing? What is happening when the function is decreasing? What is happening when the function is constant?

2. What does it say about a real-world situation if the corresponding graph is concave up? What does it mean in the situation if the graph is concave down?

3. Create an interesting story and sketch a corresponding graph. Include intervals of increase, decrease, and constancy; varying rates of change; concavity; intercepts; and maximum and minimum values.

Answer these questions and write a summary of what you learned from this investigation.

6.5. Additional Problems

1. **Graphs of situations**. Sketch a reasonable graph for each of the following situations and write a sentence or two describing your graph.

   a) The distance from the speakers at a rock concert and the loudness of the music are related.
   b) The price of a pizza depends on its diameter.
   c) The temperature of hot cocoa depends on amount of time that has elapsed since the cocoa was poured.
   d) The altitude of a fly ball hit by a batter depends on the time since the bat hit the ball.
   e) As you breathe, the volume of air in your lungs changes with time.
   f) Your head's distance from the ground is related to the time elapsed since a Ferris wheel you are riding began.

2. **Technology exploration**. Use a motion detector connected to a graphing calculator to explore relationships between distance and time or speed and time.

3. **Ceiling function**. In the solution to the Bossy the Cow problem in Chapter 1, we used the ceiling function, $f(x) = \lceil x \rceil$, the smallest integer greater than or equal to x. Sketch a graph for each of the following functions.

   a) $f(x) = \lceil x \rceil$
   b) $f(x) = \lceil x \rceil + 2$
   c) $f(x) = \lceil x + 2 \rceil$
   d) $f(x) = \lceil x \rceil - 2$
   e) $f(x) = \lceil x - 2 \rceil$
   f) $f(x) = 2\lceil x \rceil$
   g) Describe how the location of the 2 in each formula affects the graph.

6.6. Pedagogical Explorations

1. **Describe a situation.** Many everyday patterns can be described as functional relationships. For instance, the number of chair legs in your classroom is four times the number of chairs, and could be represented by the equation *l = 4c, where l is the number of chair legs and c is the number of chairs*. Think of a situation that would be familiar to students in grades K-3. Describe the situation with words and then make a table and create a graph that would represent the situation for one to ten values of the independent variable. Identify the variables and write an equation that describes the situation.

2. **Cheeseburger problem**. A fifth-grade mathematics problem is shown below.

   a) First, answer the question as it is written.

   For this week only, Shaky's Hamburger Joint is selling cheeseburgers by the bag at a price of $4.00 for a bag of five cheeseburgers. How many cheeseburgers could you buy for $20.00?

   b) Reword the question to direct children's thinking away from finding a single numerical answer and toward thinking about the relationships among the quantities in the problem.

3. **Function machine.** Make a function machine with a half-gallon milk or juice carton. Cut two rectangular slots on one side of the carton. Cut a strip of tag board or a manila folder that is slightly less that the width of the carton and about as long as the carton is tall. Crease the strip 1/2 inch from each end to form tabs for attaching the strip. Fasten the strip inside the carton above the top slot and below the bottom slot. The strip should be long enough to curve inside the carton. If you insert a 3"x5" card front-wise into the top, the curve will flip the card so that the back of the card shows when the card comes out the bottom.

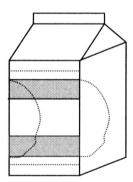

Make four sets of function cards on 3"x5"cards to use with your function machine. Each set should include 6 or more cards with numbers that fit the same rule. Use rules with different levels of difficulty. On each card write an input number on one side and the corresponding output number on the other side. You may want to mark the sides "I" for input and "O" for output.

4. **Interpreting a graph.** Interview a student in grades 4 through 8.

   a) Show the student the first graph you drew for Situation #1 in section 6.4. Explain that the horizontal axis on the graph represents the distance Rachel and her dog Spunky traveled on a walk and the vertical axis represents the time they walked. Ask the student to use the shape of the graph to describe their walk. Keep careful notes of the student's responses.

   b) Write an analysis of the interview. Describe the student's responses. Discuss what features of the graph the student interpreted appropriately. Also discuss any points the student did not appear to understand clearly.

6.7. Summary

Terminology

Concavity: The shape of the curve signifies the rate of increase or decrease of a function.

Function: A relationship between two sets, the domain and the range, such that each value in the domain corresponds to exactly one value in the range.

Increasing function: As the values of the independent variable are increasing, the values of the dependent variable are also increasing.

Intercepts: The points where the graph intersects the horizontal and vertical axes.

Decreasing function: As the values of the independent variable are increasing, the values of the dependent variable are decreasing.

Rate of change: A measure of how fast a function is increasing or decreasing.

Big Ideas

Functions are represented in many forms: words, tables, graphs, and equations all communicate information about functional relationships in different ways. Words describe functional relationships using everyday and mathematical language. Tables provide organized lists of specific pairs of input and output numbers, making it possible to see patterns of change in the data. Graphs provide overall visual displays of functions, making it easier to see trends and make predictions. Equations express functional relationships in symbolic notation and serve as formulas to determine particular values of functions.

References

Day, R. P. (1995). Using functions to make mathematical connections. In P. A. House & A. F. Coxford (Eds.), *Connecting mathematics across the curriculum* (pp. 54-64). Reston, VA: National Council of Teachers of Mathematics.

Lappan, G., Fey, J. T., Fitzgerald, W. M., Friel, S. N., & Phillips, E. D. (1998). *Variables and patterns: Introducing algebra*. Connected Mathematics series. Glenview, IL: Prentice Hall.

National Council of Teachers of Mathematics. (2000). *Principles and standards for school mathematics*. Reston, VA: Author.

University of Chicago School Mathematics Project. (1995). *Everyday Mathematics*. Evanston, IL: Everyday Learning Corporation.

Willoughby, S. S. (1997). Functions from kindergarten through sixth grade. *Teaching Children Mathematics, 6*, 314-318.

CHAPTER SEVEN: LINEAR FUNCTIONS

A linear function is one that involves a constant rate of change. This type of function is called *linear* because its graph is the set of points on a nonvertical line. Linear functions can be written as equations in the form $y = mx + b$, where m and b are real numbers. Linear relationships often appear among real-world quantities. For example, the number of chair legs in a room is linearly related to the number of chairs in the room (assuming all the chairs have four legs). Several of the growing patterns in Chapter 5 are also examples of linear relationships.

This chapter helps readers identify and describe important features of linear functions in tables, graphs, equations, and real-world situations. The next two chapters focus on the features of nonlinear functions. By approaching algebra by exploring linear and nonlinear functions, readers will develop a deeper understanding of the patterns in the relationships and their multiple representations.

Linear functions appear in various forms in elementary and middle school mathematics. Explorations of linear relationships are typically the first experiences that students have with variables as quantities that vary in relationship. Students later explore the similarities and differences between linear and nonlinear relationships.

Linear Functions in Elementary School

Children's first experiences with functions are typically with linear functions. In grades PreK-2, students use function machines (discussed in chapter 6) to investigate linear relationships between input and output values.

In grades 3-5, students explore the links among different representations of linear relationships. For example, in this lesson from *Everyday Mathematics* (University of Chicago School Mathematics Project, 1995), fifth-graders match number stories with their graphs. Then they select the rule that best fits each number story.

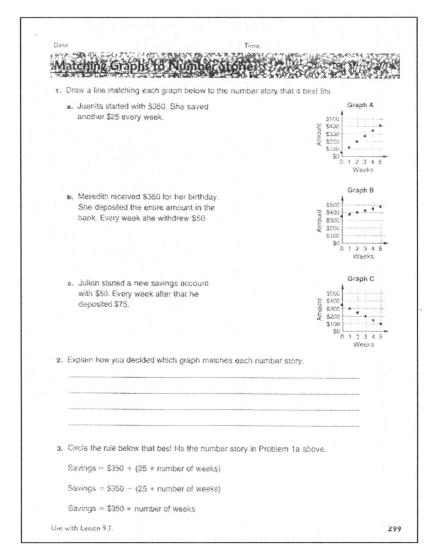

Experiences like these help students begin to see how the constant rate of change in a real-world situation is reflected in the linearity of a graph. They also challenge students to use words to describe the relationships between two variables.

Many typical elementary school activities provide opportunities for children to encounter linear functions and rate of change. For example, when elementary students plant seeds and record the growth in a table, they notice change. If the plant grows at different rates during different periods of time, a child may report: "My plant didn't grow for the first four days, then it grew slowly for the next two days, then it started to grow faster, then it slowed down again" (NCTM, 2000, p. 163). Each segment of time in the child's report represents a different rate of change, and would be represented on a graph by a line segment with a slope that is different from the slopes of the other segments. Students in grades 3-5 need experiences with rate of change to prepare them for later work with the concept of slope. It is not so important for elementary school students to be familiar with the *terminology* of functions and rate of change but rather for them to explore the *ideas*.

NCTM *Principles and Standards for School Mathematics*—Algebra (NCTM, 2000)

In prekindergarten through grade 2 all students should—

- describe quantitative change, such as a student's growing two inches in one year. (p. 90)

In grades 3–5 all students should—

- investigation how a change in one variable relates to a change in a second variable;
- identify and describe situations with constant or varying rates of change and compare them. (p. 158)

Linear Functions in Middle School

As middle school students continue the study of patterns and relationships, their study should focus on patterns that lead to linear functions. Linear functions provide a rich environment in which middle school students can refine their developing understanding of proportionality through exploration of the meaning of slope as it is reflected in stories about linear situations, in linear equations, in graphs, and in tables. They should also learn to distinguish linear relationships from nonlinear ones (NCTM, 2000).

NCTM *Principles and Standards for School Mathematics*—Algebra (NCTM, 2000)

In grades 6–8 all students should—

- identify functions as linear or nonlinear and contrast their properties from tables, graphs, or equations;
  …
- use graphs to analyze the nature of changes in quantities in linear relationships. (p. 222)

In the following set of applications from *Connected Mathematics, Moving Straight Ahead: Linear Relationships* (Lappan, Fey, Fitzgerald, Friel, & Phillips 1998), seventh-graders examine the distances traveled by three cyclists on a week-long cycling event. Notice that students are asked to translate information from a table into a graph and then interpret the graph. Later they are asked to use the information provided to write an equation for each rider and interpret the equation.

Linear Functions

Applications • Connections • Extensions

As you work on these ACE questions, use your calculator whenever you need it.

Applications

In 1–3, use the following information: José, Mario, and Melanie went on a weeklong cycling trip. The table below gives the distance each person traveled for the first 3 hours of the trip. The table shows only the time when the riders were actually biking, not when they stopped to rest, eat, and so on.

Cycling time (hours)	Distance (miles)		
	José	Mario	Melanie
0	0	0	0
1	5	7	9
2	10	14	18
3	15	21	27

1. **a.** How fast did each person travel for the first 3 hours? Explain how you got your answer.

b. Assume that each person continued at this rate. Find the distance each person traveled in 7 hours.

2. **a.** Graph the time and distance data for all three riders on the same coordinate axes.

b. Use the graphs to find the distance each person traveled in $6\frac{1}{2}$ hours.

c. Use the graphs to find the time it took each person to travel 70 miles.

d. How does the rate at which each person rides affect the graphs?

3. **a.** For each rider, write an equation that can be used to calculate the distance traveled after a given number of hours.

b. Use your equations from part a to calculate the distance each person traveled in $6\frac{1}{2}$ hours.

c. How does a person's biking rate show up in his or her equation?

This set of applications is filled with tasks and questions that challenge students to examine and describe linear relationships, making connections among multiple representations. With many such rich experiences with linear functions, middle school students can become comfortable and competent in navigating among representations of linear functions and solving linear equations.

Teachers' Knowledge of Linear Functions

So that they can promote a robust understanding of linear functions with their students, elementary and middle school teachers need to have their own deep and rich understanding of linear functions in all of their aspects and representations. In this chapter, you explore linear relationships in real-world situations and examine the connections among tables, graphs, and equations. The problems and investigations are extensions of the types of activities that appear in elementary and middle school curriculum materials.

Goals of the Chapter

In this chapter, you will—

- recognize and describe real-world situations involving linear relationships,

- recognize and describe special characteristics of linear functions represented in tables, graphs, and equations,

- write equations to represent linear functions,

- translate among various representations—words, tables, graphs, and equations—of linear functions,

- solve problems involving linear functions,

- collect real-world data and use a linear function to model the relationship.

7.1. Skate Rental

In this investigation, adapted from *Connected Mathematics, Moving Straight Ahead: Linear Relationships* (Lappan, Fey, Fitzgerald, Friel, & Phillips, 1998), you use multiple representations to explore a linear relationship between two variables.

Materials: A graphing utility or graph paper.

EXPLORE

A sixth-grade class is planning a skating party to celebrate the end of the school year. A committee of students is in charge of finding a place to rent in-line skates for a reasonable price. The committee got quotes from two companies:

> Roll-Away Skates charges $5 per person.
> Wheelie's Skates and Stuff charges $100 plus $3 per person.

Which company should the committee choose if they want to keep their costs to a minimum? Explain how you made your choice.

DISCUSS

Various representations can be used to examine this situation—equations, graphs, and tables. Which representations did you use to make your choice?

First, let's consider equations. For each company, write an equation to show the relationship between the number of people and the cost. What is the independent variable in this situation and what is the dependent variable? How can you use these equations to determine which skate-rental company to choose?

Perhaps you graphed the equations for both companies on the same set of axes. What range of values did you use for the number of people? What range of values did you use for the rental cost? How did you select these ranges? On which graph is the point (8, 40)? What does this point mean in terms of the cost to rent skates? On which graph is the point (8, 124)? What does this point mean in terms of the cost to rent skates? Find the point of intersection of the two graphs. What does this point mean in terms of the cost to rent skates?

Perhaps you made a table to show the relationship between number of people and the cost for each company. How does a table help you to see which company offers the better deal?

Can you say for sure which skate-rental company offers the better deal for the class? The number of students in the sixth grade class must be considered in determining which company offers the better deal. Suppose you have a single classroom of 30 students. Which company would you choose? Why? How can you determine this from the equations, the graph, and the table? Which company would you choose if 100 students were planning to attend the party? Why? Is there a number of students for which the two companies cost the same? How can you identify this number using the equations, the graph, and the table? If your budget for skate rental is $350, how many pairs of skates can you rent from each company?

For each of the two skate-rental companies, the relationship between the number of people and the cost is an example of a linear function. Why is this called a *linear* function? When the equations of linear functions are written in the form $y = mx + b$, the variables m and b are *parameters*; their values determine the particular relationship between x and y. What are the values of m in each equation? What do these values of m mean in terms of the cost to rent skates? How do the values of m appear in the graphs? How do the values of m appear in the table? What are the values of b in each equation? What do these value of b mean in terms of the cost to rent skates? How do the values of b appear in the graphs? How do the values of b appear in the table?

REFLECT

In this investigation, you explored the relationship between the number of people attending a skating party and the total cost to rent skates. These questions will help you summarize what you learned:

1. What are some of the advantages and disadvantages of using equations, graphs, and tables to examine linear situations?

2. Explain how to find the y-intercept of a linear relationship from an equation, a graph, and a table.

3. Summarize what you know about the graph of a linear equation of the form $y = mx + b$.

4. How are linear functions related to the arithmetic sequences we saw in Chapter 5?

Answer these questions and write a summary of what you learned from this investigation.

Linear Functions

7.2. Matching Representations of Linear Functions

In this investigation, you will explore connections among various representations— tables, graphs, and equations—of linear functions.

EXPLORE

Match each table with a graph and an equation.

Table

A.

x	y
-2	-7
-1	-5
0	-3
1	-1
2	1

B.

x	y
-2	2
-1	2
0	2
1	2
2	2

C.

x	y
-2	-2
-1	-2.5
0	-3
1	-3.5
2	-4

D.

x	y
-2	-4
-1	-3.5
0	-3
1	-2.5
2	-2

E.

x	y
-2	-1
-1	1
0	3
1	5
2	7

F.

x	y
-2	7
-1	5
0	3
1	1
2	-1

Graph

G.

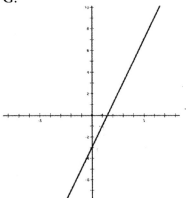

H.

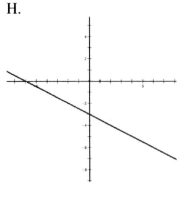

I.

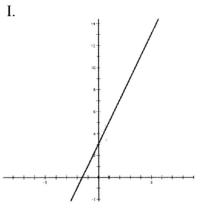

- 144 -

J.
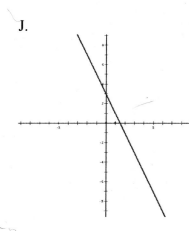

K.
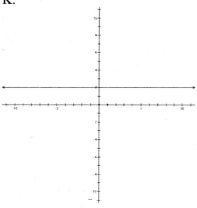

L.
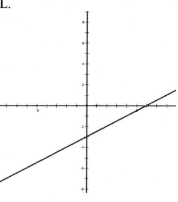

Equation

M. $y = 2x + 3$

N. $y = -2x + 3$

O. $y = 2x - 3$

P. $y = 2$

Q. $y = \frac{1}{2}x - 3$

R. $y = -\frac{1}{2}x - 3$

DISCUSS

Different people may approach this matching exercise in different ways. Discuss your selections with your class members. Explain how you made your selections. How did others in your class make their selections? Did you all agree in your selections?

Linear Functions

Two important features of a line are the *slope* and the *y-intercept*. The *slope* of the line is a measure of its steepness, indicated by the ratio $\frac{rise}{run}$ or $\frac{vertical\ change}{horizontal\ change}$. If (x_1, y_1) and (x_2, y_2) are two points on the line, then the slope can be calculated with the formula $m = \frac{y_2 - y_1}{x_2 - x_1}$. The *y*-intercept is the value of *y* at the point where the line crosses the *y*-axis.

Identify the slope and the *y*-intercept for each of the linear functions in the EXPLORE section. How does the slope appear in the table of a linear function? How does the *y*-intercept appear in the table? How does the slope appear in the equation of a linear function? How does the *y*-intercept appear in the equation?

In Chapter 6 we discussed increasing and decreasing functions. Which of the linear functions are increasing? Which are decreasing? Which are constant? How can you tell if a linear function is increasing, decreasing, or constant from the table? How can you tell if a linear function is increasing, decreasing, or constant from the graph? How can you tell if a linear function is increasing, decreasing, or constant from the equation?

In the Jumping Jacks investigation in Chapter 6, you explored the notion of rate of change. How is slope related to rate of change?

REFLECT

In this investigation, you explored connections among linear functions in tables, graphs, and equations. These questions will help you summarize what you learned:

1. If you have a table for a linear function, how can you find the graph?

2. If you have a table for a linear function, how can you find the equation?

3. If you have a graph of a linear function, how can you find the equation?

4. If you have a graph of a linear function, how can you find a table?

5. If you have an equation of a linear function, how can you find the graph?

6. If you have an equation of a linear function, how can you find a table?

7. How can you determine which one of two linear functions has the greater rate of change by looking at their graphs? How can you determine which one of two linear functions has the greater rate of change by looking at their tables? How can you determine which one of two linear functions has the greater rate of change by looking at their equations?

Answer these questions and write a summary of what you learned from this investigation.

7.3. Fahrenheit and Celsius

In this problem you derive two formulas that express the linear relationship between two different scales for measuring temperature.

EXPLORE

The relationship between degrees Fahrenheit and degrees Celsius is linear. Water freezes at 0°C and 32°F. Water boils at 100°C and 212°F. Use this information to write two formulas: One that expresses Fahrenheit temperature as a linear function of Celsius temperature, and one that expresses Celsius temperature as a linear function of Fahrenheit temperature.

DISCUSS

How did you find your formulas? Compare your methods with those of your classmates. How did you decide if your formula was correct?

What does the slope represent in each formula? What does the *y*-intercept represent?

Does it ever happen that the temperature measured in Celsius degrees is the same as the temperature measured in Fahrenheit degrees? If so, when? If not, why? Explain your answer.

REFLECT

Write a problem-solving report using the framework from Chapter 1. Explain how you determined your equation.

7.4. Identifying Linear Functions

In this investigation, you will identify linear functions in graphs, tables, equations, and real-world situations. You will also describe the special features of linear functions in each of these representations.

EXPLORE

1. Which of the following graphs represent linear functions? Explain why or why not.

a)

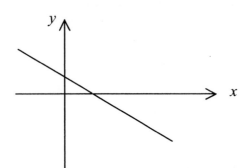

b).

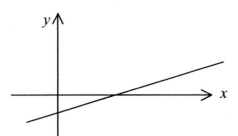

c).

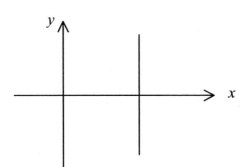

d)

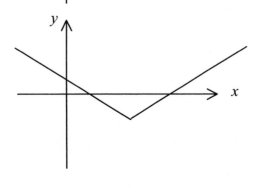

2. Which of the following tables represent linear functions? For each linear function, identify the slope and the y-intercept. For each non-linear function, explain why the function is not linear.

a)

x	-3	-2	-1	0	1	2	3	4	5
y	12	9	6	3	0	-3	-6	-12	-15

b)

x	-14	-10	-6	-2	2	6	10	14	18
y	-2	1	6	13	21	32	45	60	77

Function
Not linear

c)

x	1	2	4	8	16	32	64	128	256
y	0	5	10	15	20	25	30	35	40

d)

x	-10	-8	-6	-4	-2	0	2	4	6
y	4.0	3.5	3.0	2.5	2.0	1.5	1.0	0.5	0.0

Fuction
linear

e)

x	-16	-8	-1	5	10	14	17	19	20
y	-12	-9	-6	-3	0	3	6	9	12

3. Which of the following equations represent linear functions? For each linear function, identify the slope and the y-intercept. For each non-linear function, explain why the function is not linear.

a) $y = x - \dfrac{10}{3}$

b) $y = 4.2 - 3.2x$ $-3.2x + 4.2$

c) $y = \dfrac{x}{9} + 6$

d) $y = \dfrac{2}{x} - 10$

4. Which of the following situations can be modeled by linear functions? Explain why or why not.

a) **Painted Cubes 1**. A large cube with edges of length n units is built from small unit cubes. The faces of the large cube are painted. Write an equation for the number of small unit cubes painted on one face.

b) **Painted Cubes 2**. A large cube with edges of length n units is built from small unit cubes. The faces of the large cube are painted. Write an equation for the number of small unit cubes painted on two faces.

c) **Long-Distance Phone Company**. A phone company charges \$1.05 for the first minute of a long-distance call and 23¢ for each additional minute. Write an equation for the total cost of a long-distance call.

d) **Toothpick Pattern**. Write an explicit rule to express the relationship between the number of toothpicks and the figure number in the following growing toothpick pattern.

| **Figure 1** | **Figure 2** | **Figure 3** |

DISCUSS

Describe the special features of linear functions represented in graphs. Describe the special features of linear functions represented in tables. Describe the special features of linear functions represented in equations. Describe the special features of situations that can be modeled by linear functions.

REFLECT

In this investigation, you identified linear functions in various representations and described the special features of these representations. These questions will help you summarize what you learned:

1. How can you recognize linear functions in graphs?

2. How can you recognize linear functions in tables?

3. How can you recognize linear functions in equations?

4. How can you recognize linear functions in real-world situations?

Answer these questions and write a summary of what you learned from this investigation.

7.5. Marbles in a Glass of Water

In this investigation, you explore the relationship between the number of marbles submerged in a glass of water and the height of the water in the glass. Then you find a linear function to model this relationship.

Materials: marbles (60-100, all the same size, per group), flat-bottomed 10-16 oz. drinking glasses with vertical sides (one per group), rulers (one per group), water, graph paper (one sheet per student).

EXPLORE

Collect the Data. Construct a table like the following for recording the number of marbles in the glass and the corresponding water level.

Number of marbles										
Height of water										

Fill the glass one-third to one-half full of water. Measure and record the water level. Add marbles, at least 5 at a time, the same number each time, and record the water level each time. The marbles must remain submerged. Record the data in the table.

Graph the Data. Make a coordinate graph of your data.

Draw a Linear Approximation. After plotting your data, draw a line that fits the set of data points.

Write an Equation. Find the slope and the *y*-intercept of the line, and use these to write an equation for the line. Be sure to indicate what the variables represent.

DISCUSS

How did you decide which variable to put on the horizontal axis and which variable to put on the vertical axis? How did you select a scale for each axis?

This investigation is different from others in this chapter because the relationship between the two variables may not be perfectly linear. Why does it make sense, though, to use a linear function to model the relationship between the number of marbles and the height of the water?

Did you measure the height of the water using centimeters or inches? How might that affect your linear model? Did everyone add the same number of marbles each time?

Describe how you determined the line. Describe how you determined the slope. Describe how you determined the *y*-intercept.

REFLECT

In this investigation, you explored the relationship between the number of marbles submerged in a glass of water and the height of the water in the glass, and then you found a linear function to model the relationship. These questions will help you summarize and extend what you learned:

1. Why does it make sense to model this relationship with a linear function?

2. Describe how you found your values of m and b.

3. What does the slope of the line represent in this situation? What does the y-intercept represent in this situation?

4. How high would the water level be if 31 marbles were submerged? How many marbles are needed to make the water level approximately 13.75 cm? Show how you determined the answers to these questions.

5. How would the experiment change if you had used larger marbles? How would your line have changed if the glass had been narrower?

6. Why is it important for the glass to have vertical sides?

Answer these questions and write a summary of what you learned from this investigation.

7.6. Additional Problems

1. **Birthday money.** Sam's grandfather gave him some money as a birthday present. Sam says he will put his money in a safe place and add part of his allowance to it each week. Sam tells Clara he will save the same amount from his allowance each week. He says that after five weeks he will have a total of $175 and after eight weeks he will have $190. How much money is Sam planning to save each week? How much money did his grandfather give him for his birthday?

2. **Silver coins revisited (2).** Return to the Silver Coins Revisited (1) in Section 1.9 and reconsider the formula you wrote for the number of coins the king left the castle with if he returned with n coins.
   a) What does the slope represent in this formula?
   b) Consider the remainder of the extensions where you changed various aspects of the problem setting and found new formulae. Are there any other linear relationships in the problem?

3. **Arithmetic sequences.** Describe how linear functions are related to the arithmetic sequences you explored in Chapter 4.

4. **Hours and wage.** Mary's basic wage is $20 per week. She is also paid another $2 for each hour of overtime she works.
   a) If h represents the number of hours of overtime Mary works and if w represents her total wage, write an equation for finding Mary's total wage.
   b) Sketch a graph of this relationship with h on the horizontal axis and w on the vertical axis.
   c) Create a table of data to represent this relationship.

5. **Mowing lawns.** William spent Saturday mowing lawns. He charged $5 for small lawns and $10 for large lawns and earned $70.
   a) Sketch a graph of the relationship between the number of large lawns and the number of small lawns that William could have mowed to earn $70.
   b) Write an equation for this relationship.

Linear Functions

6. Three representations

Complete the table below to show all three representations of each linear function given.

	Table	Equation	Graph
a)			

a)

x	y

Equation: $y = 5x - 6$

b)

x	y
-3	5
-1	11
1	17
3	23
5	29

c)

x	y

Equation: $y = \dfrac{3}{7}x + 2$

d)

x	y

e)

x	y
-1	6
0	4.5
1	3
2	1.5
3	0

f)

x	y

g)

x	y

7.7. Pedagogical Explorations

1. **Modeling real-world data**. Design an investigation for elementary or middle school students to collect real-world data and use a linear function to model the relationship.

2. **Investigating students' understanding of representations of functions**.

   a) Show Table A from 7.2 Investigation: Matching Representations of Linear Functions to a student in grades 5 -8. Ask the student to select the graph that matches the table. Ask the student to explain why that choice makes sense. Ask probing questions as needed to elicit an explanation that helps you understand the students' thinking.

   b) Show Graph L to a student in grades 5-8. Ask the student to select the equation that matches the graph. Ask probing questions as needed to elicit an explanation that helps you understand the students' thinking.

   c) Write an analysis of the interview: 1) State which tables, graphs, and equations the student considered, 2) describe the student's responses, and 3) discuss what the student appears to understand and what the student appears to misunderstand.

3. **Slope**. Consider problem 4c from 7.4 Investigation: Identifying Linear Functions: *Long-Distance Phone Company. A phone company charges $1.05 for the first minute of a long-distance call and 23¢ for each additional minute. Write an equation for the total cost of a long-distance call.* Imagine that you have given this problem to a 7th grade class.

   a) Write two questions that you could pose to the class that would help you assess your students' understanding of slope in this context.

   b) Write two questions that you could pose to the class that would help you assess your students' understanding of the *y*-intercept in this context.

4. **Proportional reasoning and linear functions**. Review the Skate Rental problem in Investigation 7.1. Suppose that the sixth grade students had decided to rent in-line skates from Wheelies Skates and Stuff. They are calculating the cost of renting 75 pairs of skates. Kelsey, one of the sixth-graders calculates that it would cost or $175 to rent 25 pairs, so 75 pairs would cost 175×3, or $525. Is she right or wrong? Explain.

5. **Proportional reasoning**. This misapplication of proportional reasoning to a linear situation, illustrated in #4, is not uncommon in the middle grades as students' appreciation of the power of proportion grows.

   a) Assume that you are Kelsey's teacher. Write three questions you could ask Kelsey that would encourage her to think more about the mathematical relationship in this situation.

   b) Suppose you decide to explain to Kelsey why proportional reasoning doesn't apply in this situation. What points would you make?

7.8. Summary

Terminology

Linear function: A function that involves a constant rate of change.

Slope: A measure of the steepness of a line, indicated by the ratio $\dfrac{\text{rise}}{\text{run}}$ or $\dfrac{\text{vertical change}}{\text{horizontal change}}$.

y-intercept: the value of y at the point where the line crosses the y-axis.

Big Ideas

Linear functions are represented by equations of the form $y = mx + b$, where m and b are fixed numbers. These values, m and b, are the parameters that distinguish one linear function from another. The values of m and b can usually be determined from a table representing a linear function. The values of m and b can be used to predict important features of the graph of a linear function. The values of m and b also represent important features of real-world linear relationships.

References

Lappan, G., Fey, J. T., Fitzgerald, W. M., Friel, S. N., & Phillips, E. D. (1998). *Moving straight ahead: Linear relationships*. Connected Mathematics series. Glenview, IL: Prentice Hall.

National Council of Teachers of Mathematics. (2000). *Principles and standards for school mathematics*. Reston, VA: Author.

University of Chicago School Mathematics Project. (1995). *Everyday Mathematics*. Evanston, IL: Everyday Learning Corporation.

CHAPTER EIGHT: QUADRATIC FUNCTIONS

The term *quadratic* is derived from the Latin for "square." A quadratic function is one that can be represented by an equation of the form $y = ax^2 + bx + c$, where *a*, *b*, and *c* are real numbers and $a \neq 0$. Note that we read x^2 as "*x*-squared." Quadratic relationships are an important class of nonlinear functions, appearing in various real-world settings.

Readers have most likely encountered quadratic functions in their previous experiences with algebra. This chapter provides additional opportunities for readers to discover aspects of quadratic relationships. Explorations focus on examining patterns and describing quadratic functions represented in tables, graphs, equations, and real-world situations.

A formal study of quadratic functions is not typically addressed before Algebra I or integrated high school mathematics, but the informal exploration of quadratic relationships does appear in various forms in elementary and middle school mathematics. The patterns in nonlinear relationships are typically more difficult for students to identify, but the more experiences students have exploring the connections among various representations, the better their understanding will be.

Quadratic Functions in Elementary School

Although the language of quadratic functions does not typically appear in elementary school mathematics, students often explore patterns that involve quadratic relationships. For example, students encounter the underpinnings of quadratic relationships when they explore square numbers.

In this lesson from *Everyday Mathematics* (University of Chicago School Mathematics Project, 1995), second graders use manipulatives to build square arrays that represent numbers multiplied by themselves, and then they explore the numerical patterns in the products.

Work in a small group.

Materials   ☐ centimeter grid paper (*Math Masters*, p. 86)

☐ centimeter cubes or pennies (or both)

☐ tape

Directions

1. Each person chooses a different number from 2 to 10.

2. Build an array that shows your number multiplied by itself.
   Use pennies or centimeter cubes.

3. Draw each array on centimeter grid paper.
   Write a number model under each array.

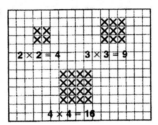

Quadratic Functions

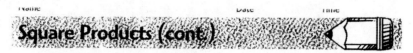

Square Products (cont.)

4. Make and record a few more arrays. On a blank sheet of paper, make a table like the one below. Begin with the smallest factors. Record them in order: 2 × 2, 3 × 3, 4 × 4, and so on.

Array (factors)	Total (products)
2 × 2	4
3 × 3	9
4 × 4	16

5. Continue working together. Build arrays with cubes or pennies for larger and larger numbers. Draw the arrays on grid paper. You may need to tape pieces of grid paper together for the larger arrays.

6. Record the factors and products for the larger numbers in your table. Look for number patterns in the list of products.

Activities such as these provide opportunities for students to explore the connections between concrete and symbolic representations of numbers and to examine patterns in nonlinear relationships.

As students move through grades 3-5, they can more closely analyze the change in area of consecutive square figures. As they describe the numerical patterns that appear they may recognize that not all patterns of growth follow a constant rate of change.

Quadratic Functions in Middle School

Quadratic functions such as the relationship between the length of the radius of a circle and the area of the circle are among the various types of nonlinear relationships that middle school students begin to explore through modeling situations and comparing their various representations.

Graphing technologies such as graphing calculators and Geometer's Sketchpad are powerful tools for examining data and moving among the various representations of functional situations. In the following example from the *Connected Mathematics, Frogs, Fleas, and Painted Cubes: Quadratic Relationships,* (Lappan, Fey, Fitzgerald, Friel, & Phillips, 1998), eighth graders use a graphing calculator to explore characteristics of the graphs of a variety of quadratic functions, including features such as the *x*- and *y*-intercepts, the line of symmetry, and maximum and minimum points.

Problem 2.4

The eight equations below were graphed on a calculator using the window settings shown. The graphs shown below and on the next page are reproduced on Labsheet 2.4.

$$y = x^2 \qquad\qquad y = x(x + 4)$$

$$y = x(4 - x) \qquad y = (x + 3)(x - 3)$$

$$y = (x + 3)(x + 3) \qquad y = (x + 2)(x + 3)$$

$$y = x(x - 4) \qquad\quad y = 2x(x + 4)$$

```
WINDOW
 XMIN=-5
 XMAX=5
 XSCL=1
 YMIN=-10
 YMAX=10
 YSCL=1
```

Do parts A–F for each equation.

A. Match the equation to its graph.

B. Label the coordinates of the x-intercepts on the graph. Describe how you can predict the x-intercepts from the equation.

C. Draw the line of symmetry on the graph.

D. Describe the shape of the graph, and label the coordinates of the maximum or minimum point.

E. Tell what features of the graph you can predict from the equation.

F. Draw and label a rectangle whose area is represented by the equation. Then, express the area of the rectangle in expanded form.

Graph 1   Graph 2

Graph 3   Graph 4

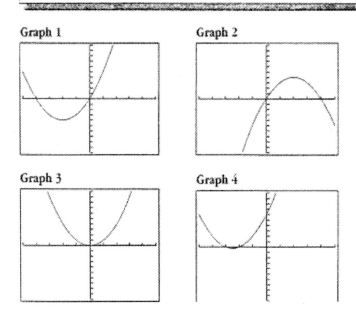

This activity helps middle school students develop their understanding of quadratic relationships by having them identify and describe connections between equations and graphs. Students are also expected to understand the meaning of special features of the graphs and to relate the graphs to concrete situations.

Teachers' Knowledge of Quadratic Functions

In this chapter, we explore quadratic relationships in real-world situations and examine the connections among tables, graphs, and equations. The problems and investigations are similar to the types of activities that appear in elementary and middle school curriculum materials.

Goals of the Chapter

In this chapter, you will—

- recognize and describe real-world situations involving quadratic relationships,

- recognize and describe special characteristics of quadratic functions represented in tables, graphs, and equations,

- write equations to represent quadratic functions,

- translate among various representations—words, tables, graphs, and equations—of quadratic functions,

- solve problems involving quadratic functions,

- collect real-world data and use a quadratic function to model the relationship.

8.1. Areas of Rectangles with Perimeter of 24

In this investigation, you will explore the relationship between the base and the area of rectangles that have a fixed perimeter of 24 inches. You will explore this relationship in various representations—a table, a graph, and an equation.

Materials: 1-inch square tiles (about 40 for each group).

EXPLORE

Shown below are several rectangles that were built with square tiles. Notice that all the rectangles have the same perimeter, 12 inches, but they do not all have the same area.

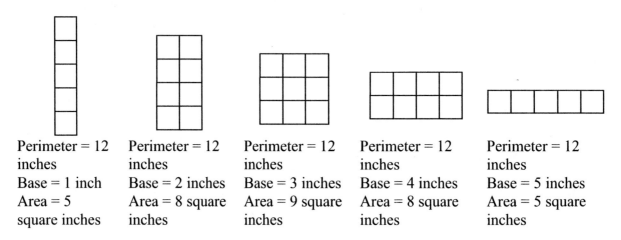

Perimeter = 12 inches
Base = 1 inch
Area = 5 square inches

Perimeter = 12 inches
Base = 2 inches
Area = 8 square inches

Perimeter = 12 inches
Base = 3 inches
Area = 9 square inches

Perimeter = 12 inches
Base = 4 inches
Area = 8 square inches

Perimeter = 12 inches
Base = 5 inches
Area = 5 square inches

Your task is a similar one, to investigate rectangles that have a perimeter of 24 inches. Use 1-inch square tiles to build as many rectangles as you can that have a perimeter of 24 inches. Sketch your rectangles. Record the base and the area of each rectangle in a table, using the base of the rectangle as the independent variable. Then use your table to sketch a graph of the relationship between base and area. Finally, write an equation to represent the area of these rectangles as a function of the base.

DISCUSS

Quadratic functions can be represented by equations of the form $y = ax^2 + bx + c$, with $a \neq 0$. Can the equation for the area of rectangles be written in this form? How did you find your equation?

In this function that relates the base to the area of rectangles with fixed perimeter, one variable depends on the other. What is the dependent variable in this relationship? What is the independent variable? If we limit the possible rectangles with perimeter of 24 inches to those that can be built with 1-inch square tiles, what is the domain of this function? What is the range? If we expand the possibilities to include rectangles using other units that have a perimeter of 24 inches, what is the domain of the function? What is the range?

Describe the patterns of change you see in the table. What patterns do you see in the values of the base of the rectangle? What patterns do you see in the values of the area? Examine the differences between the values of the area. (We will call these values the *first* differences.) Then examine the *second* differences (the differences between the first differences). What pattern do you see?

The graph of a quadratic function is called a *parabola* and has a distinctive shape that occurs often in the real world. When a baseball or a golf ball is hit into the air, it follows a parabolic path. The center of gravity of a leaping porpoise describes a parabola. So does the stream of water molecules emerging from a drinking fountain. The shape of a satellite dish is also parabolic.

Describe the shape of the graph and any special features you observe. On what intervals is the graph increasing? On what intervals is the graph decreasing? Where is the graph concave up? Where is it concave down? How can you use the graph to find the maximum possible area for a rectangle with perimeter of 24 inches? The *axis of symmetry* is the line that divides the parabola into two halves that are mirror images of each other. What is equation for the axis of symmetry in this parabola? The *vertex* of the parabola is the point that lies on the axis of symmetry. What are the coordinates of the vertex of this parabola?

What is the maximum possible area for a rectangle with perimeter 24 inches? How do you know?

REFLECT

In this investigation, you explored the quadratic relationship between the base and area of rectangles that have a fixed perimeter of 24 inches. These questions will help you summarize what you learned:

1. What is the relationship between the base and the area of rectangles that have a fixed perimeter of 24 inches?

2. Describe two ways to find the maximum area for rectangles with fixed perimeter.

3. How are tables, graphs, and equations for this quadratic function different from those of linear functions?

Answer these questions and write a summary of what you learned from this investigation.

8.2. Graphs and Equations of Quadratic Functions

In this investigation, you will use a graphing utility to explore how the graphs of quadratic functions are related to their equations.

Materials: Graphing utility.

EXPLORE

For each graph, the domain should include $-5 \leq x \leq 5$ and the range should include $-10 \leq y \leq 10$.

1. Explore the equation $y = ax^2$ by comparing the graphs of the following sets of quadratic functions. Record your observations. Then explain how the value of a affects the appearance of the graph of $y = ax^2$.

    a) $y = x^2$ and $y = -x^2$

    b) $y = x^2$, $y = 2x^2$, and $y = 4x^2$

    c) $y = x^2$, $y = 10x^2$, and $y = -10x^2$

    d) $y = x^2$, $y = \dfrac{1}{2}x^2$, and $y = \dfrac{1}{4}x^2$

2. Explore the equation $y = ax^2 + c$ by comparing the graphs of the following sets of quadratic functions. Record your observations. Then explain how the value of c affects the appearance of the graph of $y = ax^2 + c$.

    a) $y = x^2$, $y = x^2 + 1$, and $y = x^2 - 1$

    b) $y = 2x^2$, $y = 2x^2 + 6$, and $y = 2x^2 - 6$

    c) $y = -3x^2$, $y = -3x^2 + 9$, and $y = -3x^2 - 9$

    d) $y = \dfrac{1}{2}x^2$, $y = \dfrac{1}{2}x^2 + 2$, and $y = \dfrac{1}{2}x^2 - 2$

3. Explore the equation $y = ax^2 + bx$ by comparing the graphs of the following sets of quadratic functions. Record your observations. Then explain how the value of b affects the appearance of the graph of $y = ax^2 + bx$.

    a) $y = x^2$, $y = x^2 + x$, and $y = x^2 - x$

    b) $y = x^2 + x$, $y = x^2 + 2x$, and $y = x^2 + 3x$

    c) $y = 2x^2$, $y = 2x^2 + 6x$, and $y = 2x^2 - 6x$

    d) $y = -3x^2$, $y = -3x^2 + 9x$, and $y = -3x^2 - 9x$

    e) $y = \dfrac{1}{2}x^2$, $y = \dfrac{1}{2}x^2 + 2x$, and $y = \dfrac{1}{2}x^2 - 2x$

4. Explore the equation $y = ax^2 + bx + c$ by comparing the graphs of the following sets of quadratic functions. Record your observations. Then explain how the value of c affects the appearance of the graph of $y = ax^2 + bx + c$.

a) $y = x^2$, $y = x^2 + 3$, and $y = x^2 - 3$
b) $y = x^2 + x$, $y = x^2 + x + 1$, and $y = x^2 + x - 3$
c) $y = 2x^2 + 6x$, $y = 2x^2 + 6x + 4$, and $y = 2x^2 + 6x - 1$

5. Explore the graphs of the following sets of quadratic functions written in *factored form*, as the product of linear factors. Then explain how you can determine the x-intercepts of the graph from the factored form of the equation.

a) $y = x^2$, $y = x(x - 2)$, and $y = x(x + 2)$
b) $y = x(2 - x)$, $y = 2x(x + 2)$, and $y = (x + 3)(x - 3)$
c) $y = (x + 3)(x - 4)$, $y = (2x + 3)(x + 2)$, and $y = (x - 2)(x - 2)$

DISCUSS

Quadratic functions may be represented by equations of the *expanded form* $y = ax^2 + bx + c$, with $a \neq 0$. The values of a, b, and c are the parameters that distinguish one quadratic function from another. What have you learned about the values of these parameters?

Some, but not all, quadratic functions may also be represented in *factored form*, as the product of linear factors. For example, the quadratic function represented by the expanded form, $y = 2x^2 - 10x + 12$, may also be represented by the factored form, $y = 2(x - 2)(x - 3)$. The quadratic function represented by the expanded form, $y = -x^2 + 12x$, may also be represented by the factored form, $y = x(12 - x)$. The quadratic function represented by $y = 2x^2 + x + 2$, though, cannot be represented in factored form. Why not, do you suppose? What have you learned about the factored form, when it exists? In Chapter 10 we will further examine the relationship between these two forms of quadratic representations.

REFLECT

In this investigation, you examined the relationships between equations and graphs of quadratic functions. These questions will help you summarize and extend what you learned:

1. Describe as much as you can about the graph of $y = -2x^2 + 6$ *without* actually looking at the graph. Explain how you determined this information.

2. Describe as much as you can about the graph of $y = \dfrac{1}{2}x^2 - 4x$ *without* actually looking at the graph. Explain how you determined this information.

3. Describe as much as you can about the graph of $y = x^2 - 2x - 8$ *without* actually looking at the graph. Explain how you determined this information.

4. Compare and contrast the graphs of $y = (x - 4)(x + 5)$ and $y = 2(x - 4)(x + 5)$ *without* actually looking at the graphs. Explain how you determined this information.

Answer these questions and write a summary of what you learned from this investigation.

8.3. Graphs, Tables, and Equations of Quadratic Functions

In this investigation, you will use a graphing utility to explore connections among the equations, graphs, and tables of various quadratic functions.

Materials: Graphing utility

EXPLORE

1. Use a graphing utility to sketch a graph of each of the quadratic functions in a-d below. Then describe each graph. Be sure to include the vertex, x-intercepts, y-intercept, and the axis of symmetry in each description. Also indicate where the graph is increasing, decreasing, and whether it is concave up or down.

   a) $y = 3x(x+2)$

   b) $y = 5x - 2x^2$

   c) $y = (x+3)^2$

   d) $y = x^2 + 5x + 4$

2. Fill in each table below, finding the y-values, and the first and second differences in the y-values. You may find it helpful to use the Table function of a graphing calculator to find the y-values. Examine the patterns of change in the y-values and in the first and second differences for each of the tables. How are these patterns similar? How are they different?

a)　　　　　$3^2 + 6x$

x	$y = 3x(x+2)$	1st difference	2nd difference
-5			
-4	6.5		
-3	9		
-2	0	-9	
-1		-3	6
0		3	6
1		9	6
2	24	15	6
3	15	21	6
4			
5			

Quadratic Functions

b)

x	$y = 5x - 2x^2$	1st difference	2nd difference
-5			
-4			
-3			
-2			
-1			
0			
1			
2			
3			
4			
5			

c)

x	$y = (x + 3)^2$	1st difference	2nd difference
-5			
-4			
-3			
-2			
-1			
0			
1			
2			
3			
4			
5			

d)

x	$y = x^2 + 5x + 4$	1st difference	2nd difference
-5			
-4			
-3	-2		
-2	-2	0	
-1	0	2	2
0	4	4	2
1	10	6	2
2	18	8	2
3	28	10	2
4			2
5			

DISCUSS

We have seen that the graphs of quadratic functions are parabolas. The distinctive features of parabolas may also be seen in the tables of quadratic functions. For each of the functions in the EXPLORE section, describe how the U-shape of the parabola is reflected in the column of y-values in the table. That is, describe how symmetry, intervals of increase and decrease, and concavity appear in the table. Also, describe how you can determine the vertex, the x-intercepts, and the y-intercept of the parabola by examining the table.

Let's examine the relationship between the tables and the equations. Rewrite each equation in expanded form, $y = ax^2 + bx + c$. Then for each function, compare the value of a in the expanded form of the equation to the value of the second differences. What is the general relationship between these values? How can you use the second differences to find the value of a in a quadratic equation?

It is also possible to use the information in each table to determine the value of b in the equation. For each equation, find the difference between values of the function when x equals 0 and when x equals 1. That is, for each function $y = f(x)$, calculate the value of $f(1) - f(0)$. Now, how can you use the value of $f(1) - f(0)$ and the value of a to predict the value of b?

What information in the table can be used to identify the value of c in the equation?

REFLECT

In this investigation, you explored connections among the equations, graphs, and tables of various quadratic functions. These questions will help you summarize what you learned:

1. The following table represents a quadratic function. *Without* sketching a graph, use the information in the table to answer the questions below.

x	-5	-4	-3	-2	-1	0	1	2	3	4
y	-175	-120	-75	-40	-15	0	5	0	-15	-40

    a) What is the axis of symmetry for the graph of this function? Explain how you determined your answer.

    b) Is the graph concave up or concave down? Explain how you determined your answer.

    c) What is the x-intercept of the graph of this function? Explain how you determined your answer.

2. Find an equation for each of the quadratic functions represented in the following tables. Explain how you determined each equation.

Quadratic Functions

a)

x	-5	-4	-3	-2	-1	0	1	2	3
y	49	25	9	1	1	9	25	49	81

b)

x	-5	-4	-3	-2	-1	0	1	2	3
y	33	22	13	6	1	-2	-3	-2	1

c)

x	-5	-4	-3	-2	-1	0	1	2	3
y	2.5	-1	-3.5	-5	-5.5	-5	-3.5	-1	2.5

Answer these questions and write a summary of what you learned from this investigation.

8.4. Tables with a Non-Unit Change in x

In this investigation you explore how the table associated with a quadratic function changes when the values of x are not consecutive.

Materials: Graphing utility (optional)

EXPLORE

1. Fill in each table below, finding the y-values, and the first and second differences in the y-values. You may find it helpful to use the Table function of a graphing calculator to find the y-values.

    a)

x	$y = 3x^2$	1st difference	2nd difference
-8			
-6			
-4			
-2			
0			
2			
4			
6			
8			

    b)

x	$y = -2x^2$	1st difference	2nd difference
-12			
-9			
-6			
-3			
0			
3			
6			
9			
12			

c)

x	$y = 5x^2$	1st difference	2nd difference
-16			
-12			
-8			
-4			
0			
4			
8			
12			
16			

2. Examine the patterns of change in the x-values in the tables. Compare the changes in the second difference in y-values to what you would expect to find if the change in x-values was one unit. How are they different?

DISCUSS

We saw in section 8.3 that the second difference in y-values in the table for a quadratic function was related to the value of a in the expanded form of the equation, $y = ax^2 + bx + c$ when the table listed consecutive x-values. The difference between x-values in a table changes these second differences in y-values in predictable ways. How does the change in successive x-values affect the second difference in y-values?

For the functions given in the tables above, the values of b and c were 0. If they were not, how would the tables have been different?

REFLECT

In this investigation, you explored connections between the changes in x- values, the value of a, and the second differences in the table of a function $y = ax^2 + bx + c$. These questions will help you summarize and extend what you have learned:

1. How does the change in successive x-values affect the second difference in y-values in the table of a quadratic function?

2. How do you determine the equation of a quadratic function from its table if the x-values are equally spaced but not consecutive?

3. Predict the second difference in y-values in a table of values for $y = -3x^2 + 4x - 5$ if the change in successive x-values is 4. Build the table to check your prediction.

Answer these questions and write a summary of what you learned from this investigation.

8.5. Slam Dunk!

In this investigation, you describe the quadratic relationship shown in a table of data and then find an equation and a graph to represent the data.

EXPLORE

When slam-dunking, a basketball player seems to hang in the air at the height of his jump—even when he is not actually hanging on the rim! This table shows the relationship between the time t, measured in seconds, since the player started his jump and his height H, measured in feet, above the ground.

t	0.0	0.1	0.2	0.3	0.4	0.5	0.6	0.7	0.8	0.9	1.0
H	6.5	7.94	9.06	9.86	10.34	10.5	10.34	9.86	9.06	7.94	6.5

1. From the table, describe how the height of the basketball player above the ground changes over this 1-second time period.

2. Without making a graph, verify that these data represent a quadratic function.

3. Without making the graph, describe what the graph of this function would look like. Include as many important features as you can.

4. Find an equation that represents this function.

5. Now graph the function. Does the graph have the features you predicted? If not, explain.

6. What is the significance of the y-intercept in this situation?

DISCUSS

How did you verify that the data in the graph represented a quadratic function? What features of the graph were you able to predict by examining the table? How did you find the equation to represent the function?

REFLECT

Write a problem-solving report using the framework in Chapter 1.

8.6. Covering Jar Lids with Cereal

In this investigation, you explore the relationship between the diameter of a jar lid (measured in centimeters) and the number of cereal pieces required to cover the bottom of the lid. Then you will find a quadratic function to model the relationship.

Materials: spherical cereal pieces such as Cocoa Puffs (about one cup per group), cups or containers to hold the cereal for each group, a collection of jar lids (5 or 6 different sizes for each group), rulers (one per group), and a graphing utility.

EXPLORE

Collect the Data. Construct a table like the following for recording the diameter of each jar lid and the corresponding number of cereal pieces.

Diameter of jar lid							
Number of cereal pieces							

For each lid, measure the diameter by placing a ruler across the circle. Cover the bottom of the inside of each lid *with a single layer* of cereal, counting the pieces. Record your data in the table.

Graph the Data. Use a graphing utility to create a scatter plot of the data. Describe the shape of the graph.

Write an Equation. Find a quadratic equation to model the data. Graph this equation on the same set of axes as your data. What do you notice?

DISCUSS

Why is it appropriate to use a quadratic function to model the relationship between the diameter of the jar lid and the number of cereal pieces? How did you decide which variable to put on the horizontal axis and which variable to put on the vertical axis? How did you select a scale for each axis? Did you measure the diameter of each lid using centimeters or inches? How might that choice affect your graph? Describe how you found an equation to model your data.

REFLECT

In this investigation, you explored the relationship between the diameter of a jar lid and the number of cereal pieces required to fill the lid, and then you found a quadratic function to model the relationship. These questions will help you summarize and extend what you learned:

1. Would you expect the graph of this function to pass through the origin? Why or why not?

2. Does your graph pass through the origin? Why or why not?

3. Use your equation to predict the number of cereal pieces required to fill a lid that has a diameter of 12 cm, or some other size that you did not actually measure.

4. If you were to use unpopped popcorn kernels instead of cereal pieces, what effect do you think it would have on your graph?

Answer these questions and write a summary of what you learned from this investigation.

8.7. Additional Problems

1. **Familiar problems**. Which of the following problems we've seen earlier in this book involve quadratic relationships? For each one explain how you know whether or not it is quadratic. Explanations should relate to the structure of the problem situation, not the data or the equation.

   a) Painted Cubes: A large cube with edges of length n units is built from small unit cubes. The faces of the large cube are painted. Write an equation for the number of small unit cubes painted on zero faces.

   b) Painted Cubes: A large cube with edges of length n units is built from small unit cubes. The faces of the large cube are painted. Write an equation for the number of small unit cubes painted on exactly one face.

   c) Handshakes: Two teams with different numbers of players shake hands. Each player on one team shakes hands with each player on the other team. Write an equation for the number of handshakes h between a team with n players and a team with $n-1$ players.

   d) Staircases: Write an equation to express the relationship between the number of tiles and the figure number.

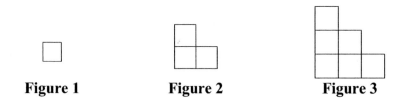

Figure 1   **Figure 2**   **Figure 3**

2. **Shooting a free throw**. A woman who is 5.6 feet tall is shooting a free throw. The path of the basketball is parabolic in shape and the ball reaches its maximum height of 11.5 feet when the ball is 10 feet from the player.
   a) Find an equation for the height of the ball as a function of its horizontal distance from the shooter.
   b) If the ball hits the front of the rim, which is 10 feet high, how far is the shooter from the rim?

3. **Three representations.** Complete the table below to show all three representations of each quadratic function given.

Table	Equation	Graph
a) 	x	y			
b) 	x	y		$y = x^2 - 4x + 3$	

c)

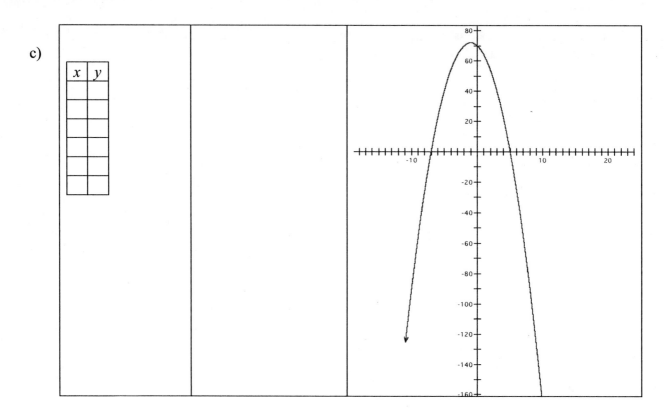

x	y

d)

x	y
-2	14
-1	3
0	-2
1	-1
2	6
3	19

e)

x	y
-2	-1
-1	-4
0	-5
1	-4
2	-1
3	4

f)

x	y

$y = 4x^2 - 16x$

4. **Writing assignment**. Write your responses to the following.

   a) Describe how you can recognize quadratic functions in graphs.
   b) Describe how you can recognize quadratic functions in tables.
   c) Describe how you can recognize quadratic functions in equations.
   d) Describe how you can recognize quadratic functions in real-world situations.

Quadratic Functions

8.8. Pedagogical Explorations

1. **Student responses**. A group of children were individually interviewed as they worked on tasks that asked them to describe sequences of numbers. All the examples in this group are quadratic sequences–in other words, sequences of numbers in which the second differences are constant. Carefully consider each student's response. Then answer the question that follows.

    a)

2	4	8	14	22

    Laura (age 8)

you add 2, 4, 6, and 8.
I got 2, and 4 added 2 and then got 4,
and 8 added 4, and the same with the rest.
(Hargreaves, Threlfall, Frobisher, Shorrocks-Taylor, 1999, p. 76)

    b)

2	5	10	17	26

    Nick (age 10)

There is 3 even numbers and 2 odd numbers.
It goes even odd even odd.
I looked at the numbers and saw that there is
even numbers and there was a odd number.
(Hargreaves, Threlfall, Frobisher, Shorrocks-Taylor, 1999, p. 77)

    c)

2	4	7	11	16
2*	3	4	5	

    Matthew (age 10)

This number pattern is not a (multiplication) table.
I found it hard to do at first but I found out that you add 1 on to the number in the gap each time.
At the top of the page I knew that 2 was in the gap on the first one and I used my fingers on the rest.
*The difference between the terms was written in by the child.
(Hargreaves, Threlfall, Frobisher, & Shorrocks-Taylor, 1999, p. 77)

In what ways could activities like this help advance children's mathematical thinking?

2. **Modeling real-world data**. Design an investigation for elementary or middle school students to collect real-world data and use a simple quadratic function to model the relationship.

3. **Comparing linear and quadratic relationships.** Square numbers are one context in which young children can explore quadratic functions. Suppose your second grade students have made a table on the chalkboard of multiples of two. Now they are making arrays with square tiles, a 2×2 array, a 3×3 array, etc., and recording the total number of tiles in another table. Without using terms such as linear or quadratic, write 3 or more questions you could ask to help your students explore the similarities and differences between a linear and a quadratic relationship.

4. **Length, width, perimeter, and area.** Materials: Square tiles and graph paper.

    a) Suppose your 6th grade students are investigating how many different rectangles can be formed that have a perimeter of 20 and integer lengths and widths. They organize all the possibilities into a table with columns for length, width, and area. Create the table for yourself and graph the data using length as the independent variable and area as the dependent variable.

    b) What is the shape of the graph? What kind of function is indicated? Write at least 5 questions you could ask your students that would guide a discussion that explored this quadratic relationship and its properties.

8.9. Summary

Terminology

Axis of symmetry: The line that divides a graph into two halves that are mirror images of each other.

Expanded form of a quadratic function: Written in the form $y = ax^2 + bx + c$, with $a \neq 0$.

Factored form of a quadratic function: Written as the product of linear factors.

Parabola: The graph of a quadratic function.

Quadratic function: A function represented by an equation of the expanded form $y = ax^2 + bx + c$, with $a \neq 0$.

Vertex of a parabola: The point of the parabola that lies on the axis of symmetry.

Big Ideas

Quadratic functions are represented by equations of the expanded form $y = ax^2 + bx + c$, with $a \neq 0$. The values of a, b, and c are the parameters that distinguish one quadratic function from another.

The values of a, b, and c can be used to predict important features of the graph of a quadratic function.

The graph of a quadratic function is called a *parabola*. The distinctive features of the graph are related to the distinctive features of the table of a quadratic function.

The values of a, b, and c can usually be determined from a table representing a quadratic function.

References

Lappan, G., Fey, J. T., Fitzgerald, W. M., Friel, S. N., & Phillips, E. D. (1998a). *Frogs, fleas, and painted cubes: Quadratic relationships*. Connected Mathematics series. Glenview, IL: Prentice Hall.

University of Chicago School Mathematics Project. (1995). *Everyday Mathematics*. Evanston, IL: Everyday Learning Corporation.

Waring, S., Orton, A., & Roper, T. Pattern and proof. In A. Orton, (Ed.), *Pattern in the teaching and learning of mathematics*, pp. 192-206. New York: Cassell.

CHAPTER NINE: EXPONENTIAL FUNCTIONS

Exponential functions are represented by equations of the form $y = a(b^x)$, where a is nonzero and b is positive but not equal to 1. Exponential functions model real-world situations involving exponential growth, such as biological population increase or the growth of a savings account paying compound interest, and the effect of medicine in the body may follow a pattern of exponential decay.

This chapter examines patterns in exponential relationships and their representation in graphs, tables, and equations. Readers compare the characteristics of exponential functions with those of linear, quadratic, and other types of functions. Among other things, they see that unlike a linear function with its steady rate of change, or a quadratic function, which may represent the product of two linear functions, the rate of change of an exponential function increases or decreases by a constant ratio.

Exponential relationships appear in elementary and middle school mathematics in the form of patterns. Repeated doubling and tripling are examples of exponential growth, and repeated halving or quartering are examples of exponential decay.

Exponential Functions in Elementary School

Elementary school students explore exponential relationships informally, without using the language and symbolism of exponential functions. For example, in this lesson from *Everyday Mathematics* (University of Chicago School Mathematics Project, 1995), second graders write the number of Wubbles after repeated doubling and after repeated halving.

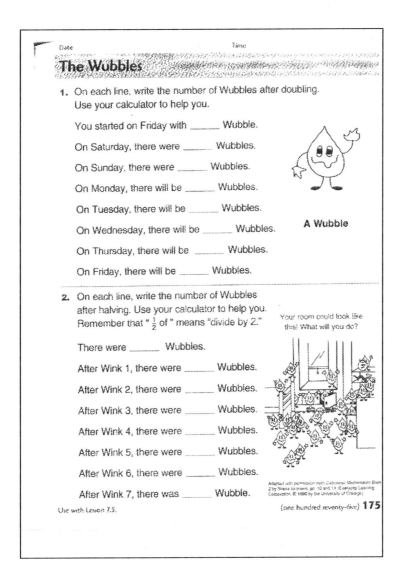

Date _____   **Time** _____

The Wubbles

1. On each line, write the number of Wubbles after doubling.
   Use your calculator to help you.

   You started on Friday with _____ Wubble.

   On Saturday, there were _____ Wubbles.

   On Sunday, there were _____ Wubbles.

   On Monday, there will be _____ Wubbles.

   On Tuesday, there will be _____ Wubbles.

   On Wednesday, there will be _____ Wubbles.

   On Thursday, there will be _____ Wubbles.

   On Friday, there will be _____ Wubbles.

   A Wubble

2. On each line, write the number of Wubbles
   after halving. Use your calculator to help you.
   Remember that " $\frac{1}{2}$ of " means "divide by 2."

   Your room could look like this! What will you do?

   There were _____ Wubbles.

   After Wink 1, there were _____ Wubbles.

   After Wink 2, there were _____ Wubbles.

   After Wink 3, there were _____ Wubbles.

   After Wink 4, there were _____ Wubbles.

   After Wink 5, there were _____ Wubbles.

   After Wink 6, there were _____ Wubbles.

   After Wink 7, there was _____ Wubble.

   Adapted with permission from *Calculator Mathematics Book 2* by Sheila Sconiers, pp. 10 and 11 (Everyday Learning Corporation, © 1990 by the University of Chicago).

Use with Lesson 7.5.   {one hundred seventy-five} **175**

This lesson helps elementary students generate patterns of exponential growth and exponential decay while practicing multiplication and division. Teachers can then ask students to describe the patterns and make predictions. Asking students to draw pictures to match the patterns and then to describe the pictures would also be a nice extension of this activity.

Exponential Functions in Middle School

Middle school students can explore the patterns of exponential relationships in tables, graphs, and equations. Making connections among these representations in the context of real-world situations helps middle school students begin to make sense of the algebraic features of nonlinear relationships.

In this lesson from *Mathematics In Context, Growth* (National Center for Research in Mathematical Sciences Education, & Freudenthal Institute, 1998), eighth graders investigate the exponential growth of a population of caterpillars and they relate the increasingly rapid rise in the number of caterpillars to the shape of a graph representing the increase. Later they will learn to distinguish the curve of exponential growth or decay from the curve of a quadratic relationship.

D. EXPLOSIVE GROWTH

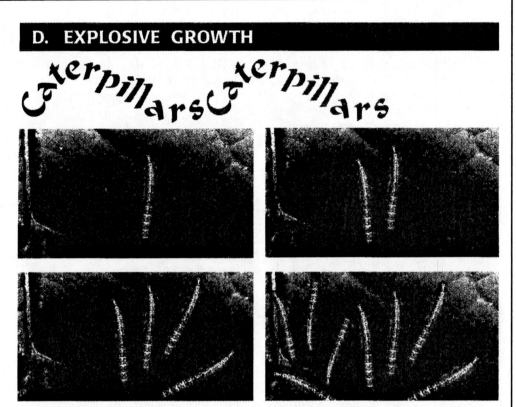

Mr. Jones has had a garden in his yard for many years. This summer he notices twice as many caterpillars on his tomato plants as last summer. He recalls that last summer there were twice as many caterpillars as in the previous summer. Mr. Jones thinks, "If this increase continues, the caterpillars will completely destroy my tomato plants next summer."

Mr. Jones is noticing a rapid growth in the number of caterpillars in his garden. This type of growth can be called *explosive growth.* Explosive growth occurs when an initial period of seemingly slow growth is followed by increasingly fast growth. The rate of growth builds up in a relatively short time.

1. Which of the three graphs shown below best represents explosive growth?

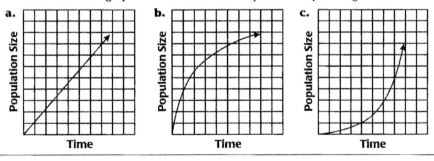

- 189 -

Exponential Functions

Growth

A caterpillar plague usually builds up over several years. In order to determine whether caterpillar growth is explosive, you need an accurate count of the caterpillar population.

The following graph shows the caterpillar population over a four-year period in Mr. Jones's garden. Year 0 is when Mr. Jones first counted the caterpillars.

Number of Caterpillars in Mr. Jones's Garden

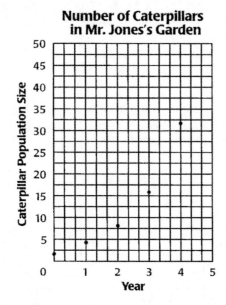

2. a. What is the starting population of caterpillars for this graph?

b. Copy the following table into your notebook and use the graph on the left to fill it in.

Year	0	1	2	3	4
Population					

c. If you draw a curve through the five points, what are you assuming about the growth during the time periods between the points?

There are two especially nice features on the second page of this lesson. First, students are asked to use a graph of the functional relationship to fill in the values of a table, thus requiring students to *read* the graph. (Traditional textbooks almost always focus on the opposite translation—using a table to construct a graph.) Second, students are asked to think about whether or not it makes sense to draw a curve through the points on the graph.

Teachers' Knowledge of Exponential Functions

In this chapter, we explore exponential relationships in real-world situations and examine the connections among tables, graphs, and equations. As in previous chapters, the problems and investigations are similar to the types of activities that appear in elementary and middle school curriculum materials.

Goals of the Chapter

In this chapter, you will—

- recognize and describe real-world situations involving exponential growth and exponential decay,

- recognize and describe special characteristics of exponential functions represented in tables, graphs, and equations,

- write equations to represent exponential functions,

- translate among various representations—words, tables, graphs, and equations—of exponential functions,

- solve problems involving exponential functions,

- collect real-world data and use an exponential function to model the relationship.

9.1. Paper Folding

In this investigation, you use paper folding to explore relationships between the number of folds and the number of resulting regions or the size of the resulting regions.

Before you begin, make a prediction. If you fold a piece of rectangular paper in half, then fold it in half again, and then fold it in half a third time, how many resulting rectangular regions will you have when you unfold the paper? Try it and see if your prediction was correct.

Materials needed: Four pieces of $8\frac{1}{2}"\times11"$ paper for each group

EXPLORE

First, repeat the folding-in-half experiment, but this time record the data in a table as you go. Begin with 0 folds. How many resulting regions are there after 0 folds? Each time you fold the paper in half, record the number of folds (that is, the number of times you have folded the paper) and the number of resulting regions. Fold the paper in half as many times as you can. Write an equation that expresses the number of regions as a function of the number of folds.

Repeat the experiment, this time folding the paper in thirds instead of halves. Record your data in a table and write an equation. (Again, the number of folds is the number of times you have folded the paper—0, 1, 2, 3, etc.)

Now repeat the folding-in-half and folding-in-thirds experiments, but instead of recording the number of resulting regions, and record the *area* of each resulting region in your table. Then, for each experiment, write an equation that expresses the area of each region as a function of the number of folds.

DISCUSS

These paper-folding experiments are situations involving *exponential* relationships. The first two experiments are examples of *exponential growth*, and the last two are examples of *exponential decay*. What patterns of change do you see in each table? How are the four tables alike? How are they different?

How are your four equations alike? How are they different? What connections do you see between your tables and your equations?

If you could fold a piece of paper in half 10 times, how many resulting regions would there be? What would be the area of each region? If you could fold a piece of paper in thirds 10 times, how many resulting regions would there be? What would be the area of each region? Explain how you found the answers to these questions.

As stated earlier, exponential functions can be represented by equations of the form $y = a(b^x)$, where a is non-zero and b is positive but not equal to 1. Based on these paper-folding experiments, what does the value of a reveal about an exponential function? What does the value of b reveal? How is the value of b in exponential growth different from the value of b in exponential decay?

REFLECT

In this investigation, you explored situations involving exponential growth and exponential decay. These questions will help you summarize what you learned:

1. How are the tables for these exponential relationships different from those in linear relationships and quadratic relationships?

2. How are equations for these exponential functions different from equations for linear functions and quadratic functions?

3. How is a table for exponential decay different from a table for exponential growth? How is the resulting equation different?

4. How are exponential functions related to the geometric sequences we saw in Chapter 5?

Answer these questions and write a summary of what you learned from this investigation.

9.2. Cuisenaire Rod Trains

In this problem, adapted from Driscoll (1999), you use Cuisenaire Rods to build trains and you determine how many different trains you can build of each length.

Materials needed: Cuisenaire rods.

EXPLORE

How many different trains can you build that have a length of 3 Cuisenaire rods (with the length of the white rod being 1 unit)? Two trains are different if you use different rods to build them or if you use the same rods but place them in a different order in the train. (For example, white-white-red and white-red-white are two different trains of length 4.) Make a table in which you record the number of Cuisenaire Rod trains you can build that have a length of 1, 2, 3, and 4, and so on, up to 10 units. Then find an equation to model the relationship between the length and the number of different possible trains.

DISCUSS

How many different trains can be built with a length of 10 units? Most likely, you did not actually build all the different trains with a length of 10 units. When could you decide to stop building the trains? How can you justify the number of possible trains of length 10 without building all of the trains?

REFLECT

Write a problem-solving report. Use the properties of Cuisenaire rod trains to explain your equation.

9.3. Exponential Functions Represented in Graphs

In this investigation, you will use a graphing utility to explore how the equations of exponential functions are related to their graphs.

Materials needed: A graphing utility.

EXPLORE

1. First you will explore how the value of b affects the appearance of the graph of $y = b^x$.

   a) Explore the equation $y = b^x$, for values of $b > 1$, by comparing the graphs of the following exponential functions. Observe domain values of $-5 \le x \le 5$ and range values of $0 \le y \le 20$. Record your observations.

   $$y = 1.25^x \qquad y = 1.5^x \qquad y = 1.75^x \qquad y = 2^x$$

   b) Explore the equation $y = b^x$, for values of $0 < b < 1$, by comparing the graphs of the following exponential functions. Observe domain values of $-5 \le x \le 5$ and range values of $0 \le y \le 2$. Record your observations.

   $$y = 0.25^x \qquad y = 0.5^x \qquad y = 0.75^x$$

2. Now you will explore how the value of a affects the appearance of the graph of $y = a(b^x)$.

   a) Explore the equation $y = a(2^x)$ by comparing the graphs of the following exponential functions. Observe domain values of $-5 \le x \le 5$ and range values of $0 \le y \le 64$. Record your observations.

   $$y = 2(2^x) \qquad y = 3(2^x) \qquad y = 4(2^x)$$

   b) Explore the equation $y = a(0.5^x)$ by comparing the graphs of the following exponential functions. Observe domain values of $-5 \le x \le 5$ and range values of $0 \le y \le 4$. Record your observations.

   $$y = 2(0.5^x) \qquad y = 3(0.5^x) \qquad y = 4(0.5^x)$$

DISCUSS

All of the equations and graphs in this investigation represent exponential functions. What similarities did you notice among the graphs? What differences did you notice?

Exponential functions are represented by equations of the form $y = a(b^x)$, where a is non-zero and b is positive but not equal to 1. The values of a and b are the parameters that distinguish one exponential function from another. Based on your observations, how does the value of b affect the appearance of the graph of $y = a(b^x)$? Which of the above equations model patterns of exponential growth? Which equations model patterns of exponential decay? In situations involving exponential growth, the value of b is called the *growth factor*, and in situations involving exponential decay, the value of b is called a *decay factor*. How can you determine whether b is a growth factor or a decay factor just by knowing its value? What relationship do you see between the graphs of $y = 0.25^x$ and $y = 1.25^x$?

How does the value of a affect the appearance of the graph of $y = a(b^x)$?

REFLECT

In this investigation, you examined the relationships between equations and graphs of exponential functions. These questions will help you summarize and extend what you learned:

1. How does the value of b affect the appearance of the graph of $y = a(b^x)$?

2. How does the value of a affect the appearance of the graph of $y = a(b^x)$?

3. How can you recognize an exponential growth pattern from a graph?

4. How can you recognize an exponential growth pattern from an equation?

5. How can you recognize an exponential decay pattern from a graph?

6. How can you recognize an exponential decay pattern from an equation?

7. Revisit sections 9.1 and 9.2, and identify the growth factor and decay factor for each of the exponential functions.

Answer these questions and write a summary of what you learned from this investigation.

9.4. Percentage Growth Rates

We have seen that exponential functions are those that model change with a constant growth or decay factor. Exponential functions may also be described as those functions that model constant *percentage* (or proportional) growth or decay. In this investigation, adapted from *Connected Mathematics, Growing, Growing, Growing: Exponential Relationships* (Lappan, Fey, Fitzgerald, Friel, & Phillips, 1998), you examine the relationship between growth factors and percentage growth rates.

EXPLORE

Sarah invested $500 in a savings account that pays a yearly interest rate of 3%. We call this 3% the *percentage growth rate* (also called the *percentage increase*). The percentage growth rate is different from the growth factor described in section 9.2.

a) Make a table showing the balance in Sarah's savings account each year for the next 10 years. (The initial investment should correspond to year 0.)

b) Sarah's friend Josh invested $1000 in a savings account that also pays a yearly interest rate of 3%. Add a row to your table showing the balance in Josh's savings account each year for the next 10 years.

c) Find the growth factor for Sarah's savings account, and write an equation for the balance S of her savings account after t years. Find the growth factor for Josh's savings account and write an equation for the balance J of Josh's savings account after t years.

d) Using your equations, find the balance S in Sarah's account after 30 years and the balance J of Josh's account after 30 years.

e) When will the balance in Sarah's account have grown to twice as much as the initial investment? When will the balance in Josh's account have grown to twice as much as the initial investment?

f) Sarah's friend Anthony invested $1000 in a savings account that pays a yearly interest rate of 2%. Add a row to your table showing the balance in Anthony's savings account each year for the next 10 years.

g) Find the growth factor for Anthony's account and write an equation for the balance A of Anthony's account after t years. How will the balance in Anthony's account compare to the balance in Sarah's and Josh's accounts after 30 years?

DISCUSS

What relationship do you see between the percentage growth rate and the growth factor? In general, if r is the percentage growth rate of an exponential function and a is the growth factor, write an equation to express the relationship between r and a.

REFLECT

In this investigation, you examined relationships between percentage growth rates and growth factors. These questions will help you summarize and extend what you learned:

1. How is a percentage growth rate of 20% per year related to a growth factor of 1.2?

2. Suppose an initial population of 100 rabbits increases by 30% each year.

   a) Predict the size of the rabbit population one year later. Explain your work.

   b) Predict the size of the rabbit population for the next five years. Explain your work.

   c) Write an equation that you could use to predict the size of the rabbit population after t years.

   d) Identify the percentage growth rate and the growth factor for this situation.

3. Suppose the equation for an exponential function is $y = 25(1.4)^x$. Find the percentage growth rate for this function.

4. Find the growth factor for each percentage growth rate.

   a) 40%
   b) 25%
   c) 5%
   d) 110%

5. Describe how the percentage growth rate is related to the growth factor and explain why they are related this way.

6. Make a conjecture describing the relationship between the *percentage decay rate* (or the *percentage decrease*) and the *decay factor*. Test your conjecture with three different examples.

Answer these questions and write a summary of what you learned from this investigation.

9.5. More Growth Factors and Decay Factors

As we discovered earlier, the constant ratio between successive y-values of an exponential function is called the growth factor or decay factor. When $y = f(x)$ is an exponential function with the independent variable x measured in increments of 1, the growth factor or decay factor from one value of x to the next can be represented by the fraction $\dfrac{f(x+1)}{f(x)}$. In this investigation, you will explore how to find the growth factor or decay factor when the independent variable is measured in increments other than 1.

Materials needed: Calculator.

EXPLORE

The tables below represent exponential functions. For each function, fill in the missing values in the table, find the growth factor or decay factor, and then write the equation in the form $y = a(b^x)$.

1.

x	y
0	
1	
2	
3	64
4	256
5	1024
6	4096
7	16384
8	65536

2.

x	y
0	2
1	
2	18
3	
4	162
5	
6	1458
7	
8	13122

3.

x	y
0	4
2	1.44
4	0.5184
6	0.186624
8	0.06718464
10	0.02418647
12	
14	
16	

4.

x	y
0	3
3	5.184
6	8.957952
9	15.47934
12	26.74830
15	

DISCUSS

First, think about and describe how you found the missing values for each table. Then describe how you used these values to determine the growth factor or decay factor. In #1, how did you use the table to determine the growth factor and the initial value of the function? In #2, the initial value is given. How did you determine the growth factor? In #3, the ratio $\dfrac{f(x+2)}{f(x)}$ is constant. How did you determine the ratio $\dfrac{f(x+1)}{f(x)}$? In #4, the ratio $\dfrac{f(x+3)}{f(x)}$ is constant. How did you determine the ratio $\dfrac{f(x+1)}{f(x)}$?

For an exponential function $y = a(b^x)$ with the independent variable x measured in increments of 1, the growth factor or decay factor is $b = \dfrac{f(x+1)}{f(x)}$. If the same exponential function has a growth factor or decay factor $B = \dfrac{f(x+k)}{f(x)}$ when the independent variable is measured in increments of k, what is the relationship between b and B? Write an equation to show the relationship between b and B.

REFLECT

In this investigation, you examined functions represented in tables and determined the growth factor or decay factor for a smaller increment of the independent variable than appeared in the given data. These questions will help you summarize and extend what you learned:

1. In an exponential function $y = f(x)$, what is the relationship between the growth factor or decay factor $\dfrac{f(x+1)}{f(x)}$ and the ratio $\dfrac{f(x+k)}{f(x)}$ when the independent variable is measured in increments of k?

2. The tables below represent exponential functions. For each function, fill in the missing values in the table, find the growth factor or decay factor, and then write the equation in the form $y = a(b^x)$.

a)

x	0	4	8	12	16	20
y	5	80	1280	20480	327680	

b)

x	0	3	6	9	12	15
y	80000	10000	1250	156.25	19.53125	

Answer these questions and write a summary of what you learned from this investigation.

9.6. Approximating Growth Factors

In this investigation, you approximate the growth factor for a set of real-world data in which the independent variable is measured in increments other than 1.

Materials needed: Calculator.

EXPLORE

The table below gives the world population (in billions) from 1950 to 2005 in 5-year intervals (Source: US Census Bureau, 2006). When modeling real world data, it is sometimes necessary to find an *approximate* exponential model.

Year	1950	1955	1960	1965	1970	1975	1980	1985	1990	1995	2000	2005
Population	2.56	2.78	3.04	3.35	3.71	4.09	4.45	4.85	5.28	5.69	6.08	6.45

(handwritten above years: 0 1 2 3 5 6 7 8 9 10 11 12)

1. Find an approximate growth factor for every *five years*, beginning with the year 1950. That is, find the average value of $\dfrac{f(x+5)}{f(x)}$.

2. Find the approximate growth factor for every *ten years*, beginning with the year 1950. That is, find the average value of $\dfrac{f(x+10)}{f(x)}$. How is this value related to the growth factor for every five years?

3. Use what you learned in #2 to find an approximate *yearly* growth factor. That is, find the average value of $\dfrac{f(x+1)}{f(x)}$.

4. Use the yearly growth factor to write an equation to predict the world population t years after 1950.

5. Use your equation to predict approximately when the population will be double the 2005 population.

DISCUSS

First, why does it make sense to find an *exponential* function and not some other type of function to model the relationship in this data?

Next, describe how you found the approximate growth factors for every five years and every ten years. How are these two growth factors related? Describe how you found the approximate yearly growth factor.

What equation did you write to predict the world population t years after 1990? How did you use your equation to predict approximately when the population would be double the 2005 population? Compare your techniques with those of your classmates.

REFLECT

In this investigation, you found a way to approximate the growth factor for a smaller increment of the independent variable than appeared in the given data. These questions will help you summarize and extend what you learned:

1. How is a yearly growth factor related to a growth factor for every five years?

2. Suppose the exponential function $N = 2500(1.6)^d$, where d is measured in decades, gives the number of individuals in a certain population.

    a) What is the yearly growth factor for this population, rounded to three decimal places?

    b) What is the growth factor for this population, rounded to two decimal places, for a century?

Answer these questions and write a summary of what you learned from this investigation.

9.7. Disappearing Ms

In this investigation, you examine the pattern of disappearing Ms in a collection of M&Ms that is repeatedly tossed in a set of trials. Then you find an exponential function to model the relationship between the trial number and the number of remaining M&Ms with an M showing.

Materials needed: A bag of approximately 100 M&Ms for each group, graphing utility.

EXPLORE

Collect the Data. Construct a table like the following to record the data.

Trial Number	0	1	2	3	4	5	6	7	8
Number of M&Ms with an M showing									

1. Dump your bag of M&Ms onto the tabletop. Important: Do not turn over any of the M&Ms and don't eat them! Count the number of M&Ms and record this number for Trial Number 0.

2. Examine the collection and *remove* the M&Ms that do *not* have an M showing.

3. Count the remaining M&Ms *with* an M showing, and record the results of the trial in the table.

4. Place the remaining M&Ms *with* an M showing back in the bag, and shake the bag. Then dump the M&Ms back onto the tabletop.

5. Repeat steps 2-4 until there are no remaining M&Ms.

Make a Graph. Use a graphing utility to create a scatter plot of the data. Describe the shape of the graph.

Find an Equation. Find an equation to model the data. Graph this equation on the same set of axes as your data.

DISCUSS

How did you decide which variable to put on the horizontal axis and which variable to put on the vertical axis? How did you select a scale for each axis? Why is it appropriate to use an *exponential* function to model the relationship between the trial number and the number of M&Ms with an M showing? Describe how you found an equation to model your data.

REFLECT

In this investigation, you examine the pattern of disappearing Ms in a collection of M&Ms that is repeatedly tossed in a set of trials, and then you found an exponential function to model the relationship. These questions will help you summarize what you learned:

1. Why does it make sense to model this relationship with an exponential function?

2. Describe how you found your values of a and b.

3. What does the value of a represent in this situation? What does the value of b represent in this situation?

Answer these questions and write a summary of what you learned from this investigation.

9.8. Sorting Functions

The following sorting activity, adapted from Cooney et al. (1996), is designed to focus your attention on different ways of categorizing functions and their representations. A set of functions appears on the next few pages, which can be photocopied and then pasted onto index cards. Each function has a letter associated with it -as indicated on the card. You will be asked to determine different ways of sorting the cards. Note that this activity includes additional types of functions beyond the three discussed in detail in this unit.

Materials needed: A set of functions pasted on index cards for each group

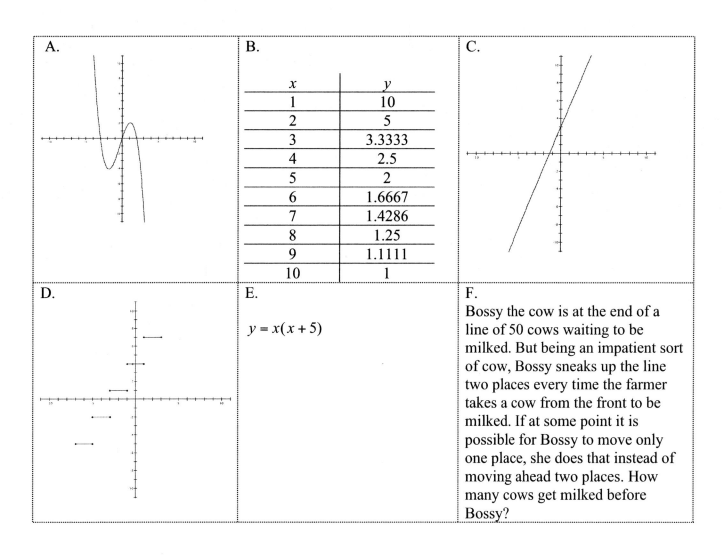

A.

B.

x	y
1	10
2	5
3	3.3333
4	2.5
5	2
6	1.6667
7	1.4286
8	1.25
9	1.1111
10	1

C.

D.

E.

$$y = x(x + 5)$$

F.

Bossy the cow is at the end of a line of 50 cows waiting to be milked. But being an impatient sort of cow, Bossy sneaks up the line two places every time the farmer takes a cow from the front to be milked. If at some point it is possible for Bossy to move only one place, she does that instead of moving ahead two places. How many cows get milked before Bossy?

G.

x	y
0	0
1	3
2	6
3	9
4	12
5	15
6	18
7	21

H.

I.

x	y
0	20
1	10
2	5
3	2.5
4	1.25
5	0.625
6	0.3125

J.

x	y
0	0
1	1
2	8
3	27
4	64
5	125
6	216
7	343

K.

L.

$y = 2x + 1$

M.

N.

On the first day of school, you notice a few patches of fungus on the leaves of the pumpkin vines in your garden. You estimate the area covered by the fungus and find that the patches cover about 1 cm^2. Suppose that the leaf area covered by this kind of fungus quadruples every day. How much area will the leaf fungus cover after 8 days?

O.

A large cube with edges of length n centimeters is built from centimeter cubes. The faces of the large cube are painted. Write an equation for the number of centimeter cubes painted on no faces.

P.

x	y
0	1
1	5
2	11
3	19
4	29
5	41
6	55
7	71

Q.

$y = \dfrac{3}{x}$

R.

$y = \lceil x \rceil$

S.	T.	U.
$\begin{array}{c\|c} x & y \\ \hline 0 & 0 \\ 1 & 1 \\ 2 & 1 \\ 3 & 2 \\ 4 & 2 \\ 5 & 3 \\ 6 & 3 \\ 7 & 4 \end{array}$	$y = 2x^3 + x^2 + x + 1$	Celia receives $20 for her birthday on January 1, puts it in her drawer, and adds $4 to it every month. On what day is the original amount of money doubled?
V. $y = 2(3^x)$	W. A family of rectangles has a fixed perimeter of 56 inches. What is the maximum possible area of the rectangle?	X. A group of volunteers worked all day helping to build a new city playground. The local pizzeria offered to supply ten pizzas for their celebration dinner. What is the relationship between the number of volunteers and the number of pizzas per person?

EXPLORE

In your groups, take turns answering the following questions. Pay attention to each other's responses.

1. Consider cards C, M, and X. What is the easiest way to sort these 3 cards into two piles? What criterion did you use?

2. Sort all 24 cards into four piles. Which criterion makes sorting the easiest?

3. Sort cards A, T, and U into two piles. In what sense is your sorting criterion different from the criterion used in exercises 1 and 2?

4. In what sense are cards D, F, and R alike?

5. In what sense are cards K, P, and W alike?

6. Select a card that satisfies each of the following analogies.

a) Card G is to card P as card C is to what card?

b) Card I is to card V as card P is to what card?

c) Card X is to card B as card F is to what card?

d) Card T is to card A as card V is to what card?

7. Sam has sorted cards E, P, and W into one pile and cards G, L, and U into another pile. What criteria did Sam likely use to sort the cards?

8. What are the 6 different types of functions involved in the card sorting activities? Draw a 6 × 4 matrix, using the letters of the functions, that organizes the types of functions and their types of representations. Label the headings of your matrix with the names of the types of functions and the names of the representations.

DISCUSS

Compare the 6 × 4 matrices you and your classmates created for #8. Did you all agree on the names of the various types of functions? Was there consensus among the groups about the entries in the matrices even if you didn't use the same names for the categories? Which types of functions were familiar? Which ones were new?

Discuss how you recognized the different types of function in the various representations. What are the particular characteristics of each type of function in a table? How can you recognize each type of function in a graph? What are the identifying features of the various word problems? How can you recognize their equations?

REFLECT

In this investigation, you used identifying characteristics of different types of functions in various representations—word problems, graphs, tables, and equations—to sort functions into categories. These questions will help you summarize what you learned:

1. Which types of functions were familiar to you? How did you recognize these familiar functions in word problems, graphs, tables, and equations?

2. Which types of functions were not so familiar to you? What strategies did you use to categorize the not-so-familiar functions?

Answer these questions and write a summary of what you learned from this investigation.

9.9. Additional Problems

1. **Fairy tale**. A children's fairy tale tells of a boy who did a great service for a king. In exchange, the king offered the boy any prize he wanted. The clever boy asked for a quantity of rice. "Put one grain of rice on the first square of a chessboard" said the boy, "and put two on the second square, then four on the third square, and keep doubling until all 64 squares of the chess board are used." Thinking this to be a modest request, the king agreed. To accommodate the boy's request, how many grains of rice would the king have to put on the 64th square of the chessboard?

2. **Identifying exponential functions in tables**. Which of the following tables represent exponential functions? For each table that represents an exponential function, find its equation.

a)

x	-3	-2	-1	0	1	2	3	4
y	2/18	2/9	2/3	2	6	18	54	163

b)

x	-3	-2	-1	0	1	2	3	4
y	0.003	0.03	0.3	3	30	300	3000	30000

c)

x	-3	-2	-1	0	1	2	3	4
y	16	8	4	2	1	1/2	1/4	1/8

d)

x	-4	-2	-1	0	1	2	4	8
y	1/64	1/16	1/4	1	4	16	64	256

3. **Writing assignment**. Write your responses to the following.

   a) Describe how you can recognize exponential functions in graphs.
   b) Describe how you can recognize exponential functions in tables.
   c) Describe how you can recognize exponential functions in equations.
   d) Describe how you can recognize exponential functions in real-world situations.

4. **Geometric sequences**. Describe how exponential functions are related to the geometric sequences you explored in Chapter 5.

5. **Animal population**. The following table shows the population P of animals as a function of time t, in years.

t	0	1	2	3	4	5	6	7	8	9	10
P	100	200	400	800	1600	3200	6400	12800	25600	51200	102400

Exponential Functions

(a) Find the growth factor for this relationship.
(b) Find an exponential equation to model the relationship between time t and population P.

6. **Freezer temperature** (Adapted from Crauder, Evans, and Noell, 1999.). A freezer maintains a constant temperature of 6° Fahrenheit. An ice cube tray is filled with tap water and placed in the freezer to make ice. The difference D between the temperature of the water T and that of the freezer was sampled every minute and recorded in the table.

Time (t)	0	1	2	3	4	5
Temperature difference (D)	69	66.3	63.7	61.2	58.8	56.5

a) Find the decay factor for this relationship.
b) Find an exponential equation to model the relationship between time t and temperature difference D.
c) Use your answer in part b to find an exponential equation to model the relationship between time t and the temperature T of the cooling water. (Hint: How can you find the value of T when $t = 0$?)
d) When will the temperature of the water reach 32 degrees Fahrenheit?

7. **Savings account** (Adapted from Crauder, Evans, and Noell, 1999.). Suppose you invest $500 into a savings account that pays a yearly interest rate of 4%.

a) Write an equation for an exponential function giving the balance in the account as a function of time since the initial investment.

b) Calculate the *monthly* growth factor, rounded to three decimal places, for this account. What is the corresponding monthly interest rate?

c) Calculate the *decade* growth factor, rounded to two decimal places.

d) Use your equation in part (a) to determine how long it will take for the account to reach $740. Explain how this is consistent to your answer to part (c).

8. **Cooling coffee.** Suppose hot coffee was poured into a cup and allowed to cool. The difference D between the coffee temperature and the room temperature was recorded every minute for 7 minutes, as shown in the following table. Find an equation to model the exponential relationship between time t, measured in minutes, and temperature difference D, measured in °C.

t	0	1	2	3	4	5	6	7
D	80	72	65	58	52	47	43	38

9.10. Pedagogical Explorations

1. **Modeling real-world data**. Design an investigation for elementary or middle school students to collect real-world data and use a simple exponential function to model the relationship.

2. **Getting paid.** Ask a third grade student if he would rather be paid for chores 25¢ a day for 10 days or 1¢ the first day, 2¢ the second day, 4¢ the third day, and so on, doubling every day. Record his answers and ask him to explain why he made that choice.

   If the child chooses 25¢, calculate the first 5 days together. Compare the totals. Say, "So the person with 25¢ per day gets more. Let's check the 4th day." Continue one day at a time until the 10th day or until the child decides that doubling one cent yields more. Observe when this realization occurs and probe if necessary to reveal the child's thinking. Ask the child how this can happen.

   Write a description of the child's thinking. Also write a statement about what you would want students to learn from this activity if it were presented to a class.

   Ask the same question of a sixth grade student. Probe the student's thinking. Compare the thinking of the students at two different grade levels.

3. **Exploring exponential functions.** Examine the activity *Explosive Growth: Caterpillars* in the Introduction of Chapter 9. Imagine that you used this activity with an 8th grade class. Identify at least 3 properties of exponential functions you would want students to notice. Write a question for each property that would encourage students to think about that property.

9.11. Summary

Terminology

Exponential function: A function represented by an equation of the form $y = a(b^x)$, where a is non-zero and b is positive but not equal to 1.

Growth factor: The constant factor that each term in an exponential growth pattern is multiplied by to get the next term. If the exponential function $y = a(b^x)$ is an increasing function, the value of b is called a growth factor.

Decay factor: The constant factor that each term in an exponential decay pattern is multiplied by to get the next term. If the exponential function $y = a(b^x)$ is a decreasing function, the value of b is called a decay factor.

Percentage growth rate: The percentage change in an exponential growth pattern from one term to the next.

Big Ideas

Exponential functions are represented by equations of the form $y = a(b^x)$, where a is non-zero and b is positive but not equal to 1. The values of a and b are the parameters that distinguish one exponential function from another.

The values of a and b can usually be determined from a table representing an exponential function.

The values of a and b can be used to predict important features of the graph of an exponential function.

The values of a and b also represent important features of real-world exponential relationships.

References

Cooney, T. J., Brown, S. I., Dossey, J. A., Schrage, G., & Wittmann, E. C.. (1996). *Mathematics, pedagogy, and secondary teacher education*. Portsmouth, NH: Heinemann.

Crauder, B., Evans, B., & Noell, A. (1999). *Functions and change: A modeling alternative to college algebra* (preliminary edition). Boston: Houghton Mifflin.

Driscoll, M. (1999). *Fostering algebraic thinking: A guide for teachers, grades 6-10*. Portsmouth, NH: Heinemann.

Lappan, G., Fey, J. T., Fitzgerald, W. M., Friel, S. N., & Phillips, E. D. (1998). *Growing, growing, growing: Exponential relationships*. Connected Mathematics series. Glenview, IL: Prentice Hall.

National Center for Research in Mathematical Sciences Education, & Freudenthal Institute. (1998). *Growth*. Mathematics in Context series. Chicago, Illinois: Encyclopaedia Britannica Educational Corporation.

National Council of Teachers of Mathematics. (2000). *Principles and standards for school mathematics*. Reston, VA: Author.

University of Chicago School Mathematics Project. (1995). *Everyday Mathematics*. Evanston, IL: Everyday Learning Corporation.

United States Census Bureau. (2006). Total midyear population for the world: 1950-2050. Retrieved September 5, 2006, from http://www.census.gov/ipc/www/worldpop.html

UNIT FOUR: LEARNING ALGEBRA THROUGH GENERALIZATION AND PROOF

THIS UNIT CONTAINS:
Chapter 10: Properties of Numbers and Operations
Chapter 11: Algebraic Proof
"Working with algebraic investigations has convinced us that problem situations based on the generalization and justification of patterns help emphasize a frequently neglected aspect of algebra – its ability to promote mathematical reasoning and an understanding of the nature of mathematical proofs."
(Friedlander & Hershkowitz, 1997, pp. 446-447)

CHAPTER TEN: PROPERTIES OF NUMBERS AND OPERATIONS

Using information from specific examples to describe general relationships is known as generalization. The act of generalizing mathematical relationships and precisely representing them with symbols is at the heart of doing mathematics (Kaput, 1999). In fact, some researchers have argued that if teachers are not in the habit of getting students to express their own generalizations, then mathematical thinking is not taking place (Mason, 1996).

When solving many of the problems in this textbook, you engage in a process of generalization—for example, discovering patterns and representing relationships with variables and symbolic expressions. Many of the patterns focus on the notion of change. For example, with the Crossing the River problem in section 1.2, you analyzed how changes in two variables (the number of adults and the number of children) affected change in a third variable (the number of trips). Also, with the growing patterns in Chapter 4, you explored the results of changes in figure numbers. The investigations in this chapter focus on a slightly different type of generalization that arises from the patterns that can be observed in operations on numbers. Instead of looking at patterns of change, you examine patterns of regularity--for example, in properties that are always true for certain types of numbers and operations.

Patterns of regularity appear throughout elementary and middle school mathematics in the study of numbers and operations. It is important for students to have multiple opportunities to examine and describe these patterns. Without this foundation, many students face major obstacles when they begin to study algebra because they fail to recognize the properties they used in arithmetic, and their restricted conceptions of arithmetic as a series of calculations may stand in the way of learning (Schifter, 1999).

Properties of Numbers and Operations in Elementary School

Traditional instruction in elementary school mathematics often consists of a teacher first demonstrating rules for computation and students then practicing the use of those rules. An alternative is to let students first invent and explain their own rules for computation. When students are given such opportunities, they typically discover patterns in numbers and operations. As children explain their reasoning, they often describe fundamental properties of arithmetic, although they may not use the formal names of these properties.

Implicit and Explicit Understanding

In the following episode from a third-grade classroom, adapted from Schifter, Bastable, and Russell (1999, pp. 84-85), David demonstrates his implicit understanding of a fundamental property of arithmetic and algebra. Without being aware of the name or definition, David incorporates the relationships implied by the distributive property into his reasoning.

Teacher: We have 18 kids here today, and each one needs 12 blocks for the next activity. How can we figure out the number of blocks to give out?

Josh: That would be 18 times 12, and I know 10 times 10 is 100, and 8 times 2 is 16, so if you add them together it would be 100 plus 16 equals 116.

David: That's wrong.

Teacher: What do you mean, David?

David: I did 18×10 and I got 180, but I thought at first I was wrong, so I double-checked. I noticed that Josh didn't do 8×10, so my answer was right. I didn't do the 2 yet, so I do 18×2. Then you add it up—$180 + 36$.

From their work with numbers and operations, elementary school children have a great deal of implicit knowledge about patterns of regularity and fundamental properties in mathematics, although they rarely have opportunities to make their knowledge explicit (Carpenter, Franke, & Levi, 2003). Most children know that when they add zero to a number, the sum is the number they started with ($a + 0 = a$, for all real numbers a). They also know that when adding two small numbers together, they can change the order of the numbers and still get the same sum ($a + b = b + a$, for all real numbers a and b). Some children, though, are not as confident that they can change the order of *large* numbers and still get the same sum. Their knowledge of the property is thus *not* explicit. The lack of explicit understanding of properties becomes a problem when students start manipulating algebraic expressions that contain variables as well as numbers. When students lack explicit understanding of the properties, the manipulations they perform on algebraic expressions are just meaningless procedures.

Children who are able to explain and justify the properties they use as they carry out arithmetic calculations are making a critical transition to algebraic thinking. By encouraging children to make generalizations explicit using words and symbols, teachers can help children form a basis for understanding both arithmetic and algebra (Carpenter, Franke, & Levi, 2003).

Conjectures

To foster the development of explicit understanding, students should be encouraged to make mathematical *conjectures*—informed guesses they have not yet proven true or false. The goal is more than just getting students to talk about mathematics. By asking students to make conjectures, we are asking them to extend their mathematical thinking and take responsibility for generating new ideas, thus helping them to *understand* the mathematics they are learning and using (Carpenter, Franke, & Levi, 2003). .

Generalization

As elementary students articulate their mathematical thinking, they begin by using everyday, familiar language. This provides a foundation on which to build connections to formal mathematical language. The mathematical communication of middle school students can be held to more stringent standards. They should be expected to present and explain their reasoning, using appropriate mathematical language and symbols (NCTM, 2000).

Table 10.1 shows a list of some children's conjectures about important mathematical ideas, the symbolic statements of these conjectures, and the names of the fundamental properties.

Table 10.1 Conjectures Based on Fundamental Properties

Children's Conjectures	Symbolic Statements	Names of Properties
When you add two numbers together, the order of the two numbers doesn't matter; you will still get the same answer.	For all real numbers a and b, $a + b = b + a$	Commutative Property of Addition
When you add three numbers together, it doesn't matter which two numbers you add together first.	For all real numbers a, b, and c, $(a + b) + c = a + (b + c)$	Associative Property of Addition
When you multiply two numbers, the order of the two numbers doesn't matter; you will still get the same answer.	For all real numbers a and b, $a \times b = b \times a$	Commutative Property of Multiplication
When you multiply three numbers, it doesn't matter which two numbers you multiply first.	For all real numbers a, b, and c, $(a \times b) \times c = a \times (b \times c)$	Associative Property of Multiplication
When you multiply two numbers, you can break the numbers into parts, and multiply the parts.	For all real numbers a, b, and c, $a \times (b + c) = a \times b + a \times c$, and $(a + b) \times c = a \times c + b \times c$	Distributive Property of Multiplication over Addition

---

**NCTM *Principles and Standards for School Mathematics*—Number and Operations
(NCTM, 2000)**

In prekindergarten through grade 2 all students should—

- develop a sense of whole numbers and represent and use them in flexible ways, including relating, composing, and decomposing numbers;
  …
- develop and use strategies for whole-number computations, with a focus on addition and subtraction;
  … (p. 78).

In grades 3–5 all students should—
  …
- recognize equivalent representations for the same number and generate them by decomposing and composing numbers;
  …
- understand and use properties of operations, such as the distributivity of multiplication over addition;
  … (p. 148).

Properties of Numbers and Operations in Middle School

Middle school students also encounter the fundamental properties shown in Table 10.1, often in explorations that include the use of variables. For example, in the following problem in *Connected Mathematics, Say It with Symbols: Algebraic Reasoning* (Lappan, Fey, Fitzgerald, Friel, & Phillips, 1998), eighth graders use a rectangular area model to explore the distributive property with whole numbers and variables.

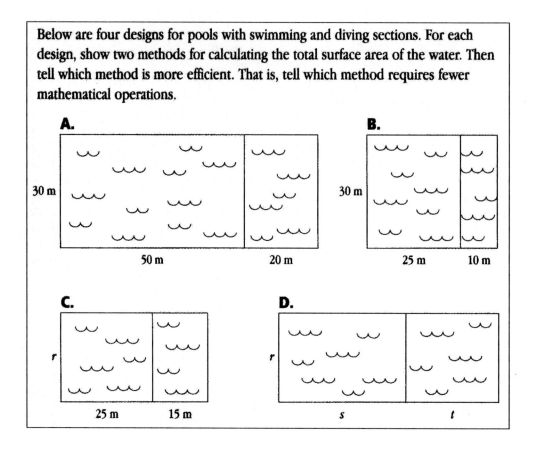

Below are four designs for pools with swimming and diving sections. For each design, show two methods for calculating the total surface area of the water. Then tell which method is more efficient. That is, tell which method requires fewer mathematical operations.

One method for finding the area of the first pool in part A is to find the area of each of the smaller rectangles and then add those quantities together: $30(50) + 30(20)$. This involves three operations. The second method is to calculate the total length of the pool and then multiply that by the width of the pool: $30(50 + 20)$. This method involves only two operations and is thus more efficient. Because the area is the same no matter which method you use, the two expressions are equivalent. This can be stated symbolically: $30(50) + 30(20) = 30(50 + 20)$, thus illustrating the distributive property.

For middle school students, patterns of regularity can play an important role in the meaningful development of rules for computation of fractions, decimals, and integers. Too often, though, the rules are introduced prematurely, without first providing adequate opportunities for students to informally explore the concepts underlying the procedures. Unfortunately, the rules do not help students think about the operations and what they mean. Also, because there are so many different rules, students often get confused about when to use each one. However, when students are given opportunities to invent their *own* rules, they make fewer errors and they develop a better understanding of the numbers and the operations (Van de Walle, 2007).

Middle school students' invented rules for operations with fractions, decimals, and percentages often make use of familiar number properties. An invented rule for multiplication of fractions may use the distributive property. For example, $\frac{3}{4} \times 2\frac{1}{2}$. A student who understands that $2\frac{1}{2}$ is

the same as $2 + \frac{1}{2}$ may multiply $\frac{3}{4} \times 2$ and $\frac{3}{4} \times \frac{1}{2}$ and then add the results (Van de Walle, 2007).

NCTM *Principles and Standards for School Mathematics*—Number and Operations (NCTM, 2000)

In grades 6–8 all students should—

• work flexibly with fractions, decimals, and percents to solve problems;

…

• use the associative and commutative properties of addition and multiplication and the distributive property of multiplication over addition to simplify computations with integers, fractions, and decimals;

… (p. 214).

Teachers' Knowledge of Properties of Numbers and Operations

This chapter focuses on the notion of algebra as generalized arithmetic. The investigations provide opportunities to explore the patterns and properties that exist in numbers and operations. Implicit mathematical ideas will be made explicit as teachers express generalizations using words and symbols. Although some of the investigations in this chapter are similar to those in elementary and middle school mathematics, the last investigation is particularly designed to provide a challenge and thus a new perspective.

Goals of the Chapter

In this chapter, you will—

• use words and symbols to make conjectures about numbers and operations;

• use variables as generalized numbers;

• examine and describe properties of numbers and operations.

10.1. Which Does Not Belong?

In Table 10.1, you saw some children's conjectures that were based on fundamental properties of operations on real numbers. In this investigation, you use words and symbols to write additional conjectures about operations on real numbers.

EXPLORE

For each of the following groups of equations, select the one that does not belong with the other three. Then use words to write a conjecture that describes the pattern you see in the other three equations. Then use variables to write a general rule, a symbolic statement, to describe this pattern. Be sure to declare what the variables represent.

Group 1
a) $3 + 0 = 3$

b) $0 + \frac{1}{2} = \frac{1}{2}$

c) $-5 + 0 = -5$

d) $1 + 4 = 5$

Group 2

a) $4 \times \frac{1}{4} = 1$

b) $-\frac{1}{2} + \frac{3}{2} = 1$

c) $-\frac{2}{3} \times -\frac{3}{2} = 1$

d) $.25 \times 4 = 1$

Group 3
a) $6 \times 1 = 6$
b) $1 \times (-2) = -2$

c) $1 \times \frac{3}{2} = \frac{3}{2}$

d) $2 \times \frac{1}{2} = 1$

Group 4
a) $3 + (-3) = 0$

b) $-\frac{1}{2} + \frac{1}{2} = 0$

c) $4 \times 0 = 0$

d) $5.7 + (-5.7) = 0$

DISCUSS

The patterns you identified and described represent additional fundamental properties of operations on real numbers. What are the names of these properties? Later in this chapter we will explore these properties in relation to other sets of numbers.

Word problems are important tools for helping students develop new mathematical ideas. When carefully designed, word problems can connect the concrete experiences of students' real lives to the abstract symbolism of the mathematics classroom. For example, which of the properties in the Explore section is illustrated by the following two word problems?

Problem 1: Aaron has 4 bags of apples. There is 1 apple in each bag. How many apples does Aaron have altogether?

Problem 2: Kate walked 1 hour at a rate of 6 miles per hour. How many miles did Kate walk?

Give an example of two or more word problems that could be used to help elementary or middle school students focus on the ideas behind each of the other properties in the Explore section.

In Section 1.9, we discussed five uses of variables. How are variables used in this investigation?

REFLECT

In this investigation, you used words and symbols to write conjectures about operations on real numbers. These questions will help you summarize and extend what you learned:

1. Write a set of four "Which Does Not Belong?" symbolic statements for each of the properties shown in Table 10.1.

2. Write a set of two word problems that could help elementary students focus on the idea behind the commutative property of addition. For example, write a word problem that could be represented by $23+14$, and another one that could be represented by $14+23$.

3. Write a set of two word problems that could help elementary students focus on the idea behind the commutative property of multiplication. For example, write a word problem that could be represented by 3×8, and another one that could be represented by 8×3.

Answer these questions and write a summary of what you learned from this investigation.

Generalization

10.2. Building Rectangles with Algebra Tiles

Algebra tiles are manipulatives that are often used as concrete models for algebraic ideas. A set of algebra tiles typically has multiple copies of three different rectangular pieces: a small square, a large square, and a rectangle with the same width as the small square and the same length as the large square. This model uses the fact that every rectangle has length, width, and area.

Call the length and width of the small square 1 unit. Then the area of the small square is 1 square unit. The length of the side of the large square is *not* a whole number multiple of the length of the small square. In other words, it is not possible to line up a collection of squares to be the same length as the rectangle. Thus, we cannot determine the length of the rectangle, so we will call the length x units. Because the width of the rectangle is 1 unit and the length is x units, then the area of the rectangle is x square units. The length and width of the large square are the same as the length of the rectangle, so we will also call the length and the width of the large square x units. So the area of the large square is x^2 square units.

If you were asked to use algebra tiles to form a rectangle that had dimensions $x + 2$ units on one side and $x + 3$ units on the other, you might build the following rectangle.

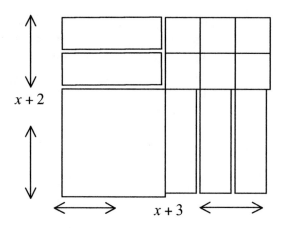

To determine the area of the rectangle, we find the area of all of the pieces that were used to build the rectangle. The area of the large square is x^2 square units, the area of each rectangular piece is x square units, and the area of each small square is 1 square unit, so the total area of the rectangle is $x^2 + x + x + x + x + x + 1 + 1 + 1 + 1 + 1 + 1$ or $x^2 + 5x + 6$ square units.

Each of the three types of pieces (small square, large square, and rectangle) can also appear in two different colors, one color representing positive values and the other color negative values. When working with positive and negative values, it is important to remember that when opposites of the same size are added together, the result is zero. For example, $3 + (-3) = 0$, $2x + (-2x) = 0$, or $x^2 + (-x^2) = 0$. You will also need to remember rules for multiplying positive and negative numbers. What do you remember about these rules?

Let's build a rectangle with dimensions $x + 2$ and $x - 3$. Keep in mind, $x - 3$ is the same as $x + (-3)$. This rectangle will have the same shape as the one above, but this one will be built of different colors.

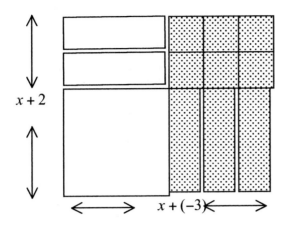

The area of this rectangle is $x^2 + 2x + (-3x) + (-6)$ or $x^2 - x - 6$.

In this investigation, you will use algebra tiles to build rectangles. For some rectangles, you will be given the length and the width, and asked to find the area. For others, you will be given the area and asked to find the length and the width.

Material needed: Algebra tiles with two different colors to represent positive and negative values.

EXPLORE

1. For each of the following, use algebra tiles to build a rectangle with the given dimensions. Name the tiles used to build the rectangle, and add the values of all the tiles together to find the area. Draw a picture of each rectangle, labeling the dimensions of the rectangle and the value of each tile.

    a) The dimensions are $x + 3$ and $x + 4$.

    b) The dimensions are $2x + 3$ and $2x + 4$.

    c) The dimensions are $-2x$ and $x + 4$.

    d) The dimensions are $x + 5$ and $x - 2$.

    e) The dimensions are $x - 2$ and $x - 1$.

    f) The dimensions are both $3x - 4$.

Generalization

2. For each of the following, use algebra tiles to build a rectangle with the given area. Then determine the dimensions of the rectangle. Draw a picture of each rectangle, labeling the dimensions of the rectangle and the value of each tile.

a) The area of the rectangle is $x^2 + 6x + 8$.

b) The area of the rectangle is $2x^2 + 7x + 6$.

c) The area of the rectangle is $2x^2 + 5x - 3$.

d) The area of the rectangle is $4x^2 + 9x + 2$.

DISCUSS

Jerome Bruner (1966) described a theory of learning that identified three stages of representation: (1) enactive (or concrete), (2) iconic (or pictorial), and (3) symbolic (or abstract). Bruner suggested that students must engage in explorations that progress through these three stages to develop understanding of mathematical concepts. Applying that theory, now that you have used algebra tiles (enactive) and drawn pictures (iconic) to explore the relationships between the dimensions of a rectangle and its area, we can associate the concrete and pictorial representations with more symbolic (abstract) ones by writing equations to represent the relationships.

In general, the relationships between the dimensions of a rectangle and its area can be expressed with either one of these two equations: Length × Width = Area or Area = Length × Width. For example, an equation to represent the relationships in the rectangle with dimensions $x - 3$ and $x - 2$ would be $(x - 3)(x - 2) = x^2 - 5x + 6$. Similarly, an equation to represent the relationships in the rectangle with area $2x^2 - 7x - 4$ would be $2x^2 - 7x - 4 = (2x + 1)(x - 4)$. What equations can you write for each of the rectangles in the Explore section? These two examples illustrate two mathematical procedures typically taught in Algebra I. The first example illustrates "multiplying binomials (algebraic expressions with two terms)" and the second illustrates "factoring trinomials (algebraic expressions with three terms)." When these procedures are taught without first giving students opportunities to explore the concepts in their concrete and pictorial forms, students may simply memorize the procedures (e.g., FOIL—first, outside, inside, last) and thus develop a rather shallow understanding of the concepts.

How did the algebra tiles help you explore the mathematical concepts underlying these procedures? What insights did you gain from using the tiles? Why was it important to draw and label the pictures of the rectangles?

Go back to Chapter 1 and review the five uses of variables discussed in section 1.9. How are variables used in this investigation?

REFLECT

In this investigation, you used algebra tiles to build rectangles, drew pictures to represent the rectangles, and used algebraic symbols to represent the relationship between the dimensions and the area of each rectangle. These questions will help you summarize and extend what you learned.

1. Describe how explorations in building rectangles with algebra tiles are related to the procedures of multiplying binomials and factoring trinomials.

2. Describe how these explorations are related to the area model of the distributive property shown in the introduction to this chapter.

3. Some trinomials, such as $x^2 + 4x + 6$ cannot be factored. How can you explain this using algebra tiles? Find another trinomial that cannot be factored.

4. Describe the kinds of tiles and list the numbers of each kind of tile that would be needed to build a model of the product $(x + 1)(x + 1)(x + 1)$ cubic units. Draw a picture of the model. [Hint: This will require a *volume* model (a three-dimensional model), not an *area* model (a two-dimensional model).]

Answer these questions and write a summary of what you learned from this investigation.

Generalization

10.3. Properties of Sets and Operations

In this investigation, you will explore properties for various operations defined on various sets.

EXPLORE

1. Recall the set of *whole numbers* is W = {0, 1, 2, 3, 4,...}. Let * be an operation on the set of whole numbers defined as follows: When * is applied to two whole numbers, the result is the sum of the second number and twice the first number.

    a) Find 3 * 5. Find 2 * 4.

    b) Is it possible to apply * to the numbers 2, 5, and 6 all at the same time? Why or why not?

    c) If a and b are whole numbers, is a * b a whole number? How do you know?

    d) If a and b are whole numbers, is a * b the same as b * a? How do you know?

    e) If a, b, and c are whole numbers, is (a * b) * c the same as a * (b * c)? How do you know?

2. Let @ be an operation on the set of whole numbers defined as follows: When @ is applied to two whole numbers, the result is twice the second number subtracted from the first number.

    a) Find 7 @ 2. Find 8 @ 1.

    b) Is it possible to apply @ to the numbers 10, 4, and 1 all at the same time? Why or why not?

    c) If a and b are whole numbers, is a @ b a whole number? How do you know?

    d) If a and b are whole numbers, is a @ b the same as b @ a? How do you know?

    e) If a, b, and c are whole numbers, is (a @ b) @ c the same as a @ (b @ c)? How do you know?

3. Recall the set of *integers* is Z ={..., -3, -2, -1, 0, 1, 2, 3, ...}. Let + denote traditional addition.

    a) Find 7 + -2. Find -8 + -1.

    b) Is it possible to apply + to the numbers –10, 4, and –1 all at the same time? Why or why not?

    c) If a and b are integers, is a + b an integer? How do you know?

d) If *a* and *b* are integers, is *a* + *b* the same as *b* + *a*? How do you know?

e) If *a*, *b*, and *c* are integers, is (*a* + *b*) + *c* the same as *a* + (*b* + *c*)? How do you know?

4. Let S be the set of *odd integers*, {... -7, -5, -3, -1, 1, 3, 5, 7, 9,...}, and let × denote traditional multiplication.

   a) If *a* and *b* are in S, is *a* × *b* in S? How do you know?

   b) If *a* and *b* in S, is *a* × *b* the same as *b* × *a*? How do you know?

   c) If *a*, *b*, and *c* are in S, is (*a* × *b*) × *c* the same as *a* × (*b* × *c*)? How do you know?

   d) Is there a number *n* in S such that *a* × *n* is always the same as *a*? If so, what is the number *n*?

5. Let # be an operation on the finite set of objects S = {W, X, Y, Z} defined by the following table:

#	W	X	Y	Z
W	W	X	Y	Z
X	X	Y	Z	W
Y	Y	Z	W	X
Z	Z	W	X	Y

   a) If *a* and *b* are in S, is *a* # *b* in S? How do you know?

   b) If *a* and *b* in S, is *a* # *b* the same as *b* # *a*? How do you know?

   c) If *a*, *b*, and *c* are in S, is (*a* # *b*) # *c* the same as *a* # (*b* # *c*)? How do you know?

   d) Is there a number *n* in S such that *a* # *n* is always the same as *a*? If so, what is the number *n*?

DISCUSS

Let us introduce some terminology to describe the operations and properties you have just explored.

Binary Operations

All of the above operations were examples of *binary operations*. An operation is binary if it can only be applied to two elements of the set at one time. Not all operations are binary operations.

Generalization

For example, consider the set of integers and let * be the operation defined as "choose the smallest of these numbers." We see that * can be applied to more than two elements of the set of at one time. For instance, when * is applied to the numbers 5, -2, and 6, the result is –2. Similarly, when * is applied to the numbers –1, 0, and –3, the result is –3. Thus, * is not a binary operation.

Definition: A *binary operation* * on a set A, assigns to each pair of elements *a* and *b* from A, a unique result *a* * *b*. If every pair of elements from A is assigned a result, then the binary operation is *defined on A*.

Closure Property

A set is *closed* under a given operation if, when you perform the operation on any two elements of the set, the result is an element of the set. This must always be true no matter which two elements of the set you use. If the result is an element outside the set, then the operation is *not closed*.

Which of the examples above describe sets closed under the given operation? Explain your reasoning.

Commutative Property

A set is commutative under a given operation if the order in which you perform the operation on any two numbers in the set is irrelevant; that is, you get the same result regardless of the order of the two numbers. This property can be expressed algebraically as follows: A set is commutative under the operation * if $a * b = b * a$, for any two elements *a* and *b* in the set.

Which of the examples above describe operations that are commutative on the given sets? Explain your reasoning.

Associative Property

A set is associative under a given operation if when you perform the operation on any three elements of the set, you get the same result regardless of the sequence in which you perform the operation. This property can be expressed algebraically as follows: A set is associative under the operation * if $(a * b) * c = a * (b * c)$, for any three elements *a*, *b*, and *c* in the set.

Which of the examples above describe operations that are associative on the given sets? Explain your reasoning.

Identity Element

A set has an *identity* under a given operation if the set has a unique element, say *I*, such that when you perform the operation on *I* and any other element, say *x*, in the set, the result of the operation is x. Algebraically, this can be expressed as follows: A set has an identity I under the operation * if, for any element x in the set, $I * x = x * I = x$.

Which of the examples above describe sets that have identity elements for the given operation? Explain your reasoning.

Inverse of an Element

An element, x, belonging to a set, has an *inverse* if there is another element, y, in the set such that when you perform the given operation on x and y, the result is the identity, I. Algebraically, this can be expressed as follows: An element x has an inverse under the operation * in a given set with identity I if there is an element y in the set such that $x * y = y * x = I$. If such an element exists, then y is the inverse of x, and x is the inverse of y.

Which of the examples above describe sets that have inverse elements under the given operation? Explain your reasoning.

Go back to Chapter 1 and review the five uses of variables discussed in section 1.9. How were variables used throughout this investigation? How were they used in the table in example #5 above?

REFLECT

In this investigation, you explored binary operations defined on specific sets of numbers or objects. These questions will help you summarize and extend what you learned:

1. Consider the set of *natural numbers*, $N = \{1, 2, 3,...\}$. Is N closed under addition? Is N closed under multiplication? Is N closed under subtraction? Is N closed under division?

2. Does the set N have an additive identity element? If so, what is it? Does the set N have a multiplicative identity element? If so, what is it?

3. Consider the set of *rational numbers*, $Q = \{\frac{a}{b}$ where a and b are integers and $b \neq 0\}$. Is addition associative on set Q? Is multiplication associative on Q? Is subtraction associative on Q? Is division associative on Q? Explain your responses.

4. Does the set Q have an additive identify? If so, what is it? Does Q have a multiplicative identity? If so, what is it?

5. Define two new binary operations, one that is closed and one that is not closed, on a set of your choosing. Indicate which is which and explain your reasoning.

6. Define two new binary operations, one that is commutative and one that is not commutative, on a set of your choosing. Indicate which is which and explain your reasoning.

Generalization

Answer these questions and write a summary of what you learned from this investigation.

10.4. Additional Problems

1. **Using algebra tiles to multiply binomials**. Use algebra tiles to model the product of the following pairs of binomials. Draw a picture to show how you determined each product.

    a) $(2x-1)(x+4)$
    b) $(2x+1)(3x-1)$
    c) $(2+x)(3-x)$
    d) $(1-3x)(3+x)$

2. **Using algebra tiles to factor trinomials**. Use algebra tiles to build rectangles to represent the following trinomials. Draw a picture to show how you can use the tiles to determine the factors of each trinomial.

    a) x^2-5x+6
    b) $2x^2+x-3$
    c) $3+2x-x^2$
    d) $2-3x-2x^2$

3. **Binary operation ***. Let * be a binary operation on the finite set of objects {A, B, C, D} defined by the following table:

*	A	B	C	D
A	D	C	B	A
B	C	A	D	B
C	B	D	A	C
D	A	B	C	D

    a) Is the set closed under *? How do you know?
    b) Is the set commutative under *? How do you know?
    c) Is the set associative under *? How do you know?
    d) Does the set have an identity under *? If so, what element is the identity?
    e) Does each element of the set have an inverse under *? If so, identify the inverses.

Generalization

4. **Binary operation** °. Let ° be a binary operation on the finite set of objects {A, B, C, D} defined by the following table:

°	A	B	C	D
A	A	C	B	D
B	C	D	A	B
C	B	A	D	C
D	D	B	C	A

a) Is the set closed under °? How do you know?
b) Is the set commutative under °? How do you know?
c) Is the set associative under °? How do you know?
d) Does the set have an identity under °? If so, what element is the identity?
e) Does each element of the set have an inverse under °? If so, identify the inverses.

10.5. Pedagogical Explorations

1. **Child's invented algorithms**: A student explained her strategy for adding 56 + 39.

Marta:	Well, 5 and 3 is 8.
Ms. L.:	[*Interrupting*] Where are the 5 and the 3?
Marta:	Okay, it's 50 and 30. That's like 5 tens and 3 tens. So it's 8 tens; that's 80. And 80 and 6 is 86, and 4 more is 90, and 5 more onto that is 95.

    Her explanation implies the following steps:
    a) $56 + 39 = (5 \times 10 + 6) + (3 \times 10 + 9)$
    b) $\qquad = (5 \times 10 + 3 \times 10) + (6 + 9)$
    c) $\qquad = (5 + 3) \times 10 + (6 + 9)$
    d) $\qquad = 8 \times 10 + (6 + 9)$
    e) $\qquad = 80 + (6 + 9)$
    f) $\qquad = (80 + 6) + 9$
    g) $\qquad = 86 + 9$
    h) $\qquad = 86 + (4 + 5)$
    i) $\qquad = (86 + 4) + 5$
    j) $\qquad = 90 + 5$
    k) $\qquad = 95$

    For each step, identify the property of the base-10 system or the property of operations that justifies the step. Some steps may require more than one property. (Adapted from Carpenter, Franke, & Levi, 2003)

2. **Interview a student**. This activity could be used to assess your students' ability to make generalizations about number patterns. (Bell, 1976, in Harding, 1999). Answer the questions yourself and then ask the same questions of a student in grades 4-8. Write an account of the interview, including the questions you ask and especially the student's responses. Ask more questions if the student's reasoning is not clear. Write a paragraph about what you have learned from the interview about the student's ability to generalize.

    Start with a number; double it; and add the next number. For example, start with 6; double it to get 12; and add the next number, 13. The result is 25.
    Do a few more examples. Note the starting numbers and the resulting finishing numbers.
    Do the reverse, i.e., for a given finishing number, find the starting number.
    Can you finish on 13? What starting number do you need?
    Can you finish on 21?
    Can you finish on 14?
    Find some rules about what numbers you can or can't get as finishing numbers.
    Find also a rule for finding the starting number for a given finishing number.
    For each rule, say whether it is always true for whole numbers or only sometimes true.

3. **Writing number sentences**. Review the conjectures in Table 10.1. Choose one of the conjectures and write a series of 5 number sentences that would support children's

development of the conjecture you chose. Write a paragraph explaining how the number sentences you wrote would support the development of children's understanding of the property.

4. **A fourth grader at work** (adapted from Carpenter, Frank, & Levi, 2003). Is the student in the following vignette using generalization? If so, by referring to the line numbers to explain where and how you think the student is using generalization. If there is more than one instance of generalization, identify each one.

1 Fourth-grader Jamie thoughtfully shuffles some 1-centimeter
2 cubes around on a centimeter grid sheet. "Look at this," she
3 says. "A rectangle three cubes wide and four cubes tall has
4 the same number of cubes as a rectangle four cubes wide
5 and three cubes tall. It's the same with a rectangle five cubes
6 wide and seven cubes tall and a rectangle seven cubes wide and
7 five cubes tall.
8 Teacher: How could you write down what you see?
9 Jamie: Like this (she writes): $3 \times 4 = 4 \times 3$ $5 \times 7 = 7 \times 5$
10 It makes sense because I can turn this 3 by 4 rectangle around
11 so that it will look just like the 4 by 3 rectangle. I think that
12 whenever you multiply one number times another, you can get
13 the same answer if you switch them around and multiply the
14 second number times the first.
15 Teacher: I see what you mean.
16 Jamie: In fact, if I use w for width and h for height of the rectangles
17 I can show what I mean with $w \times h = h \times w$. It works no
18 matter what w and h are.
19 Teacher: That makes sense.
20 Jamie: See, if I make a rectangle with w equal to 2 and h equal to 5
21 and another one with w equal to 5 and h equal to 2, then
22 $2 \times 5 = 5 \times 2$.
23 Teacher: Good thinking.

10.6. Summary

Terminology

Generalization: The use of information from specific examples to describe general relationships.

Conjecture: An informed guess that has not been proven true or false.

Big Ideas

Children who are able to explain and justify the properties they use as they carry out arithmetic calculations are making a critical transition to algebraic thinking. To foster the development of explicit understanding, students should be encouraged to make mathematical *conjectures*— informed guesses they have not yet proven true or false.

References

Bruner, J.S. (1966). *Toward a theory of instruction.* New York, NY: W. W. Norton.

Carpenter, T. P., Franke, M. L, & Levi, L. (2003). *Thinking mathematically: Integrating arithmetic and algebra in elementary school.* Portsmouth, NH: Heinemann.

Driscoll, M. (1999). *Fostering algebraic thinking: A guide for teachers, grades 6-10.* Portsmouth, NH: Heinemann.

Friedlander, A., & Hershkowitz, R. (1997). Reasoning with algebra. *Mathematics Teacher, 6,* 442-447.

Harding, B. (1999). Proof and justification: A primary teaching perspective. *Mathematics Teaching, 169,* 12-16.

Kaput, J. (1999). Teaching and learning a new algebra. In E. Fennema & T. Romberg (Eds.), *Mathematics classrooms that promote understanding* (pp. 133-155). Mahwah, NJ: Lawrence Erlbaum.

Lappan, G., Fey, J. T., Fitzgerald, W. M., Friel, S. N., & Phillips, E. D. (1998). *Say it with symbols: Algebraic reasoning.* Connected Mathematics series. Glenview, IL: Prentice Hall.

Mason, J. (1996). Expressing generality and roots of algebra. In N. Bednarz, C. Kieran, & L. Lee (Eds.), *Approaches to algebra: Perspectives for research and teaching* (pp. 65-86). Dordrecht: Kluwer.

National Council of Teachers of Mathematics. (2000). *Principles and standards for school mathematics*. Reston, VA: Author.

Schifter, D. (1999). Reasoning about operations: Early algebraic thinking in grades K-6. In L. V. Stiff & F. R. Curcio (Eds.), *Developing mathematical reasoning in grades K-12* (pp. 62-81). Reston, VA: National Council of Teachers of Mathematics.

Schifter, D., Bastable, V., & Russell, S. J. (1999). *Building a system of tens: Casebook*. Parsippany, NJ: Dale Seymour.

Van de Walle, J. A. (2007). *Elementary and Middle School Mathematics*: Teaching Developmentally (Sixth Edition). Boston: Pearson Education.

CHAPTER ELEVEN: ALGEBRAIC PROOF

Mathematical reasoning encompasses explanation, argumentation, justification, and proof, none of which can be separated from communication. As you saw in Chapter 10, generalization involves *inductive reasoning*, the use of information from specific examples to draw a general conclusion. Inductive reasoning is an important tool for doing mathematics. Inductive reasoning can lead students to form conjectures and can help students answer the question, "*What* is always true?" Another type of reasoning, however, is needed to answer the question, "*Why* does this always work?" Answering this question requires *deductive reasoning*, a method of drawing conclusions from given true statements by using rules of logic.

The result of deductive reasoning may be a mathematical *proof*, a formal way of verifying that a particular generalization is valid. A proof is a convincing argument, a coherent string of thoughts that persuades others that a mathematical result is valid. According to Driscoll (1999), convincing arguments must meet three criteria:
- Convincing arguments leave nothing to inference.
- Convincing arguments are tied to the original context of the problem.
- Convincing arguments stand up to any challenge.

A proof can serve numerous functions in mathematics, including 1) verification of the truth or falsity of a statement, 2) explanation of *why* something is true or false, 3) discovery or invention of new results, 4) construction of an empirical theory, and 5) incorporation of a well-known fact into a new framework, thus providing a fresh perspective (Hanna, 2000). Although the uses of proof vary widely, most students first encounter the concept of proof as it is used to verify and explain.

Algebraic Proof in Elementary School

The increased emphasis placed on reasoning and proof in response to the *Principles and Standards for School Mathematics* (NCTM, 2000) has contributed to a shift away from the typical rule-oriented emphasis on skill development and procedural proficiency toward a view that reasoning must be a central aspect in all areas and at all levels of mathematics instruction.

NCTM *Principles and Standards for School Mathematics*—Reasoning and Proof (NCTM, 2000)

Instructional programs from prekindergarten through grade 12 should enable all students to—

- recognize reasoning and proof as fundamental aspects of mathematics;
- make and investigate mathematical conjectures;
- develop and evaluate mathematical arguments and proofs;
- select and use various types of reasoning and methods of proof. (p. 56)

Understanding of proof develops slowly, with time and for most students, appropriate nurturing. According to Mingus and Grassl (1999), , "An early and broad introduction to proofs that parallels students' cognitive development from concrete to formal reasoning may be the best way to foster their understanding of the process of proof" (p. 438).

Yackel and Hanna (2003) add, "Students as early as the primary grades of elementary school, given a classroom environment constituted to support mathematics as reasoning, can and do engage in making and refuting claims, use both inductive and deductive modes of reasoning, and generally treat mathematics as a sense-making activity—that is, they treat mathematics as reasoning" (p. 234).

Algebraic Proof in Middle School

Whereas elementary students' mathematical proofs may be limited to words, pictures, and numbers, middle school students may also use variables and algebraic expressions in their mathematical arguments.

NCTM *Principles and Standards for School Mathematics—Variables and Algebraic Expressions* (NCTM, 2000)

In the middle grades, students should have frequent and diverse experiences with mathematics reasoning as they —
- examine patterns and structures to detect regularities;
- formulate generalizations and conjectures about observed regularities;
- evaluate conjectures;
- construct and evaluate mathematical arguments. (p. 262)

In this lesson from *Connected Mathematics, Say It with Symbols: Algebraic Reasoning* (Lappan, Fey, Fitzgerald, Friel, & Phillips, 1998, p. 40), eighth graders write algebraic expressions to describe three different methods for finding the area of a trapezoid and then verify that the expressions are equivalent.

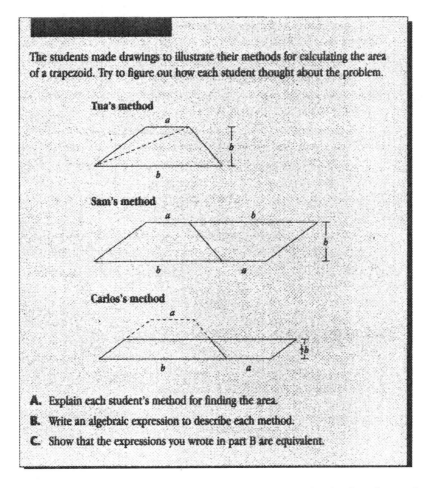

The students made drawings to illustrate their methods for calculating the area of a trapezoid. Try to figure out how each student thought about the problem.

Tua's method

Sam's method

Carlos's method

A. Explain each student's method for finding the area.

B. Write an algebraic expression to describe each method.

C. Show that the expressions you wrote in part B are equivalent.

Consider what students learn from solving this problem. Not only do they learn the formula for the area of a trapezoid, but they also learn about the processes of conjecture and proof. Parts A and B require the use of words and algebraic expressions to describe three conjectures and part C requires an algebraic proof.

Teachers' Knowledge of Algebraic Proof

Proof is considered to be an essential component of the discipline of mathematics and the practice of mathematicians (Knuth, 2002). Yet proof may be something that many teachers and students associate only with high school geometry. This chapter provides you with several opportunities to explore *algebraic* proof. These investigations will help you to appreciate more fully the power of algebra to express mathematical relationships and justify mathematical reasoning.

Again, we encourage you to work in groups to complete the activities. It is especially important for students and teachers to receive feedback on the mathematical language they use to describe their generalizations. Although elementary and middle school students may use informal language to express their mathematical ideas, elementary and middle school *teachers* should be comfortable using formal mathematical terminology as well.

Goals of the Chapter

In this chapter, you will—

- evaluate mathematical arguments;

- generalize algebraic relationships using words and equations;

- write proofs to verify algebraic relationships.

11.1. Analyzing Children's Proofs

An important aspect of effective mathematics teaching is the ability to understand students' thinking about mathematical ideas. Healy and Hoyles (2000) designed a task to investigate 14- and 15-year-old students' conceptions of proof in algebra. In this investigation, we pose a similar task to you.

EXPLORE

Arthur, Bonnie, Ceri, Duncan, Eric, and Yvonne were trying to prove whether the following statement is true or false: "When you add any two even numbers your answer is always even." Rank their proofs in order from most convincing to least convincing. Be prepared to discuss your decisions.

<table>
<tr>
<td colspan="2">

Arthur's answer

a is any whole number

b is any whole number

$2a$ and $2b$ are any two even numbers

$2a + 2b = 2(a + b)$

So Arthur says it's true.
</td>
<td colspan="2">

Bonnie's answer

$2 + 2 = 4$	$4 + 2 = 6$
$2 + 4 = 6$	$4 + 4 = 8$
$2 + 6 = 8$	$4 + 6 = 10$

So Bonnie says it's true.
</td>
</tr>
<tr>
<td colspan="2">

Ceri's answer

Even numbers are numbers that can be divided by 2. When you add numbers with a common factor, 2 in this case, the answer will have the same common factor.

So Ceri says it's true.
</td>
<td colspan="2">

Duncan's answer

Even numbers end in 0, 2, 4, 6, or 8. When you add any two of these, the answer will still end in 0, 2, 4, 6, or 8.

So Duncan says it's true.
</td>
</tr>
<tr>
<td colspan="2">

Eric's answer

Let x = any whole number,

y = any whole number.

$x + y = z$

$z - x = y$

$z - y = x$

$z + z - (x + y) = x + y = 2z$

So Eric says it's true.
</td>
<td colspan="2">

Yvonne's answer

So Yvonne says it's true.
</td>
</tr>
</table>

DISCUSS

Compile the rankings of the class and compare your decisions with those of your classmates.

How do you define an *even number*? How does your definition affect the way you analyze the students' arguments?

In their research, Healy and Hoyles (2000) asked 14- and 15-year-old students to choose the proof that would be closest to their own and to choose the one they thought their teacher would prefer. The research revealed that the students valued explanatory arguments such as Duncan's but they thought their teachers would prefer algebraic proofs such as Arthur's and Eric's. The students also thought they would likely create a proof similar to Bonnie's empirical proof, even though they believed it would not receive the highest marks from their teacher. Why do you think that students value proofs expressed with algebraic symbols when proofs in plain English apparently make more sense to them?

The students' teachers were also asked which argument would be most like their own and which would receive the best score. The teachers most often chose algebraic arguments for their own approach, but indicated in interviews that they also considered a narrative proof to be an effective proof that would receive a good grade. Do you agree with the teachers?

What is a good proof? Healy and Hoyles (2000) suggest the following criteria for evaluating a mathematical argument:
- Does it contain any mistakes?
- Does it show that the statement is *always true*?
- Does it show *only* that the statement is true for some even numbers?
- Does it show *why* the statement is true?
- Is it an easy way to *explain* to someone who is unsure?

Evaluate each of the six students' arguments according to these criteria.

The term *justification* is broader than *proof* and may also include less formal attempts at mathematical verification. Carpenter, Franke, and Levi (2003) observed elementary school children's attempts to verify that mathematical statements were true, and they identified three levels of attempted justification:
- *Appeal to authority*: "Mr. Jones told us last year that when you multiply by 10 you just put a zero at the end (p. 87)." By appealing to authority, children actually avoided mathematical justification.
- *Justification by example*: Children relied on specific examples to justify their general conclusions. In other words, they used inductive reasoning rather than deductive reasoning. Justification by example is sometimes referred to as an *empirical argument* because the conclusion is based on a limited amount of empirical evidence (Healy & Hoyles, 2000).
- *Generalizable arguments*: Generalizable arguments explain why something must always be true or why something is impossible. Children did not commonly provide generalizable arguments, but older children began to see the limits of justification by example. Some children used concrete manipulatives to provide convincing arguments that went beyond justification by example.

At which of the above three levels would you place Arthur's, Bonnie's, Ceri's, Duncan's, Eric's, and Yvonne's justifications?

REFLECT

In this investigation, you examined the arguments made by various children to verify a conjecture. These questions will help you summarize and extend what you learned.

1. Write your own proof for this conjecture: "When you add any 2 odd numbers, the answer is always even."

2. Now show how Arthur, Bonnie, Ceri, Duncan, Eric, and Yvonne might prove the same conjecture.

Answer these questions and write a summary of what you learned from this investigation.

11.2. Department Store Discount

This problem involves the relationship between a discount and sales tax. You make a conjecture and write an algebraic proof.

EXPLORE

Dewey's Department Store is having a storewide 15% discount sale. Sales tax is 7%. As a customer, would you prefer to receive the discount first then have sales tax added, or would you prefer to have sales tax figured first and then the discount taken? Make a conjecture and then write an algebraic proof to verify that your conjecture is true for all items in the store.

DISCUSS

Was your initial conjecture correct or did you find that you had to revise your conjecture?

Warning: A common error in writing algebraic proofs is to begin with the assumption that two algebraic expressions are equal and then to apply operations to both sides of the equation until the expressions on both sides are identical. We should *not*, however, assume that what we are trying to prove is true. Instead our purpose is to verify the truth. A useful algebraic technique is to begin with one of the two expressions and perform operations on it until it is transformed into the other expression, thus proving that the two expressions are indeed equal. Did you make this error when writing your proof?

How were variables used in this problem?

REFLECT

Write a problem-solving report using the framework from Chapter 1. Be sure to discuss your initial conjecture.

11.3. Changing Rectangles

In this investigation, adapted from Friedlander and Hershkowitz (1997), you explore relationships between the area and perimeter of different rectangles, make conjectures using words and algebra, and write algebraic proofs.

EXPLORE

1. **Area**. Each rectangle has been changed so that it is no longer a square. Investigate the relationship between the areas of each pair of rectangles.

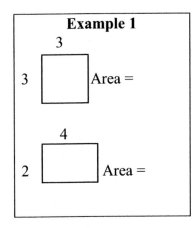
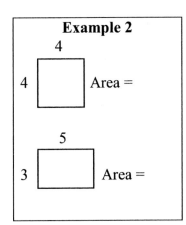
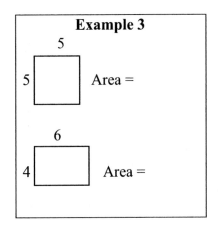

   a) Create some additional examples of this relationship and find the areas.

   b) Describe the relationship between the areas of each pair of rectangles using *words*, not symbols.

   c) Use algebraic symbols to write a general rule that describes the relationship.

   d) Using the algebraic symbols, show how you would convince others that your rule *always* works. (In other words, write an algebraic proof.)

2. **Perimeter**. Again, each rectangle has been changed so that it is no longer a square. Investigate the relationship between the perimeters of each pair of rectangles.

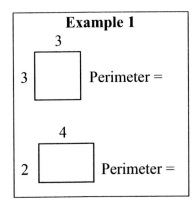
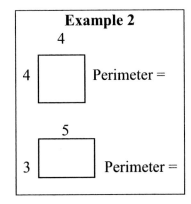
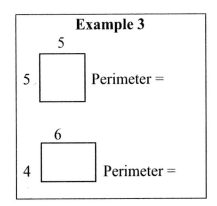

Algebraic Proof

    a) Create some additional examples of this relationship and find the perimeters.

    b) Describe the relationship between the perimeters of each pair of rectangles using *words*, not symbols.

    c) Use algebraic symbols to write a general rule that describes the relationship.

    d) Using the algebraic symbols, show how you would convince others that your rule *always* works. (In other words, write an algebraic proof.)

DISCUSS

Spend some time discussing the various ways you and your classmates used words to describe these relationships. It might be helpful to write several people's statements on the board so that you can compare and contrast them. You may find that some people's statements are clearer, some more descriptive, some more concise, some more sophisticated, and some more elegant. Are there differences in the use of mathematical terminology?

Are there as many differences in the ways people used algebraic symbols to describe the relationships as there were in the statements in words? How are the verbal statements related to the algebraic ones?

Also, spend some time looking at proofs written by your classmates. The final task in both of these problems is essentially to prove the equality of two algebraic expressions. Remember to *not* begin your proof by assuming the two expressions are equal.

You may notice that the algebraic rules and proofs written by you or some of your classmates contain words along with the algebraic expressions. For example, words are used to define what the variables represent. Other words and phrases, sometimes as simple as "if," "then," or "consider this," serve as transitions and contribute to the readability of algebraic rules and proofs.

REFLECT

Write a problem-solving report using the framework from Chapter 1.

11.4. Numerical Relationships

In this investigation, also adapted from Friedlander and Hershkowitz (1997), you explore numerical relationships in fractions and three-digit whole numbers, make conjectures using words and algebra, and write algebraic proofs.

EXPLORE

1. **Fraction Pairs**. Investigate the following relationship between subtraction and multiplication of special pairs of fractions.

Example 1	Example 2	Example 3
$\dfrac{1}{2} - \dfrac{1}{3} =$	$\dfrac{1}{3} - \dfrac{1}{4} =$	$\dfrac{1}{4} - \dfrac{1}{5} =$
$\dfrac{1}{2} \times \dfrac{1}{3} =$	$\dfrac{1}{3} \times \dfrac{1}{4} =$	$\dfrac{1}{4} \times \dfrac{1}{5} =$

a) Find some additional examples of this relationship and perform the operations.

b) Describe the relationship using *words*, not symbols.

c) Use algebraic symbols to write a general rule that describes the relationship.

d) Using the algebraic symbols, show how you would convince others that your rule *always* works for these special pairs of fractions. (In other words, write an algebraic proof.)

e) Explore this rule for other types of pairs of fractions, that is, fractions whose denominators are *not* consecutive integers. Does this rule work for other types of pairs of fractions?

2. **Reversals**. Investigate the following relationship between the results of subtraction and addition of pairs of three-digit numbers in which the order of the digits in the second number is reversed.

Example 1	Example 2	Example 3
$321 - 123 =$	$724 - 427 =$	$953 - 359 =$
$198 + 891 =$	$297 + 792$	$594 + 495 =$

a) Find some additional examples of this relationship and perform the operations.

b) Describe the relationship using *words*, not symbols.

c) Use algebraic symbols to write a general rule that describes the relationship.

d) Using the algebraic symbols, show how you would convince others that your rule *always* works for such pairs of three-digit numbers. (In other words, write an algebraic proof.)

DISCUSS

This problem and others in this chapter highlight the difference between inductive and deductive reasoning. What parts of this problem involved inductive reasoning? What parts involved deductive reasoning?

As with the previous investigation, it is a valuable exercise to examine the various ways you and your classmates used words to describe the mathematical relationships. What kinds of mathematical terminology were used in your descriptions? Did everyone use the same terms or were different terms used to express the same ideas?

How did the patterns in the numbers appear in the algebraic expressions in your proofs?

REFLECT

Write a problem-solving report using the framework from Chapter 1.

11.5. Sums of Consecutive Integers

In this investigation, adapted from Driscoll (1999), you explore some number patterns, make conjectures, and write proofs.

EXPLORE

$7 = 3 + 4$ $\qquad\qquad$ $9 = 2 + 3 + 4$ $\qquad\qquad$ $22 = 4 + 5 + 6 + 7$

These number sentences are examples of sums of consecutive integers. The number 7 is shown as the sum of two consecutive integers. The number 9 is shown as the sum of three consecutive integers. The number 22 is shown as the sum of four consecutive integers. In this activity, you explore what numbers can and cannot be made by sums of consecutive integers.

1. For each number from 1 to 35, find *all* the ways to write it as a sum of two or more consecutive integers. [Note: Include negative integers and 0 in your sums.]

2. What can you discover about sums of consecutive integers? Explore and record three or more discoveries.

3. Without doing any calculations, predict whether each of the following numbers can be made with two consecutive integers, three consecutive integers, four consecutive integers, and so on. Explain why you made the predictions you did.

   a. 45
   b. 57
   c. 62

4. Use the discoveries you made in question 2 and the predictions you made in question 3 to come up with shortcuts for writing the following numbers as the sum of two or more consecutive integers. Describe the shortcuts you created and tell how you used them to write each of the following numbers as the sums of consecutive integers.

   a. 45
   b. 57
   c. 62

Algebraic Proof

DISCUSS

Share with your classmate the conjectures you made in question 2 and the shortcuts you discovered in question 4.

As with the growing patterns in Chapter 4, you may have seen *recursive* relationships that helped you answer questions about this problem, for instance, that helped you predict which numbers can be written as the sum of four consecutive integers. It is helpful, though, to find an *explicit* method for predicting whether a given number, say 4,706, can be written as the sum of four consecutive integers. Put into words an explicit rule for describing the kind of number that can be written as the sum of four consecutive integers. Then write an algebraic expression to represent this kind of number. How can this algebraic expression be used to write a rule for finding the four consecutive integers? State this relationship as a conjecture and then write a proof of the conjecture.

As you discovered, sums of consecutive integers are rich with patterns, and sometimes patterns of patterns. For example, what numbers can be written as the sum of three consecutive integers? What numbers can be written as the sum of five consecutive integers? What numbers can be written as the sum of seven consecutive integers? Write algebraic expressions to represent these kinds of numbers and then describe how these algebraic expressions can be used to write rules for finding the various consecutive integers. State these relationships as conjectures and write proofs of the conjectures.

What numbers can be written as the sum of two consecutive integers? What numbers can be written as the sum of six consecutive integers? Write algebraic expressions to represent these kinds of numbers and then describe how these algebraic expressions can be used to determine the algebraic expressions for the various consecutive integers. State these relationships as conjectures and write proofs of the conjectures.

What did you discover about powers of two? Write a conjecture and a proof of the conjecture.

REFLECT

In this investigation, you explored patterns in sums of consecutive integers. These questions will help you summarize and extend what you learned.

1. In words, describe the numbers that can be written as the sum of three consecutive integers, and describe how the consecutive integers can be found. Then use symbols to state this formula as a conjecture. Finally, write a proof to verify that the formula is valid. Do the same for the numbers that can be written as the sum of five consecutive integers. What overall pattern do you see among the statements regarding numbers written as the sums of odd numbers of consecutive integers?

2. In words, describe the numbers that can be written as the sum of four consecutive integers, and describe how the consecutive integers can be found. Then use symbols to state this formula as a conjecture. Finally, write a proof to verify that the formula is valid. What

overall pattern do you see among the statements regarding numbers written as the sums of even numbers of consecutive integers?

Answer these questions and write a summary of what you learned from this investigation.

11.6. Additional Problems

1. **Number tricks**. Investigate each of the following processes for several different starting numbers. For each process, write a generalization, "The result is always…" Then write a proof of why this always works.

   A. Pick a number.
      Add 3.
      Multiply by 2.
      Subtract 1.
      Add your number.
      Add 4.
      Divide by 3.
      Subtract your number.
      Multiply by 4.
      What is the result?

   B. Pick a number.
      Add 2.
      Multiply by 5.
      Subtract your number.
      Add 2.
      Divide by 4.
      Add 7.
      Subtract your number.
      Divide by 2.
      What is the result?

2. **Explorations**. The following conjectures can be used to provide elementary and middle school students opportunities to explore algebraic proof (Driscoll, 1999; Mingus & Grassl, 1999). How would you prove them?

   a) There is no largest integer.
   b) There are just as many even numbers as odd numbers.
   c) There are just as many positive fractions a/b as there are integers.
   d) The squares of 1, 2, 3, .. 19 end in 0, 1, 4, 5, 6, or 9.
   e) Any six-digit number of the form abc, abc is divisible by 13.
   f) The number $n^3 - n$ is always even.
   g) $\dfrac{1}{2} < \dfrac{1}{101} + \dfrac{1}{102} + ... + \dfrac{1}{200} < 1$

3. **Sums of consecutive integers**. Think about your work with sums of consecutive integers. For instance: What did you discover about the sum of any three consecutive integers? What did you discover about the sum of any five consecutive positive integers? What did you discover about the sum of any seven consecutive positive integers? Can you prove or disprove the following (Bremigan, 2004)?

   a) The sum of n consecutive positive integers is a multiple of n when n is prime, and it is not a multiple of n when n is composite.
   b) The sum of n consecutive positive integers is a multiple of n when n is odd, and it is not a multiple of n when n is even.

4. **Trapezoids.** Solve the trapezoids problem in the textbook reproduction at the beginning of this chapter.

11.7. Pedagogical Explorations

1. **Interview**. Present the task from Investigation 11.1 to one or more 14- or 15-year-old students. Compare these responses to those of your classmates.

2. **Vignette**. Consider the following vignette from *Thinking Mathematically* (Carpenter, Franke, & Levi, 2003). Alicia is justifying the conjecture: When you add two numbers, you can change the order of the numbers you add, and you will still get the same number.

   Alicia: It's like this. If you have 7 plus 5 [*puts out a set of 7 blocks and to the right of it a set of 5 blocks*], look you can move them like this [*moves the set of 5 blocks so that they are to the left of the set of 7 blocks*]. Now it's 5 plus 7, but it's still the same blocks. It's going to be the same when you count them all. It doesn't matter which you count first; it's still going to be the same.

   Ms. P.: Okay, I see how that works for 7 and 5, but how do you know that is true for all numbers?

   Alicia: It doesn't matter how many are in the groups. It could be any number. You are just moving them around like I did there; they are still the same blocks no matter what number you use (Carpenter, Franke, & Levi, 2003, p. 89).

   In the example above, Alicia used a single example modeled with blocks to justify the conjecture about all numbers.

   a) Discuss whether and/or how she generalized the single example to all numbers.

   b) Discuss the teacher's role in developing Alicia's reasoning.

3. **Justification**. Locate the article "Why, Why Would I Justify?" by John Lannin, David Barker, and Brian Townsend, on pages 438-443 in the May 2006 issue of *Mathematics Teaching in the Middle School*.

   a) Read the article carefully, particularly the descriptions and examples of empirical justification, generic examples, and deductive justification.

   b) Solve the Poster problem presented in the article in Figure 4 on page 441. Then write and clearly label three justifications for your rule. Make one an empirical justification, another a generic example, and make your third justification a deductive justification.

   c) Exchange justifications with a classmate and discuss whether you agree about the classifications.

11.8. Summary

Terminology

Deductive reasoning: A method of drawing conclusions from given true statements by using rules of logic.

Inductive reasoning: The use of information from specific examples to draw a general conclusion.

Proof: A convincing argument, a coherent string of statements that convinces others that a mathematical result is valid.

Big Ideas

The increased emphasis placed on reasoning and proof in response to the *Principles and Standards for School Mathematics* (NCTM, 2000) has contributed to a shift away from the typical rule-oriented emphasis on skill development and procedural proficiency toward a view that reasoning must be a central aspect in all areas and at all levels of mathematics instruction.

Proof is considered to be an essential component of the discipline of mathematics and the practice of mathematicians. Although the uses of proof vary widely, most students first encounter the concept of proof as it is used to verify and explain.

References

Bremigan, E. G. (2004). Is it always true? From detecting patterns to forming conjectures to constructing proofs. *Mathematics Teacher, 97*(2). 96-100.

Carpenter, T. P., Franke, M. L, & Levi, L. (2003). *Thinking mathematically: Integrating arithmetic and algebra in elementary school.* Portsmouth, NH: Heinemann.

Driscoll, M. (1999). *Fostering algebraic thinking: A guide for teachers, grades 6-10.* Portsmouth, NH: Heinemann.

Friedlander, A., & Hershkowitz, R. (1997). Reasoning with algebra. *Mathematics Teacher, 6,* 442-447.

Hanna, G. (2000). Proof, explanation and exploration: An overview. *Educational Studies in Mathematics, 44,* 5-23.

Healy, L. & Hoyles, C. (2000). A study of proof concepts in algebra. *Journal for Research in Mathematics Education, 31,* 396-428.

Knuth, E. J. (2002). Proof as a tool for learning mathematics. *Mathematics Teacher, 95.* 486-490.

Lannin, J, Barker, D., & Townsend, B. (2006). Why, why should I justify? *Mathematics Teaching in the Middle School, 11,* 438-443.

Lappan, G., Fey, J. T., Fitzgerald, W. M., Friel, S. N., & Phillips, E. D. (1998). *Say it with symbols: Algebraic reasoning.* Connected Mathematics series. Glenview, IL: Prentice Hall.

Mingus, T. T. Y., & Grassl, R. M. (1999). Preservice teacher beliefs about proofs. *School Science and Mathematics, 99*(8), 438-444.

National Council of Teachers of Mathematics. (2000). *Principles and standards for school mathematics.* Reston, VA: NCTM.

Yackel, E., & Hanna, G. (2003). Reasoning and Proof. In J. Kilpatrick, W. G. Martin, & D. Schifter, (Eds.), *A Research Companion to Principles and Standards for School Mathematics.* pp. 227-236. Reston, VA: NCTM.